Transforming Education

'Bates' book is ambitious and different. It explores the everyday life of schools in relation to and as manifesting global meanings and processes – the transformation of education. It uses complexity theory to think in novel ways about transformation and its alternatives. If you want to look beyond the tired clichés of globalisation then this book would be a very good place to start.'

Stephen J. Ball, Karl Mannheim Professor of Sociology of Education, Institute of Education, University College London, UK

'This book makes an important contribution to the discussion about what matters in education and thus how we run our schools and teach our children. Drawing on the sciences of complexity and social theory, Agnieszka Bates offers a powerful and original critique of the dominant approaches to school improvement. A must-read for educationalists and policymakers interested in alternatives to the current obsession with targets and "delivery".'

Chris Mowles, Professor of Complexity and Management, Director of the Doctor of Management Programme, University of Hertfordshire, UK

Transforming Education challenges the current global orthodoxy that 'educational transformation' can be achieved through a step-by-step implementation of centralised, performance-based strategies for school improvement.

Complex responsive processes theory is utilised in an original way to critique leadership myths and explore the alternative, deeper meanings of educational transformation. The theory opens up new forms of understanding about how ordinary practitioners negotiate the meanings of 'improvement' in their everyday practice. It is in the gap between the emergence of these local interactions and the predetermined designs of policymakers that educational transformation can be lost or found.

This book is an essential read for education professionals and students interested in the fields of complexity, education policy, leadership and management.

Dr Agnieszka Bates lectures in Education at the School of Education and Lifelong Learning, University of East Anglia, UK.

Transforming Education

Meanings, myths and complexity

Agnieszka Bates

Routledge
Taylor & Francis Group
LONDON AND NEW YORK

First published 2016
by Routledge
2 Park Square, Milton Park, Abingdon, Oxon OX14 4RN

and by Routledge
711 Third Avenue, New York, NY 10017

Routledge is an imprint of the Taylor & Francis Group, an informa business

© 2016 Agnieszka Bates

The right of Agnieszka Bates to be identified as author of this work has been asserted by her in accordance with sections 77 and 78 of the Copyright, Designs and Patents Act 1988.

All rights reserved. No part of this book may be reprinted or reproduced or utilised in any form or by any electronic, mechanical or other means, now known or hereafter invented, including photocopying and recording, or in any information storage or retrieval system, without permission in writing from the publishers.

Trademark notice: Product or corporate names may be trademarks or registered trademarks, and are used only for identification and explanation without intent to infringe.

British Library Cataloguing in Publication Data
A catalogue record for this book is available from the British Library

Library of Congress Cataloging-in-Publication Data
Names: Bates, Agnieszka, 1963–
Title: Transforming education: meanings, myths, and complexity/ Agnieszka Bates.
Description: Abingdon, Oxon; New York, NY: Routledge is an imprint of the Taylor & Francis Group, an Informa business, [2016] | Includes bibliographical references and index.
Identifiers: LCCN 2015023378| ISBN 9781138920132 (hardback) | ISBN 9781315687346 (e-book)
Subjects: LCSH: Education – Philosophy. | Educational change – Philosophy.
Classification: LCC LB14.7 .B356 2016 | DDC 370.1 – dc23LC record available at http://lccn.loc.gov/2015023378

ISBN: 978-1-138-92013-2 (hbk)
ISBN: 978-1-315-68734-6 (ebk)

Typeset in Galliard and Gill Sans
by Florence Production Ltd, Stoodleigh, Devon, UK

Printed and bound in Great Britain by
CPI Group (UK) Ltd, Croydon, CR0 4YY

Dedicated to my father, Jan, and in loving memory
of my mother, Barbara.

Contents

List of figures ix
List of tables x
Acknowledgements xi
Abbreviations xii

PART I
The universe of complexity thinking 1

1 Educational transformation in the global age 3

2 (Un)certainty and the myth of control 21

3 Complex responsive processes theory 47

4 Researching complexity 71

PART II
'Global' policies and local interactions 95

5 The myth of 'spectacular' solutions: the *Literacy* and *Numeracy Strategies* and their (un)desirable consequences 97

6 Everyday practice and the myth of perpetual crisis 121

7 Rethinking policy, strategy and educational leadership 147

PART III
Complex responsive processes theory and educational ends 169

8 'Tremendous power', ethics and responsibility 171

9	Educational beginnings and ends	191
	Appendix	205
	Index	207

Figures

3.1	Conceptual framework of complex responsive processes theory	52
4.1	Research paradigms and their relative orientations	74
4.2	Analysis and interpretation of the empirical data	83
8.1	Page layout in the *Home-School Liaison Book*	174

Tables

2.1	Key assumptions of the 'sciences of certainty' and the 'complexity sciences'	25
5.1	Key events in the development of the *National Strategies* for primary education	99
5.2	'Element of chance' in accounts of Ofsted inspection at GLP	114

Acknowledgements

I wish to express my deepest gratitude to the following people for their vital contributions to the creation of this book. To my research participants for their valuable time and the gift of their data. To the research community of the Complexity and Management Conference for generating an abundance of insightful ideas and inspiration. To Ben Littlewood for his incisive comments in the drafting of Chapter 2. To all the children I have taught during my twelve years as a primary practitioner, for reminding me that each day may be a new beginning. To Jenny Bates for her boundless encouragement and understanding. Last but by no means least, I wish to give special thanks to Dr Norman Brady for his unstinting support and insightful critique throughout the writing of this book.

I am also grateful to W.W. Norton & Company, Inc. for permission to use an excerpt from METAMORPHOSES by Ovid, translated by Charles Martin, Copyright © 2004 by Charles Martin.

Abbreviations

BCG	Boston Consulting Group Matrix
BERA	British Educational Research Association
CBI	Confederation of British Industry
CDA	Critical Discourse Analysis
CEO	Chief Executive Officer
CPR	Cambridge Primary Review
DCSF	Department for Children, Schools and Families
DfE	Department for Education
DfEE	Department for Education and Employment
DfES	Department for Education and Skills
GERM	Global Educational Reform Movement
IEA	International Association for the Evaluation of Educational Achievement
KPIs	Key Performance Indicators
KS1	Key Stage 1
KS2	Key Stage 2
LA	Local Authority
LEA	Local Education Authority
LLUK	Lifelong Learning UK
NCSL	National College for School Leadership
NCTL	National College for Teaching and Leadership (formerly NCSL)
NLE	National Leader of Education
NLS	National Literacy Strategy (DfEE 1998)
NNS	National Numeracy Strategy (DfEE 1999)
NPM	New Public Management
NPQH	National Professional Qualification for Headship
OECD	Organisation for Economic Co-Operation and Development
Ofsted	Office for Standards in Education
PISA	Programme for International Student Assessment
PSR	Public Service Reform
PWC	PricewaterhouseCoopers
RCT	Randomised Controlled Trials

RRSA	Rights Respecting School Award
SATs	Standard Assessment Tasks (when first introduced), currently referred to as Standard Attainment Tests
SESI	School Effectiveness and School Improvement
SWOT	Strengths, Weaknesses, Opportunities and Threats
QCA	Qualifications and Curriculum Authority
QTS	Qualified Teacher Status
TALIS	Teaching and Learning International Survey
TDA	Training and Development Agency
TLP	Transnational Leadership Package
TTA	Teacher Training Agency
TUC	Trades Union Congress
UNICEF	United Nations Children's Fund
UPN	Unique Pupil Number

Part I

The universe of complexity thinking

Chapter 1

Educational transformation in the global age

> Thus when the God, whatever God was he,
> Had form'd the whole, and made the parts agree,
> That no unequal portions might be found,
> He moulded Earth into a spacious round . . .
> A creature of a more exalted kind
> Was wanting yet, and then was Man design'd:
> Conscious of thought, of more capacious breast,
> For empire form'd, and fit to rule the rest.
>
> (Ovid AD8/1998: 4–5)

'Transforming education' as a global aim

This book ventures into the world of complex responsive processes to explore the rich possibilities and complexities of 'transforming education' and to explain how the meanings of educational transformation have become narrowly circumscribed by successive education policymakers.[1] Here, the abstract prescriptions of policy are juxtaposed with the ideas and activities arising from the conversations of groups of educational professionals, which provide meaning and purpose to their everyday practice. However, in recent times, 'educational transformation' has become synonymous with hegemonic regimes of performativity. Complex responsive processes theory explains why blueprints for 'transformation' cannot simply be encoded in policy documents and transmitted to schools for their mechanical implementation. The meanings of 'transformation' emerge through the myriad day-to-day responses of school leaders and teachers to these policies, the outcomes of which are uncertain. Complex responsive processes theory, therefore, challenges many of the assumptions of policymakers about the relationship between systems, organisations and the people who work in them.

The need to challenge official notions of 'transformation' now seems imperative as the hegemony of performativity threatens to become a global orthodoxy. Approaches to creating 'effective', 'modern' education systems in many countries are increasingly dependent on standardisation, national curricula, student performance data and accountability as 'policy drivers'. Regular cycles of international comparative surveys are conducted by organisations such as the Organisation for Economic Co-operation and Development (OECD), for example, the Programme for International Student Assessment (PISA). These instruments of comparative analysis claim to identify policy drivers that may be utilised by diverse national governments to construct education policy (OECD 2009). In addition to PISA, a new programme of comparative of surveys was developed in 2009 by the OECD, the Teaching and Learning International Survey (TALIS). The main aim of the first round of TALIS has been to provide an evaluation of how effectively the national education systems of participating countries meet the demands of the global, 'knowledge-based economy'. TALIS 2009 asserts that the main task of many countries has been to transform 'traditional' models of education into 'modern' systems. Its key findings state that:

> in many countries, education is still far from being a knowledge industry in the sense that its own practices are not yet being transformed by knowledge about the efficacy of those practices.
>
> (OECD 2009: 3)

The TALIS blueprint for transforming education is predicated on creating 'knowledge-rich', 'evidence-based' education systems to be achieved often at the expense of traditional educational practices and values. Far from providing a definitive solution, however, characterising education as a 'knowledge industry' raises some unsettling questions. What are the implications of an industrial model of modern education for school leaders, teachers and children? What is meant here by 'knowledge' and 'evidence'? Is breaking with tradition necessary to transform education?

The enduring appeal for policymakers of the idea of 'transforming' education may be rooted in the meaning of transformation as a marked change in nature, form or appearance (*Oxford English Dictionary* 2014). The goal of transformative change can be found in the quotation from Ovid's *Metamorphoses* in the epigraph to this chapter. Creating order out of chaos and leaving the newly formed whole under the rule of someone endowed with special attributes of consciousness and thought is presented here as the ultimate state of transformation. A similar goal can be discerned in the idea of creating modern 'knowledge-rich', 'evidence-based' education systems. Ovid's myth of creation is premised on three assumptions. First, that it is possible to design and engineer an improved social order, analogous to the 'spacious round' moulded from 'unequal portions'. Second, that the task of completing the transformation relies on a 'spectacular' individual, granted godlike power over its enactment. Third, that the act of creation and subsequent control over the new order are essentially 'masculine'. These ideas could be interpreted simply as an articulation of a specific historical worldview and social relations in Ovid's lifetime. However, as explained later in this chapter, these assumptions continue to inform some of the 'modern' approaches to transforming education and social change in general, thus constraining transformation within a particular finite set of possibilities.

Transformation as a 'new' orthodoxy

In the context of education reform in England, 'transformation' has entered the policymakers' lexicon in recent years to signal changes aimed at raising the standards of pupil performance in national, 'high-stakes' tests and improving England's position in international comparisons, such as PISA. The intent behind England's approach to transforming education has been described by a senior figure in the Department for Education and Skills (DfES) as a move to 'crack, once and for all, the historic problems of the English education system' (Arnold 2004: i). Implicit here is the assumption that the inadequacy of the system demands a radically 'new' model of schooling to replace it.

A closer look at the discourse of transformation implies that it has been used by policymakers to mean a 'new' alternative to the 'school effectiveness and school improvement movement' (SESI) of the 1990s. SESI framed education reform in terms of pupil attainment measured by incremental, year-on-year improvement in national tests results in literacy, numeracy and science (Ouston 2003). Although test scores continue to be the most significant national, as well as global, measure of schools' performance, the policies of the New Labour governments (1997–2010) introduced the idea of transformation by expressing their objectives for education as 'transforming' standards and skills, as well as 'transforming' children's life chances, aspirations and opportunities. Numerous references to transformation in the *Five Year Strategy for Children and Learners* (DfES 2004) convey a sense of 'real change and improvement', accomplished 'quickly'. For example, as claimed by the DfES, between the New Labour coming to power in 1997 and 2004:

> As well as transforming life-chances, our reforms have shattered myths about education and shown that it is possible to make real change and improvement quickly at every phase and stage of learning.
>
> (p. 14)

The specific reforms referred to here were introduced under the name of the *National Strategies* for primary education: *National Literacy Strategy* (DfEE 1998) and *National Numeracy Strategy* (DfEE 1999). The idea of transformation at 'every phase and stage of learning' was subsequently transferred to the reform of secondary, as well as further and higher education sectors (DfES 2003; LLUK 2008; Cabinet Office Strategy Unit 2009).[2] The discourse on 'transforming education' developed post 2010 by the Coalition government emphasised competitive levers and structural changes. Measures such as improving teacher quality, modernising curricula and making schools more accountable through a better use of school performance data have been cited as policies for making England 'one of the world's top performers' (DfE 2010a: 7). The structural transformation of education by the Coalition has relied on converting state schools into 'academies' and 'free schools', modelled on the Swedish free schools and American charter schools.[3] While it is claimed that 'struggling' and 'failing' schools will be 'transformed through conversion to Academy status' (p. 14), the meaning of 'transformation' appears confined to statements of school status and improved scores in national tests.

The tendency towards assigning new labels to familiar, ongoing policy objectives has been accompanied by a 're-labelling' of the roles of educational leaders (Gunter 2004). As noted by Gunter and Forrester (2009), the role of the headteacher in England has recently been re-labelled as 'leadership of schools' and no longer requires the Qualified Teacher Status (QTS). This has opened up opportunities for non-educational professionals to become Chief Executive Officers in schools, which are being increasingly re-conceptualised as business enterprises. In accordance with the vision for transforming education, school leadership has been framed as the ability to 'manage people and money with the creativity, imagination and inspiration to lead transformation' (DfES 2004: 109).

The reliance on 'spectacular' leaders, combined with a strong orientation towards standardisation, numeracy and literacy, centrally prescribed curricula, testing regimes, attainment targets and competition align English education policy with the policy directions characteristic of the Global Educational Reform Movement, or 'GERM'. As pointed out by Sahlberg (2011: 99), GERM constitutes a 'new educational orthodoxy' that has spread across the UK, the United States, Canada, Australia, some Scandinavian countries and many countries in the developing world. GERM is often promoted by private donors and consultants, international development agencies and venture philanthropists who offer financial support to public education systems, but also insist on transferring management practices and values from the business world into education (Hargreaves and Shirley 2009; Ravitch 2010; Ball 2012). Within the standardisation-oriented approaches characteristic of GERM, school headteachers and principals have been elevated to a key role in improving schools through the micromanagement of teaching and learning in line with reform strategy (Sahlberg 2004).

This context has provided conditions for the emergence of the 'Transnational Leadership Package', or the TLP (Thomson, Gunter and Blackmore 2014). The TLP consists of normative policy prescriptions, underpinned by 'effectiveness studies' and focused primarily on the need of national governments to raise their competitiveness in the global economy. Often designed by non-educational experts, or simply exported to education from the corporate world, the TLP is sold across international markets in the form of generic leadership techniques that confine the role of teachers and other practitioners[4] working in schools to 'tactical localised delivery' (p. x). The TLP could, therefore, be seen as yet another manifestation of education conceptualised as a global 'knowledge industry' (OECD 2009).

The local school in a global network

What, then, do these global tendencies mean for a 'local' school[5] in England? What are the complex processes through which policies for transformation are enacted in the everyday life of primary schools? As suggested by existing international research evidence (Ball *et al.* 2012; Hursh 2008, 2013; Polesel *et al.* 2014) and original empirical data presented in this book, despite its rhetorical function, the idea of transforming education into a 'knowledge industry' (OECD 2009) may lead to profound changes in the nature of relationships within the 'local' school, though the changes may not mean a better educational experience for school children.

Before we explore these issues in more detail, let us first consider the different people who belong to the school community: teachers, leaders and other adults working in the school, the children and their families, Local Authority[6] employees, as well as members of the local community involved in the school on a voluntary basis. Just as with educational leaders, the roles and identities of these diverse members of the school community are also being re-labelled. For example, the increasingly businesslike discourse of education reform and much of the TLP literature refer to them as 'stakeholders' (Hill and Matthews 2010; NCSL 2011; Wallace and Tomlinson 2012). With the rise of a neoliberal vision of English education as a quasi-market, parents are being increasingly reconstructed as consumers and reduced to the functions of 'choice and voice' (Bates 2013). The focus on pupil performance data as a key reform driver has led to the development of the Unique Pupil Number (UPN) system, which enables officials in Whitehall to 'see' the progress of any child in England on their computer screens, 'at a push of a button' (DfE 2010b; Lawn 2011). Teachers and school leaders are often referred to as the 'school workforce' and reduced to the role of 'implementers', in need of periodic 'remodelling' (Gunter 2007). A substantial body of research on policy evaluation is similarly reductive, in depicting school leaders, teachers and support staff as 'cardboard cut-out sense-makers, just too linear and too rational, too focused and logical, too neat and asocial' (Ball *et al.* 2012: 5). As explained below, complex responsive processes theory challenges these reductionist tendencies in favour of understanding people as embodied, complex and inherently social, simultaneously (trans)formed by and (trans)forming others.

The key problem with a system envisioned as a 'knowledge industry' is that the main task of school leaders and teachers is reconceptualised as the implementation of improvement policies in order to maximise 'educational outcomes' rather than development of child-centred pedagogical relations. For example, as emphasised by TALIS 2009, a 'rich' knowledge and evidence base is meant to assist teachers in 'implementing change' (OECD 2009: 3). This may, in turn, alter the nature of educational professionalism by replacing child-centred orientations with a focus on the performance of the 'abstract child' (Bates 2013) who, from the policy perspective, can be reduced to a UPN. A modern, effective teaching and learning environment is defined here in teacher- and leader-centric ways. This is exemplified by the policy themes selected for the most recent cycle of TALIS 2013, which focused on school leadership; teacher training; teachers' pedagogical beliefs, attitudes and teaching practices; teacher self-efficacy and job satisfaction and the climate in schools and classrooms (OECD 2013). These themes are suggestive of a teacher- and leader-centred enquiry framed within the distinctive disciplinary knowledge and methodologies of psychology. This seems to embrace an ostensibly de-politicised, corporate-managerial focus on employee work conditions, which over-simplifies the complex dynamic of social interactions to a fixed set of variables such as training, efficacy, motivation and job satisfaction. The TALIS 2013 policy themes appear to push children to the margins of what is essentially an adult-centred world. The knowledge meant to transform education into a 'knowledge industry' is thus taken out of its political and socio-economic context and narrowly focused on effectiveness within an instrumentalist, 'objective' scientific perspective. The climate in schools and classrooms created with this kind of knowledge may be of 'cold, calculating purposefulness', with little scope for developing a deeply empathetic engagement with children (Honneth 2006: 91). For the children, therefore, an experience of being educated within a 'knowledge industry' may mean a fundamental misrecognition of their needs (Honneth 1995).

In summary, the reference to 'meanings' in the title of this book signals multiple, multifaceted meanings of 'transforming' education. These meanings depend not only on the underpinning definitions, assumptions, knowledge, intentions and interests, but also on complex connections between the global and the local and in particular on how 'global' policy messages are taken up in a 'local' school, with what consequences in the short and long term. I will refer to the meanings and messages of the national policy texts, comparative international research and the TLP as 'mainstream', to reflect the breadth of their reach and distinguish them from those conveyed by complex responsive processes theory discussed later in the chapter. Let us now consider the 'mythology' developed to justify mainstream messages about educational transformation.

Mythologies of transformation

The 'new orthodoxy' for achieving educational transformation proclaims two intentions: first, to 'shatter myths about education' by making 'real' improvement 'quickly' (DfES 2004: 14), and second, to develop a modern knowledge base about conditions contributing to learning environments, which 'verifies – and dispels – many of the myths that exist about teachers today' (OECD 2014a: 19). Both intentions, however, reveal myth-making tendencies of their own. The references to shattering and dispelling myths about education convey the notion of myth as a widely held but false belief (*Oxford English Dictionary* 2014). This notion, however, does not explain the paradox of relying on myth in evidence-based approaches to transforming education (OECD 2009), nor the 'magico-mythical' thinking underpinning mainstream theories of leadership (Mowles 2011). In his semiological analysis of contemporary 'mythologies', Barthes (2000: 131) explains that myth is a system of communication, a message conveyed in a particular way, for a particular purpose. Barthes explains the ubiquitous presence of myth in Western mass culture as based not on its relationship to 'truth' but on its use. Its use, in turn, is linked to the ability of myth to distort reality by transforming historical contingencies into universal necessities. For example, the specific historical space-time that provided the context to Ovid's myth of creation is rendered timeless and universal rather than contingent. As a message, therefore, the myth of creation is not about its 'truth' value, but its usefulness in legitimating a view of the world and social hierarchies predominant in Ovid's times. To return to our focus on transforming education, three 'myths' in particular appear to have been used in policymakers' discourse on education: the myth of control, the myth of 'spectacular' solutions and the myth of perpetual crisis. All three seem to be embedded in Ovid's myth of creation.

The myth of control is linked to a specific perception of what the social world is like and what counts as valid, reliable and relevant knowledge of this world. For example, knowledge about the working conditions of teachers in participating countries generated by the TALIS programme is claimed to aim at policy relevance, robustness, reliability, generalisability, comparability, efficiency and cost-effectiveness (OECD 2014a). These aims position a TALIS researcher as a 'scientific', expert observer motivated by a benign intention to assist policymakers in improving education. This position resonates with Ovid's image of 'God-the-scientist', guided by some 'objective' law for making parts of the world 'agree'. Both narratives can be read as stemming from a belief in universal laws, which can be applied to produce a controlled effect. Both seem to erase the motive that inspires 'God-the-scientist' and a TALIS researcher to seek laws for changing the world. When we focus on the practice of science, not just scientific knowledge, the motive underpinning the image of the benign 'objective' scientist will need to be carefully examined. As explained further in Chapter 2, the myth of control epitomises assumptions of the 'sciences of certainty', which are rooted in a normative positivist view of knowledge and its usefulness in maintaining control over aspects of the world.

The second myth supporting policies for educational transformation is the myth of 'spectacular' solutions. The myth can be traced to the desire to be able to 'crack once and for all' deep-seated educational problems and to 'make real change and improvement quickly' (DfES 2004: 14). In the global education reform context, 'spectacular' solutions are driven by economic imperatives and consist of generic tools and techniques for increasing productivity borrowed from the business world. They rely on a 'spectacular' leader, endowed with privileged insight and understanding, not unlike Man in Ovid's myth of creation: 'conscious of thought' and 'for empire form'd'. The influence of the myth of 'spectacular' solutions seems to be particularly strong within the model of 'transformational leadership'. A transformational leader inspires the followers to exceed the expected performance by 'empowering' them and raising their levels of commitment and work satisfaction (Bass 1985, 1998). Developed and evaluated as highly effective in military settings, the model has recently been transferred to other settings (Avolio and Yammarino 2002; Bass and Riggio 2006). Transformational leaders are often endowed with sovereign power, making them 'fit to rule the rest':

> *Transformational leaders* demonstrate the elixir of human understanding ... [they] can reform organizations in magic ways. Leaders using this style create an environment where every person is empowered to fulfill his or her highest needs and becomes a member of a productive learning community.
>
> (Hoyle 2006: 2)

The myth of 'spectacular' solutions diminishes the importance of ordinary everyday practice and many mundane local interactions which, over time, do bring about profound change, for good or ill. That the 'magic' solutions of a transformational leader may or may not be taken up by the followers could be because the followers may not share the leader's rationale for 'spectacular' solutions in the first place. Which brings us to the third myth often called upon in order to justify policies for transforming education: the myth of perpetual crisis.

As exemplified by the Coalition government's *Case for Change* (DfE 2010c: 3), the narrative of perpetual crisis is based on the perceived deficiencies within the current system, as well as radical 'shifts in technology and the global economy'. The sense of urgency is evoked through references to governments across the world responding to the 'new economic reality' of globalisation by reforming their education systems in order to train a highly skilled competitive workforce. Education is thus being made accountable for the country's economic competitiveness and tasked not just with performing to standards, but also with 'outperforming' others. To support the notion of outperformance, the *Case for Change* cites President Obama, who stated that 'the countries that out-teach us today will out-compete us tomorrow' (DfE 2010c: 4). In Ovid's terms, the myth of perpetual crisis seems to originate in a particular kind of deficiency – the fact that a 'creature of a more exalted kind' is 'wanting yet' – a highly skilled individual fit to continually outperform the rest.

There are, however, some notable contradictions in the narratives of perpetual crisis. The discourse of crisis and the resulting 'urgent' need to reform education started in the UK a few decades ago and intensified in the 1990s, leading to what some researchers labelled the 'policy hysteria'. As pointed out by Stronach and MacLure (1997: 88), the 'policy hysteria' refers to a flux of successive waves of reforms, often inconsistent and incoherent, 'designed to respond to crises that were formulated in terms more imaginary than real . . . and so destined to fail'. For example, in the eight years between 1996 and 2004, 459 policy documents related to teaching primary literacy were issued, averaging more than one document every week (Hofkins and Northen 2009). As argued by Ball (2013: 4), 'the pressures and expectations and ferment of policy are enormous'. It is also probable that the proliferation of often incoherent policies has contributed to the mood of perpetual crisis, rather than providing a remedy for the supposed deficiencies of the system (Barker 2010). This can be exemplified by the striking lack of logic in the DfES (2004: 9) claim to a 'real', 'quick' success of their policies and the resulting need for even more policies, 'so we have to sustain progress, with new and more radical reforms'. Despite the myth of 'spectacular' new solutions, the policy discourse seems to be stuck on incremental improvement in pupil test scores as the key lever of reform. Ironically, the 'policy hysteria' has so far failed to ensure a higher PISA ranking for England (OECD 2014b). As schools are tasked with pursuing, often 'unattainable', continuous improvement in examination results (Barker 2010: 100) and implementing 'fast policies', a paradoxical situation has emerged. Here teachers and leaders 'are expected to be familiar with, and able to enact, multiple (and sometimes contradictory) policies that are planned for them by others and they are held accountable for' (Ball *et al.* 2012: 9).

This tendency to rely on myths may be explained in terms of their usefulness in justifying and legitimating policies for transforming education. As pointed out by Barthes (2000: 170), such usefulness is predicated on the way in which myth 'empties reality', how it 'abolishes the complexity of human acts' and 'gives them the simplicity of essences'. For example, the myth of 'spectacular' solutions eclipses all possible alternatives to economic efficiency and resorts to a simplistic model of transformational leadership to reform organisations into 'productive' learning communities. The complex organisational reality that encompasses power relations, politics and ideology, dynamic of inclusion and exclusion, conflict, compliance and resistance has thus been 'emptied' and replaced with a simple 'essence' of 'transformation'. As Barthes points out, as soon as the mythical discourse has been spoken or written, it is 'frozen into something natural: it is not read as a motive, but a reason' (p. 154). Consequently, to be able to understand a myth requires an opposite reading – not for a reason for the message conveyed in a myth, but a motive underpinning the message. This point will be developed further in Chapter 6.

'Self-transforming' education and complex responsive processes theory

In the light of myth-making tendencies and negative consequences of the mainstream approaches to transforming education outlined above, this book turns to an alternative meaning of 'transformation'. George Herbert Mead's (1956) theory of social change defines transformation as a profound, progressive change in the minds of individuals and the quality of social relations. This understanding is different from the mainstream meanings in that transformation here denotes a profound change in 'nature' (and not just 'form' or 'appearance'), which affects how we think and perceive the world and others and how we relate to each other. It is progressive in the sense that we can speak of transformation when the quality of social relations has improved, based on individuals' increasing ability to 'enter into the attitude of others' (Mead 1956: 40). The recognition of the perspectives of others provides the conditions for the emergence of qualitatively different social relations, when our decisions and actions cease to be based solely on what they mean for us. The meaning of our actions needs to be continually discerned anew through everyday empathetic connection to others (Honneth 1995). Mead's account opens an alternative understanding of a 'self-transforming' change that arises from *within* educational practice and involves profound changes in our 'selves'.

Contrary to Ovid's myth of creation, this transformative process cannot be 'cracked once and for all' and 'engineered' by a policymaker or another 'spectacular' leader endowed with godlike insight and power, but rather emerges from many ordinary local interactions. Also unlike in the myth of creation and its iterations in the successive waves of the 'policy hysteria', transformation emerges within long timeframes, leaving us always in the midst of the processes of continuity and change. Consequently, an assumption that it is possible to create a modern education system through a wholesale adoption of a new model, as assumed by the 'new orthodoxy', is both misleading and potentially damaging, for it is the traditional ways of working that provide us with a system of meaning and a foundation from which novel approaches may emerge.

Mead's insights have been taken up by complex responsive processes theory (Griffin 2002; Shaw 2002; Stacey 2007, 2010, 2012; Mowles 2011, 2015), which provides the conceptual framework for the analyses presented in this book and is discussed in detail in Chapter 3. The key insight of complex responsive processes theory in relation to our discussion so far is that a 'global order arises from, but is not reducible to, the sum of all activity that comprises interacting agents acting locally' (Mowles 2014: 166). Human interaction is always complex, emergent and essentially unpredictable, especially in the long term. Because the meaning of policies arises in the school leaders' and teachers' responses, policymakers are unable to predetermine in advance or fully control the enactment[7] of their policies. This, in turn, calls for an alternative to the command and control approach to policy: by paying attention to what 'transforming' education means for the 'local' school and 'real' people (rather than the 'cardboard cut-out' adults and the UPN children), policymakers could contribute to creating conditions for novel understandings of 'modern' education to emerge.

In paying attention to the processes that contribute to continuity and change, complex responsive processes theory provides understandings that transcend the mainstream approaches to transforming education characteristic of the GERM (Sahlberg 2011). The generative potential of these understandings is rooted in the process of emergence described above. The theory itself is an 'emergent project', based on the continuing work of Ralph Stacey and his colleagues and aimed at developing a 'whole spectrum of theories of human organization' (Griffin 2002: x). This aim has been realised through making transdisciplinary connections between the complexity sciences and sociological, psychological and philosophical insights of writers who provide important conceptual resources for understanding the complexities of human relating. These writers include Mead (1934, 1956), Elias (1978, 1991), MacIntyre (1985), Honneth (1995, 2006) and Arendt (1998) among others and are drawn upon throughout this book. Hence, complex responsive processes theory offers a rich body of knowledge and insight that can illuminate policy and practice in novel ways and 'complexify' the simple (and potentially misleading) blueprints for creating 'evidence-based', 'knowledge-rich' education systems. A modern education system cannot be 'evidence-based' if its policies are legitimated through myths. It cannot be 'knowledge-rich' if it myopically focuses on particular disciplines and methodologies, such as those privileged by the TALIS programme, as if they provided the final, and uncontested, answers. An education system cannot be transformed in novel, genuinely progressive ways through the application of standardised levers that ignore the complex realities of everyday interactions among 'real', embodied children, women and men who learn and work in the 'local' school. The remainder of Chapter 1 outlines the scope and structure of this book, highlighting the distinctive insights into the debates on transforming education offered by complex responsive processes theory.

The scope and structure of this book

This book is divided into three parts. Part 1, *The universe of complexity thinking* (Chapters 1–4), is primarily concerned with explaining complexity theory and its research methodology. Part 2, *'Global' policies and local interactions* (Chapters 5–7), examines education policies and notions of leadership and presents evidence of their enactment in two case study schools. Part 3, *Complex responsive processes theory and educational ends* (Chapters 8 and 9), considers alternative possibilities for educational transformation.

Taking each chapter in turn, Chapter 2 explains the distinction between the 'sciences of certainty' and the 'complexity sciences' and how they may affect approaches to policymaking and policy enactment. The 'sciences of certainty' assume a mechanistic social reality, viewing change as predictable and control maintained on the basis of simple 'if . . . then . . .' causality. In the context of technological invention, the 'sciences of certainty' are able to produce a controlled effect. For example, the complicated mechanism of a jet engine is made up of parts that are designed and controlled to work in highly predictable ways. The whole is made to work by making all component parts work, so that the overall effect is a predictable total of the sum of the parts. The 'complexity sciences' reveal the universe beyond the mechanistic Newtonian world, in which such reductive analyses and universal laws no longer apply, neither do the distinctions between subject/object, fact/value, matter/meaning, knowledge/knower or nature/culture. In doing so, the 'complexity sciences' provide an authoritative theoretical platform for questioning the myth of control and its use in legitimating the 'new orthodoxy' discussed above. Some readers may find parts of Chapter 2 on the discussion of the 'complexity sciences' challenging. For example, the section entitled *In dialogue with nature and the 'quantum revolution'* provides a detailed overview of some important developments within quantum physics and the insights they offer into the 'nature of nature' and the nature of knowledge (Barad 2007). This section may be of particular interest to the more scientifically inclined reader. It may, however, be skipped by readers who wish to proceed directly to the discussion of distinctive meanings of transforming education offered by the 'sciences of certainty' and the 'complexity sciences'.

Chapter 3 guides the reader into the world of complex responsive processes to explain how transformation emerges from local interactions among interdependent (mutually dependent) people involved in their everyday activities and conversations. Contrary to step-by-step rules for policy implementation and idealised leadership models, local interactions in organisations include 'daily conversation, gossip, political negotiations, power plays, acts of resistance and pursuit of personal agendas' (Stacey 2010: 124). This means that, in trying to introduce change, we need to constantly engage in negotiations with the intentions and actions of others. In explaining continuity and change, complex responsive processes theory embraces the 'complexity sciences' as well as sociological, philosophical and psychological knowledge illuminating the complexities of human organising. This book, therefore, seeks to contribute rich, transdisciplinary understandings of complex responsive processes theory to the existing knowledge and research in the areas of 'policy sociology' (Ball 1997, 2013), policy studies (Rizvi and Lingard 2010) and critical studies in educational leadership (Thomson *et al.* 2014).

As we shall see in Chapter 4, the book also offers examples of how empirical research can be conducted within the new, 'emerging' research paradigm of complexity (Cohen *et al.* 2011: 28; Fenwick *et al.* 2011). The 'complexity sciences' underline holistic research focused on details that elude the measurement and simplification characteristic of the evidence-based approaches embraced by the TALIS and SESI research. The research methodology aligned with complex responsive processes theory highlights the importance of local patterns of conversation as simultaneously expressing and enacting change in schools and classrooms. The chapter also considers the opportunities offered by case study research for deeper understandings of complex educational settings and processes. This makes case studies relevant and significant in other contexts of a similar nature, as well as in improving 'the soundness of future policy decisions' (Simons 2009: 170).

The next four chapters draw on the empirical data to shed some light on 'local' responses to 'global' policies. The focus of Chapter 5 is on the accounts of the enactment of the *National Strategies* for literacy and numeracy (DfEE 1998, 1999) narrated by teachers, leaders and other practitioners working in two case study schools. Designed and disseminated as a 'spectacular' solution, the *National Strategies* promised to 'crack' the problem of low standards by delivering a significant rise in pupil literacy and numeracy test results by 2002. While most practitioners who participated in the research espoused the belief that 'standards have risen', some of them experienced significant dissonance between their perceptions of policy aims and how they coped, not always successfully, with an over-prescriptive curriculum and accompanying resources. The chapter concludes with accounts of Ofsted inspections, which highlight the asymmetrical power relations between inspectors and practitioners and the 'game playing' nature of these encounters.

Chapter 6 examines education reform in the context of the neoliberal ideology, which continued to shape government policy in England during the Coalition government 2010–2015. The myth of perpetual crisis refers to the now well-established 'global' orthodoxy that weaknesses in national economic performance are inextricably bound up with weaknesses in educational performance, hence government preoccupation with high-stakes tests and international comparisons. In this context, school leaders and teachers in the case study schools constantly re-ordered their priorities in response to what they perceived as government 'tinkering'. The case study findings open up a complex world in which practitioners struggle to assimilate changes that frequently clash with their personal identities as educational professionals.

Chapter 7 explores the contrast between policymakers' constructs of school leadership and the research participants' understandings of leadership in everyday practice. In government narratives, school leaders have become idealised as Chief Executive Officers or entrepreneurial individuals who 'inspire' and 'empower' teachers and pupils to excel. In contrast, the testimonies of practitioners highlighted the difficulties of leading school improvement in a climate of continuous change and uncertainty. *Management by values* receives particular attention here, as policymakers' values of excellence and competitiveness are mediated by the complex professional identities of school leaders and their teams. The challenge for the educational leader is to understand the complex nature of values and the ethical limits to deploying values in an idealised, monolithic culture of excellence.

Chapter 8 presents insights into the relationship between power, ethics and responsibility offered by complex responsive processes theory. The distinctive insights into power relations are premised here on the complexity concept of interdependence (mutual dependence). 'Power figurations' among interdependent humans are based on mutual need rather than the will to control. The case study findings reveal a tension between the normative modus operandi imposed on schools by policy stipulations and the capacity of practitioners to preserve teacher–child relations as mutual and essentially human. In a data-driven target culture, the *child-learner* is being reconstructed as a *child-worker*, divorced from intrinsic modes of learning and misrecognised as an abstract statistic. The ethical loss entailed in this reconstruction stems from prioritising accountability for school performance statistics over responsibility for 'real' children.

Chapter 9 draws together the main themes and research findings and considers them in relation to contested meanings of 'transformation'. It revisits the myths presented in the book to emphasise the ways in which they deny the complexity of existence and create ideological accounts of reality, at the same time disowning ideology (Barthes 2000). The enduring appeal of myth rests on its power to make the meaning and purpose of our lives intelligible. Paradoxically, however, the presence of myth in our culture is also rooted in its power to impose a particular normative order onto the world. The 'mythical intent' behind transforming education into a 'knowledge industry' seeks to affirm economic efficiencies as the ultimate purpose of 'modern' education. While economic means and ends have become central to the grand narrative of the GERM, education has its own beginnings and ends. These educational beginnings and ends, however, may emerge only after the mythical content and intent of transforming education into a global 'knowledge industry' has been demystified.

Notes

1   The term 'policymakers' is used in this book to refer to a fluid network of agencies and individuals who design or influence education policy. As Gunter and Forrester (2009) point out, in the English context policymakers include ministers and other officials in the Department for Education (DfE), think tanks, the government-funded National College for Teaching and Leadership (NCTL), private-sector consultants as well as some advisors from universities, local government and schools.
2   This book concentrates on the manifestations of the global policy trends for 'transforming' education in the primary school context. However, complex responsive processes theory explanations of the interplay between the local and the global may be applicable to other education sectors.
3   The Academies Programme was announced by the New Labour in 2000 and aimed at improving education through more diverse provision, parental choice and voice, as well as 'positive' influence of private sponsors (Gunter 2011). It was accelerated by the Coalition, by often forcing schools to convert to academy status against the wishes of the school and the parents (Ball 2013). The Coalition also funded new 'free schools', based on the Swedish and American models. Like academies, free

schools are independent of Local Authority control, directly accountable to the Secretary of State for Education and not required to abide by the National Curriculum and national agreements on the working conditions for teachers. They 'could' be run for profit in the future (Eaton 2012).
4   The term 'practitioners' is used in this book to refer to adults working in schools in teaching, leadership, pupil support and administrative roles.
5   In the UK context, the 'local' school is a state school, serving the local community. Although the book will at times refer to UK policy and context, its main focus on the English setting reflects the location of two case study schools from which the empirical data are drawn. The aim here is to address the processes which connect the global and the local, rather than differences in education policy and practice in Scotland, Wales, Northern Ireland and England.
6   Within the English education system, most state primary and secondary schools are directly accountable to their local council (the Local Authority), while the DfE, led by the Secretary of State for Education (Education Secretary), provides legislation to be implemented by schools in the form of policies (set out in White Papers and Education Acts) and strategies (for example the *National Literacy Strategy* and the *National Numeracy Strategy*).
7   The distinction between policy 'implementation' and 'enactment' in this book reflects that made by Ball *et al.* (2012: 3–4), who define policy enactment as complex interactions 'between diverse actors, texts, talk, technology and objects (artefacts) which constitute ongoing responses to policy . . . There are minute and mundane negotiations and translations which go on . . . [p]olicy is not 'done at one point in time; in our schools it is always in the process of "becoming"'. Policy enactment thus defined resonates with the core concepts of complex responsive processes theory of continuity and change as emergent from local interactions (Chapter 3).

References

Arendt, H. 1998. *The Human Condition* (2nd edn). Chicago, IL and London: The Chicago University Press.

Arnold, R. 2004. *Transforming Secondary Education: The Beacon Council Scheme: Round 4*. Slough: National Foundation for Educational Research.

Avolio, B.J. and Yammarino, F.J. (eds) 2002. *Transformational and Charismatic Leadership: The Road Ahead*. Boston, MA: JAI.

Ball, S.J. 1997. Policy sociology and critical social research: A personal review of recent education policy and policy research, *British Educational Research Journal*, 23(3): 257–274.

Ball, S.J. 2012. *Global Education Inc.: New Policy Networks and the Neo-Liberal Imaginary*. London and New York: Routledge.

Ball, S.J. 2013. *The Education Debate* (2nd edn). Bristol: The Policy Press.

Ball, S.J., Maguire, M. and Braun, A. 2012. *How Schools Do Policy: Policy Enactments in Secondary Schools*. London and New York: Routledge.

Barad, K. 2007. *Meeting the Universe Halfway: Quantum Physics and the Entanglement of Matter and Meaning*. Durham, NC and London: Duke University Press.

Barker, B. 2010. *The Pendulum Swings: Transforming School Reform*. Stoke on Trent: Trentham Books.

Barthes, R. 2000. *Mythologies*. (A. Levers, Trans.). London: Vintage Books.

Bass, B.M. 1985. *Leadership and Performance Beyond Expectations*. New York: Free Press.

Bass, B.M. 1998. *Transformational Leadership: Industrial, Military, and Educational Impact.* Mahway, NJ: Lawrence Erlbaum Associates.
Bass, B.M. and Riggio, R.E. 2006. *Transformational Leadership* (2nd edn). Mahwah, New Jersey: Lawrence Erlbaum Associates.
Bates, A. 2013. Transcending systems thinking in education reform: Implications for policy-makers and school leaders, *Journal of Education Policy*, 28(1): 38–54.
Cabinet Office Strategy Unit. 2009. *Unleashing Aspiration: The Final Report of the Panel on Fair Access to the Professions.* London: Crown Copyright.
Cohen, L., Manion, L. and Morrison, K. 2011. *Research Methods in Education* (7th edn). Abingdon: Routledge.
DfE. 2010a. *The Importance of Teaching: The Schools White Paper 2010.* Available at: www.ictliteracy.info/rf.pdf/Schools-White-Paper2010.pdf (accessed 15 March 2012).
DfE. 2010b. *Unique Pupil Numbers (UPNs) – Policy and Practice: Guidance for Local Authorities and Schools.* Available at: www.education.gov.uk/researchandstatistics/datatdatam/upn/a0064607/upn-policy-and-practice-guidance (accessed 27 August 2012).
DfE. 2010c. *The Case for Change.* London: Crown Copyright.
DfEE. 1998. *The National Literacy Strategy: Framework for Teaching.* London: DfEE.
DfEE. 1999. *The National Numeracy Strategy: Framework for Teaching Mathematics.* London: DfEE.
DfES. 2003. *A New Specialist System: Transforming Secondary Education.* London: DfES.
DfES. 2004. *Five Year Strategy for Children and Learners.* Norwich: The Stationery Office.
Eaton, G. 2012. Gove reveals plan for profit-making schools. *New Statesman*, 29 May. Available at: www.newstatesman.com/blogs/staggers/2012/05/gove-reveals-plan-profit-making-schools (accessed 20 September 2013).
Elias, N. 1978. *What Is Sociology?* New York: Columbia University Press.
Elias, N. 1991. *The Symbol Theory.* London: Sage.
Fenwick, T., Edwards, R. and Sawchuk, P. 2011. *Emerging Approaches to Educational Research: Tracing the Sociomaterial.* London and New York: Routledge.
Griffin, D. 2002. *The Emergence of Leadership: Linking Self-Organisation and Ethics.* London and New York: Routledge.
Gunter, H.M. 2004. Labels and labelling in the field of educational leadership, *Discourse: Studies in the Cultural Politics of Education*, 25(1): 21–41.
Gunter, H.M. 2007. Remodelling the school workforce in England: A study in tyranny, *Journal of Critical Education Policy Studies*, 5(1): 73–93.
Gunter, H.M. (ed.) 2011. *The State and Education Policy: The Academies Programme.* London: Continuum.
Gunter, H.M. and Forrester, G. 2009. School leadership and education policy-making in England, *Policy Studies*, 30(5): 495–511.
Hargreaves, A. and Shirley, D. 2009. *The Fourth Way: The Inspiring Future for Educational Change.* Thousand Oaks, CA: Corwin.
Hill, R. and Matthews, P. 2010. *Schools Leading Schools II: The Growing Impact of National Leaders of Education.* Nottingham: National College Publishing.
Hofkins, D. and Northen, S. (eds) 2009. *Introducing the Cambridge Primary Review.* Cambridge: University of Cambridge.
Honneth, A. 1995. *The Struggle for Recognition: The Moral Grammar of Social Conflicts* (J. Anderson, Trans.). Cambridge: Polity Press.

Honneth, A. 2006. *Reification: A Recognition-Theoretical View*. Available at: http://tannerlectures.utah.edu/lecture-library.php#h (accessed 14 March 2014).

Hoyle, J.R. 2006. 'Leadership Styles'. In English F. (ed.) *Encyclopedia of Educational Leadership and Administration*. Thousand Oaks, CA: Sage, 595–598. Sage Reference Online.

Hursh, D. 2008. *High-Stakes Testing and the Decline of Teaching and Learning: The Real Crisis in Education*. Lanham, MD: Rowman & Littlefield.

Hursh, D. 2013. Raising the stakes: High-stakes testing and the attack on public education in New York, *Journal of Education Policy*, 28(5): 574–588.

Lawn, M. 2011. Governing through data in English education, *Education Enquiry*, 2(2): 277–288.

LLUK. 2008. *Workforce Strategy for the Further Education Sector in England, 2007–2012: Transforming the Future FE Workforce to Become a Force for Change*. Available at: http://webarchive.nationalarchives.gov.uk/20081007160501/http://lluk.org/fe-workforce-strategy.htm (accessed 20 November 2014).

MacIntyre, A. 1985. *After Virtue: A Study in Moral Theory* (2nd edn). London: Bloomsbury.

Mead, G.H. 1934. *Mind, Self, and Society from the Standpoint of a Social Behaviourist*. Chicago, IL and London: The University of Chicago Press.

Mead, G.H. 1956. *On Social Psychology*. Chicago, IL: Chicago University Press.

Mowles, C. 2011. *Rethinking Management: Radical Insights from the Complexity Sciences*. Farnham: Gower.

Mowles, C. 2014. Complex, but not quite complex enough: The turn to the complexity sciences in evaluation scholarship, *Evaluation*, 20(2): 160–175.

Mowles, C. 2015. *Managing in Uncertainty: Complexity and the Paradoxes of Everyday Organizational Life*. London and New York: Routledge.

NCSL. 2011. *National Professional Qualification for Headship Competency Framework*. Available at: www.gov.uk/government/uploads/system/uploads/attachment_data/file/284573/npqh-competency-framework.pdf (accessed 5 May 2014).

OECD. 2009. *Creating Effective Teaching and Learning Environments: First Results from TALIS*, TALIS, OECD Publishing. Available at: http://dx.doi.org/10.1787/9789264068780-en (accessed 28 April 2014).

OECD. 2013. *Teaching and Learning International Survey TALIS 2013: Conceptual Framework*. Available at: www.oecd.org/edu/school/TALIS%20Conceptual%20Framework_FINAL.pdf (accessed 7 May 2015).

OECD. 2014a. *TALIS 2013 Results: An International Perspective on Teaching and Learning*, TALIS, OECD Publishing. Available at: http://dx.doi.org/10.1787/9789264196261-en (accessed 7 May 2015).

OECD. 2014b. *PISA 2012 Results in Focus: What 15-Year-Olds Know and What They Can Do with What They Know*. Available at: www.oecd.org/pisa/keyfindings/pisa-2012-results-overview.pdf (accessed 7 May 2015).

Ouston, J. 2003. 'School Effectiveness and School Improvement: Critique of a Movement'. In Preedy, M., Bennett, N. and Wise, C. (eds) *Strategic Leadership and Educational Improvement*. London: Sage, 252–264.

Ovid. AD8/1998. *Metamorphoses* (J. Dryden, *et al.*, Trans., S. Garth, ed.). Ware: Wordsworth Editions Limited.

Oxford English Dictionary. 2014. Available at: www.oed.com (accessed 13 April 2015).

Polesel, J., Rice, S. and N. Dulfer. 2014. The impact of high-stakes testing on curriculum and pedagogy: A teacher perspective from Australia, *Journal of Education Policy*, 29(5): 640–657.

Ravitch, D. 2010. *The Death and Life of the Great American School System. How Testing and Choice are Undermining Education*. New York: Basic Books.

Rizvi, F. and Lingard, B. 2010. *Globalizing Education Policy*. Abingdon: Routledge.

Sahlberg, P. 2004. Teaching and globalisation, *Managing Global Transitions*, 2(1): 65–83.

Sahlberg, P. 2011. *Finnish Lessons: What Can the World Learn from Educational Change in Finland?* New York and London: Teachers College.

Shaw, P. 2002. *Changing Conversations in Organizations: A Complexity Approach to Change*. London: Routledge.

Simons, H. 2009. *Case Study Research in Practice*. London: Sage Publications.

Stacey, R.D. 2007. *Strategic Management and Organisational Dynamics: The Challenge of Complexity* (5th edn). Harlow: Pearson Education Limited.

Stacey, R.D. 2010. *Complexity and Organisational Reality: Uncertainty and the Need to Rethink Management after the Collapse of Investment Capitalism* (2nd edn). London: Routledge.

Stacey, R. 2012. *Tools and Techniques of Leadership and Management*. Abingdon: Routledge.

Stronach, I. and MacLure, M. 1997. *Educational Research Undone: The Postmodern Embrace*. Buckingham: Open University Press.

Thomson, P., Gunter, H. and Blackmore, J. 2014. 'Series Foreword'. In Gunter, H.M. *Educational Leadership and Hannah Arendt*. London and New York: Routledge, vi–xii.

Wallace, M. and Tomlinson, M. 2012. 'Contextualizing Leader Dynamics: How Public Service Leaders Endeavour to Build Influence'. In Preedy, M., Bennett, N. and Wise, C. (eds) *Educational Leadership: Context, Strategy and Collaboration*. Milton Keynes: The Open University, 145–159.

Chapter 2

(Un)certainty and the myth of control

> and all things were at odds with one another,
> for in a single mass cold strove with warm,
> wet was opposed to dry and soft to hard,
> and weightlessness to matter having weight.
> Some god (or kinder nature) settled this
> dispute by separating earth from heaven,
> and then by separating sea from earth
> and fluid aether from the denser air;
> and after these were separated out
> and liberated from the primal heap,
> he bound the disentangled elements
> each in its place and all in harmony.
>
> (Ovid AD8/2004: 15–16)

In this chapter, we will consider the distinction between the 'sciences of certainty' and the 'complexity sciences' and the different meanings they bring to bear on policymaking and school leadership. As explained in Chapter 1, the 'new orthodoxy' for achieving educational transformation relies on reforms aimed at raising standards measured against international benchmarks. The science of international comparisons tends to utilise an 'apparatus' consisting of research tools such as the TALIS. The TALIS researchers assert that their survey provides a 'groundbreaking instrument' enabling 'countries to see their own teaching profession in the light of what other countries show can be achieved' (OECD 2009: 3). As we shall see later, comparative analyses encourage a particular way of 'seeing' school teachers and leaders, simultaneously obscuring other perspectives from view. They are aligned with the 'sciences of certainty', which focus scientific enquiry on practical application and control of the natural and social worlds and are an expression of instrumental rationality.

The desire for control seems to be deeply ingrained in Western culture. As suggested in the contemporary translation of Ovid's myth of creation cited above, control is premised on the binary logic of separating and categorising: 'disentangling' elements from the chaotic disorder of the 'primal heap'. This mythical blueprint for making the world a better-ordered place is also a recurring theme in education policy. As discussed below, the roots of the 'new orthodoxy' in the 'sciences of certainty' lead to reductive management techniques, which may be 'analytical, concrete, logical, convincing and wrong' (Mowles 2011: 16). The 'complexity sciences' call into question issues of control and challenge the 'complexity reduction' accompanying the political desire for 'making education into a perfectly controllable and perfectly predictable technology' (Osberg and Biesta 2010: 1). They also focus on the entanglement of subject/object, fact/value, matter/meaning, knowledge/knower and nature/culture (Barad 2007). The chapter begins by introducing the distinction between the 'sciences of certainty' and the 'complexity sciences'. This is followed by a discussion of the key assumptions made by the 'sciences of certainty' and the 'complexity sciences' in relation to the nature of the world (ontology), the nature of knowledge (epistemology) and their implications for understanding educational change (Table 2.1). Particular emphasis is placed on how complexity understandings of uncertainty, the nature of knowledge and change over time challenge the myth of control at the heart of the 'new orthodoxy' for transforming education.

The 'sciences of certainty' and the 'complexity sciences'

By the 'sciences of certainty', Stacey (2010) refers to the 'classic' natural sciences first developed in the sixteenth and seventeenth centuries by Galileo and Newton in parallel with the rationalist philosophical tradition advanced by Descartes. These founding figures of the Enlightenment, or the 'age of reason', maintained the primacy of reason in discovering universal truths about an objectively knowable reality. Accordingly, the natural scientific method advanced in the eighteen and nineteenth centuries, relies on careful observation and formulation of hypotheses. The hypotheses are tested empirically and, when proved to be valid, presented in the form of mathematical formulae. For example, the laws of classical Newtonian mechanics are expressed as differential equations that explain rates of change over time and can, therefore, be applied to predicting regularities (Stewart 1997). These regularities can then be used for controlling the 'passive nature' (Prigogine 1996: 12), analogous to the God-shaped order in Ovid's myth. Many universal laws of the Newtonian world 'work' when important features of the environment are disregarded, 'separated out' and then re-ordered, 'each in its place and all in harmony'.

Take, for example, the equation for the motion of a pendulum: $T = 2\pi \sqrt{L/g}$, where 'T' denotes the time taken for a full swing, 'L' the length of string and 'π' and 'g' are constant values. This is a linear equation that shows the relationship between a cause – the length of string – and its perfectly predictable effect – the time it takes the pendulum to complete a full swing. The regularity of the swing, first calculated by Galileo, makes the pendulum an accurate timekeeper and was later applied by Newton and other scientists to measure local gravitational acceleration (Nelson and Olsson 1985). However, the equation is valid only for small angles and excludes such conditions affecting the motion of the pendulum as the friction at the pivot and air resistance. Similarly, many other laws of the sciences of certainty 'work' when two elements are investigated in isolation from others, or when complexity is reduced to small units and controlled in mechanistic, highly technical ways:

> In technology we don't so much understand the universe as build tiny universes of our own, which are so simple that we can make them do what we want. The whole object of technology is to produce a controlled effect in given circumstances. We *make* our machines so that they will behave deterministically.
>
> (Stewart 1997: 36)

Stewart emphasises that the technological paradigm does not apply to many natural phenomena and, above all, to the behaviour of people. Since 'Newton could not predict the behaviour of three balls, could Marx predict that of three people?' (p. 33). The essential unpredictability of the consequences of the collective activities of diverse social groups is demonstrated by the global credit crunch of 2008. For example, Friedman (2009: 152) argues that the complex causes leading to the collapse of the financial sector in the United States and globally were extremely difficult to predict and can best be discerned 'with the luxury of hindsight'. One of the key causes identified by a number of commentators was an increase in the lending of subprime mortgages in the context of increasingly lax mortgage underwriting (Jordan and Jain 2009; MacKenzie 2011). However, there were also other contributing causes, in particular weak regulation leading to a large-scale sidelining of 'important gatekeepers', combined with other factors that eventually magnified the system's 'calamitous mortgage related losses' (MacKenzie 2011: 1778). In popular understandings of chaos theory, the credit crunch illustrates the 'butterfly effect', whereby a small change in initial local conditions, such as the flapping of butterfly wings in Brazil, may set off a chain of events leading to a large-scale phenomenon, such as a tornado in Texas.

As noted by Smith and Jenks (2006: 5), however, thinking about 'a small flap here' as the cause of 'an almighty force elsewhere' implies a simple cause-simple effect, or a reduction of complex non-linear instability of global weather systems to linear causality. As Smith and Jenks put it, it is the number of variables, interactions and possibilities that contribute to the difficulty to predict, 'not some magical magnifier' (p. 5). The key point here is that, in the context of human organising, uncertainty does not just entail an inability to reliably predict the future. As noted by Stacey (2010: 3), it also means that 'is it not at all clear what is currently going on and even what happened some time ago is open to many interpretations'. The unpredictability of complex dynamics emergent within complex systems is a key focus of study in the 'complexity sciences'.

The 'complexity sciences' are termed variously as 'complexity theory' (Mason 2008; Osberg and Biesta 2010; Fenwick *et al.* 2011), 'complexity thinking' (Davis and Sumara 2006) or the 'sciences of uncertainty' (Stacey 2010). Stacey's (2010) reference to the 'complexity sciences' emphasises that there is no single science of complexity but rather a number of disciplines that move away from linear relationships such as those captured in the formula for the swing of the pendulum. They include the physics of dissipative structures (thermodynamics) developed by Prigogine (1996) among others, evolutionary biology (Kauffman 1993; Maturana and Varela 1998), quantum mechanics (Barad 2007) and the new mathematics of chaos (Stewart 1997), which models complex systems dynamics within these disciplines.[1] The complexity sciences challenge the sciences of certainty for failing to account for many phenomena, both natural and social, which emerge as a result of instabilities and irregularities, such as weather patterns, ecosystems and fluctuations in the economy. As pointed out by Stewart, some of the irregular phenomena were not even 'seen' by Newtonian scientists, for example the behaviour of gas particles. In order to explain the seemingly 'chaotic' behaviour of gases, mathematicians ended up with two sets of laws, one for ordered and one for disordered patterns of behaviour – differential equations and statistical calculations, respectively. However, what we perceive as 'chaos' has been defined as 'lawless behaviour governed entirely by law' (Stewart 1997: 12). The mathematics of chaos is able to model what appears to be random or chaotic behaviour by using iteration, a repeated application of the same formula to the output of the previous calculation. In the course of many iterations, small errors or seemingly insignificant differences (often not taken into account by the sciences of certainty) may accumulate to lead to huge differences over time, such as the credit crunch. Because order and chaos are intertwined in subtle yet fundamental ways, Stewart urges caution about the prevalent Western view of the universe as a 'regular clockwork machine' and assumption that 'deterministic equations always lead to regular behaviour' (p. 16).

The belief in a predesigned order, or a universal 'Plan of Creation' is also challenged by the theory of evolution and its reworking by Kauffman (1993: 6), who posits two processes at play in the emergence of biodiversity: Darwinian natural selection and self-organisation. The origins of the great variety of species and the maintenance of order in complex biological systems rely on the spontaneous emergence of order (self-organisation), constrained by natural selection, which in turn yields species able to adapt more successfully to the environment. Another important contribution of Darwin's theory is replacing the study of individuals with the study of populations, whereby 'slight variations ... taking place over a long period of time, can generate evolution at a collective level' (Prigogine 1996: 20). As we shall see below, in contrast to the widespread view of knowledge as an outcome of an individualistic pursuit, the

Table 2.1 Key assumptions of the 'sciences of certainty' and the 'complexity sciences'

	Sciences of certainty	Complexity sciences
View of scientific knowledge	Knowledge as 'outcome': 'discovered' and presented in the form of universal laws	Knowledge as 'process': becoming increasingly complex and interconnected
Assumptions about the scientist	Autonomous, objective 'spectator', independent of the 'apparatus'	Interdependent, entangled in the scientific 'apparatus'
Assumptions about the world (the 'nature of nature')	Made up of objects that are classifiable and divisible to smaller units	Constantly evolving, the total greater than the sum of the parts
Understanding of social and educational change and 'transformation'	Mechanistic, manipulated, leveraged and delivered. Modelled by linear or differential equations where the final outcome is directly related to the initial input	Self-organising, emergent, dependent on iteration within complex conditions. A small error or difference in initial conditions may lead to significant difference in results after many iterations

complexity view of the processes of knowledge creation provides two important insights: first, that whatever knowledge we possess, we owe to others, and second, that there is no 'final truth of the matter, only increasingly diverse ways of interacting in a world that is becoming increasingly complex' (Osberg, Biesta and Cilliers 2008: 213). These and other key assumptions and insights of the complexity sciences crucial to developing an alternative understanding of educational transformation, are summarised in Table 2.1 and discussed in the remainder of this chapter.

The moon as a goddess and a process view of knowledge

Darwin's theory of evolution made a vital contribution to understanding knowledge as a process, challenging the more static, outcome-oriented approach of the sciences of certainty. The sciences of certainty tend to emphasise the products of knowledge creation: information, tools and techniques that are directly applicable to practice. Because they are abstracted from the conditions of their creation, they hide the processes that lie 'at the heart of the most significant episodes of scientific development' (Kuhn 1996:140). In contrast, a more dynamic perspective on knowledge characteristic of the complexity sciences pays attention to science as practice and not just scientific 'facts'. It also emphasises the provisional nature of knowledge. As pointed out by Norbert Elias (1978: 23), there was a time when 'people imagined that the moon was a goddess', while today, many generations later:

we have a more adequate, more realistic idea of the moon. Tomorrow it may be discovered that there are still elements of fantasy in our present idea of the moon, and people may develop a conception of the moon, the solar system and the whole universe still closer to reality than ours.

(p. 23)

Knowledge can thus be seen as never complete and always evolving, especially when we resist the tendency to rely on the relatively short time span of human life as the 'principal frame of reference' (Elias 1991: 30). It is 'the timeframe of humanity' or time distances of a larger order of generations that provide a framework for a more realistic evaluation of what may, in our lifetime, appear to be groundbreaking and finite.

Within the timeframe of humanity, it is possible to see how the natural sciences, philosophy, art, literature and political thought of a given time are closely interwoven as interdependent (mutually dependent) domains of thought and activity. For example, Cartesian rationality emerged in parallel with the sciences of the Enlightenment. Descartes' thought turned to scepticism as a tool for freeing rational enquiry from hitherto largely undisputed compliance with medieval church dogma. The only universal that defied his radical doubt was *'cogito ergo sum'* – 'I think therefore I am'. As pointed out by Descartes (2005: 16), ' "I think therefore I am" was so certain and assured that all the most extravagant suppositions brought forward by the sceptics were incapable of shaking it'. Descartes' world is 'full of "things" with determinate substance, defined and measured in accordance with the principles of mathematics and physics' (Bates 2013: 356–7). This world of 'things' is organised into dualistic categories such as subject-object, mind-matter, nature-culture, emotions-reason. Unprecedented technological progress sprung from a combination of the Cartesian rational-analytical mindset, Newtonian mechanics and mathematical knowledge of the time. Differential equations, used to explain and predict regularities, coexisted with regular rhyme and rhythmic patterns in poetry, as in John Dryden's translation of Ovid's *Metamorphoses* in the epigraph to Chapter 1. In the political sphere, laws of a highly stratified, hierarchical society kept social mobility (and deviation from such 'regularity') to a minimum (Elias 1994). The scientific progress of the 'civilised' Western mind can thus be viewed as rooted in the bedrock of the sciences of certainty.

The evolution of the idea of the moon as a goddess prompts an evaluation of the 'age of reason' in light of some of its long term consequences. Many generations later, a paradoxical darkness of the Enlightenment is becoming apparent. The Cartesian conception of man as '*homo clausus*', a 'little world in himself' who 'finds himself confronted as a thinking ego within his own head by the entire external world' (Elias 1994: 472–3), has been iterated as instrumental rationality, a prevailing mode of confronting our (post)modern world (MacIntyre 1985). The rise of instrumentalist, rational-bureaucratic forms of administration contributed to 'breakdowns of civilisation', such as the Holocaust

(Elias 1996). The industrialisation of the Newtonian clockwork world created a paradigm that promotes economic expansion and leads to environmental pollution, while the recent developments within biogenetic technologies provide opportunities for turning the genetic code of living matter into capital (Braidotti 2013). The origins of these contemporary phenomena are complex and their entangled roots will probably be better understood in the future with the benefit of hindsight. Similarly, it may take the time span of several generations to ascertain the as yet unpredictable long-term consequences of the vision of education as a 'knowledge industry' (OECD 2009). In recognition of complexity and ambiguity, Elias (1991) points out that, through the civilising process started in the 'age of reason', we have got ourselves into 'certain entanglements unknown to less civilised peoples'. However, we also know that:

> these less civilized peoples are for their part often plagued by difficulties and fears from which we no longer suffer, or at least not to the same degree ... It may be that, through clearer understanding, we shall one day succeed in making accessible to more conscious control these processes which today take place in and around us not very differently from natural events, and which we confront as medieval people confronted the forces of nature.
>
> (p.xiv)

As suggested by the paradigm changes discussed below, a clearer understanding may emerge from a recognition of the limits to our knowledge and ability to predict the future.

Paradigms, scientists and their apparatus

Classic natural sciences separate or 'disentangle' the knower (scientist) and the known (knowledge to be discovered) from the apparatus and the socio-political context, analogous to the re-ordering of the 'passive nature' in Ovid's myth of creation. An 'apparatus' comprises instruments of observation, measuring tools and other equipment used by the scientist in the process of experimentation. The view of the scientist prevalent in the sciences of certainty is that of an objective observer, detached (in the physical and ideological sense) from the world (s)he studies (Stacey 2007). As explained in this section, however, the processes of knowledge production are complex and 'messy'. The growth of knowledge within a particular discipline is frequently disrupted or challenged and the uses to which scientific discoveries are put, often ethically controversial.

The traditional view of science was challenged in 1962 by Thomas Kuhn, a physicist, historian and philosopher of science who, with the concept of a paradigm, introduced a new way of looking at the practice of science. In the postscript to the second edition of his controversial book, *The Structure of Scientific Revolutions*, Kuhn (1970: 175) defined the paradigm as 'the entire constellation of beliefs, values, techniques, and so on shared by the members of a given community'. This definition contains two important assumptions: first, that beliefs and values are intertwined with techniques or methods as part of the scientific process and second, that the process is a community endeavour. In tracing the growth of scientific knowledge within the timeframe of humanity, Kuhn noticed that it progressed through a combination of slow, cumulative developments and rapid, 'revolutionary' transformations, when a new paradigm came to replace the existing one:

> when paradigms change, the world itself changes with them. Led by a new paradigm, scientists adopt new instruments and look in new places. Even more important, during revolutions scientists see new and different things when looking with familiar instruments in places they have looked before.
>
> (Kuhn 1996: 111)

One of Kuhn's examples of paradigmatic change is the Copernican revolution. Following the development of the seminal heliocentric model of the Solar System by Copernicus, astronomers 'saw new things when looking at old objects with old instruments' as if they 'lived in a different world' (p. 117).

To come back to the example of the motion of the pendulum discussed above, Kuhn explains how Galileo's work brought a paradigmatic shift in understanding the dynamics of objects falling within the gravitational field of the Earth. Unlike Aristotle, who also investigated the pendulum, but saw it as a falling body, Galileo saw a pendulum as a 'swinging stone', a body that 'almost succeeded in repeating the same motion over and over again ad infinitum' (pp. 119–120), and it is this perception that led him to novel understandings. Based on seeing a body in constrained fall, the Aristotelian investigation of the pendulum focused on the weight of the stone, the height to which it was raised, the time required to come to a rest and the resistance of the medium. Galileo deployed different conceptual categories, developed in medieval times to the study of oscillatory motion. These included measurements of weight, radius, time per swing and angular displacement, eventually leading to the law of the pendulum swing ($T = 2\pi \sqrt{L/g}$) described above. Like the post-Copernican astronomers who 'saw new things when looking at old objects', Galileo saw the pendulum, rather than a falling body, because of the descriptions of oscillatory motion developed by his medieval predecessors. Newton's interpretation of Galileo's work provides an interesting illustration of the limits to knowledge created within a specific paradigm. As pointed out by Kuhn (p. 139), Newton credited Galileo with the discovery of the constant force of gravity acting on falling objects and producing motion proportional to the square of the time, even though Galileo 'said nothing of the sort'. Quite the opposite, his work rarely referred to forces. Kuhn concludes that, by giving Galileo credit for an answer to a question that Galileo's paradigm did not allow to be posed, Newton's interpretation 'hides the effect of a small but revolutionary reformulation in the questions that scientists asked about motion as well as in the answers they felt they were able to accept' (pp. 139–140).

Although Kuhn's concept of a paradigm shift maintains the knower-world-instrument separation, it begins to move towards a less normative view of science. He points out that the science prevalent at any given time, or 'normal science', often discourages debate of 'what makes a particular problem or solution legitimate' (p. 46) and may also suppress 'fundamental novelties because they are necessarily subversive of its basic commitments' (p. 5). Kuhn begins to intertwine beliefs, values, perceptions and historically conditioned conceptual constraints with 'objective' techniques and methods as inextricable elements of scientific enquiry. He thus highlights the complex nature of science as practice. Kuhn's challenge of the view of knowledge as 'outcome' rather than process, is iterated in his critique of science textbooks, which often obliterate the practices at the heart of significant events in the history of scientific development. Instead, textbooks seem to convey to the reader 'what the contemporary scientific community thinks it knows', creating an impression that knowledge is developed by gathering together a series of individual discoveries and inventions (p. 140).

Kuhn's notion of the scientist departs from the self-centred perspective of the Cartesian *homo clausus*. However, his focus on seeing the familiar differently also promulgates a traditional view of knowledge as 'accurate representation' whereby the scientist seeks to discover pre-existing facts about 'passive nature' (Rorty 1979; Barad 2007). In the light of the complexity sciences, a more radical paradigm shift may be required, open to the possibility that the processes of knowledge production may be even more complex and ambiguous. We will, therefore, turn to an important, albeit controversial, reformulation of the 'nature of nature' and the nature of scientific practice by Karen Barad (2003, 2007, 2014), a philosopher with a doctorate in theoretical particle physics. As signalled in Chapter 1, the following section focuses on developments within quantum physics that are revolutionising scientific knowledge, with some profound implications for our understanding of the nature of knowledge. This detailed overview of some of the discoveries and debates contributing to the 'quantum revolution' (Heisenberg 1958) underpins the core argument of the present chapter, relating to the nature of knowledge within the complexity sciences. However, an understanding of the key assumptions of the sciences of certainty and the complexity sciences presented in Table 2.1 above is sufficient as a platform for proceeding to the section *'Education revolution' and the 'science of getting things done'*.

In dialogue with nature and the 'quantum revolution'

Barad (2007) draws on the 'philosophy-physics' of Niels Bohr, awarded the Nobel prize in 1922 for his model of the atom, as well as the post-humanist philosophy of Judith Butler, Donna Haraway and Michel Foucault. Her aim is to develop a framework consistent with Bohr's contribution to the 'quantum revolution' and simultaneously embrace the current philosophical thinking. Barad's work advances our discussion of the distinctions between the sciences of certainty and the complexity sciences by elaborating the nature of knowledge (epistemology) and the 'nature of nature' (ontology). If education is to be transformed by the knowledge about the efficacy of educational practices (OECD 2009), then a number of Barad's insights into the nature and application of knowledge merit careful consideration. We will, therefore, have a closer look at her argument concerning the entanglement of subject/object, knowledge/knower and nature/culture and the resulting inseparability of ontology, epistemology and ethics in the scientific enquiry, spawned by the developments in the field of quantum physics. This will be followed by an alternative definition of scientific 'apparatus' and a performative, as opposed to representationalist, perspective on knowledge. In alignment with the central thesis of the complexity sciences, at the heart of these insights is an understanding of the 'nature of nature', which challenges the view developed by the sciences of certainty. In contrast to the 'passive nature' found in Ovid's myth of creation and iterated in the Newtonian-Cartesian paradigm, the complexity sciences assume that 'the world affects us and our instruments, that there is an interaction between the knower and the known' (Prigogine 1996: 153). By extrapolation, the scientific process may be not so much about discovering nature but 'our dialogue with nature' (Prigogine 1996: 153) in which the materiality of nature and the apparatus actively interact in the scientific process (Barad 2003). This active interaction is exemplified by Bohr's work in the field of quantum physics.

Barad (2007) explains that one of the greatest puzzles faced by Bohr in relation to the 'nature of nature' was the nature of light and matter, with the scientific community split around the question of the wave-particle duality. According to classical physics and Newton's 'corpuscular' theory, light was a particle. Consequently, light would have the measurable properties of any macroscopic moving object: position and momentum. The 'corpuscular' theory was challenged in the nineteenth century by James Clerk Maxwell who posited the wave nature of light. Efforts to determine the 'true ontological nature of light' included passing light through a grating with two-slits, with light forming a 'diffraction pattern' (similar to the patterns made when sea waves combine and overlap on passing through two openings in a breakwater structure) and hence exhibiting wavelike behaviour (Barad 2003: 815). However, when the apparatus is modified, experiments show that light also exhibits particle-like characteristics. The modification of apparatus enables a determination of which of the two slits a given 'particle of light' (a photon) passes through, since particles can only go through a single slit one at a time, unlike waves. The result of conducting this modified experiment is that the diffraction pattern is destroyed, confirming the particle nature of light.

One of the problems linked to the wave-particle duality examined by Bohr and fellow physicists was measuring the position and momentum of subatomic particles (electrons). In this regard, Bohr's mentee Werner Heisenberg upheld the 'uncertainty principle', which stated that the more we know about a particle's position, the less we know about its momentum (Barad 2007). In contrast, Bohr argued for the complementarity explanation: the nature of the particle depended on the apparatus used in experimentation. The 'complementarity principle' undermined the very foundations of Newtonian physics by positing that objects do not have measurement-independent properties, but rather their properties are specific physical (material) arrangements that are 'defined by the circumstances required for their measurement' (Barad 2007: 109). To illustrate the 'complementarity principle', Bohr developed a 'thought experiment' to determine the position and momentum of a moving electron. Because of the physical constraints of the measuring apparatus, the electron's position was determinate (defined meaningfully) when it was measured using a fixed apparatus. In contrast, its momentum could be defined by a moveable apparatus, capable of measuring movement on impact, when the electron was hit by a photon (a light quantum). A photon from a camera flash would bounce off the electron, hit the movable platform, with the movement of the platform being a measure of the electron's momentum. It follows that, unlike in the Newtonian mechanics that measures both the position and momentum of macroscopic (relatively 'large') objects, the values of complementary variables, that is position and momentum, are not 'simultaneously determinate' (p. 118). The implications of Bohr's 'complementarity principle' for understanding the 'nature of nature' as dependent on the measurement are profound:

> every measurement involves a particular choice of apparatus, providing the conditions necessary to give meaning to a particular set of variables, at the exclusion of other essential variables, thereby placing a particular embodied cut delineating the object from the agencies of observation.
>
> (p. 115)

The 'indeterminacy' and 'complementarity' principles represent two distinct perspectives on the wave-particle duality, with implications that go deeper than those of Aristotle's and Galileo's perceptions of the pendulum. While Heisenberg takes issue with what we can or cannot know, or the epistemological question, Bohr is interested in the ontological question about the nature of reality. In arguing that particles 'do not *have* determinate values of position and momentum simultaneously', he calls into question 'an entire tradition in the history of Western metaphysics: the belief that the world is populated with individual things with their own independent sets of determinate properties' (p. 19). More importantly, the properties that become determinate are not controlled by the will of the experimenter but by the specific materiality of the experimental apparatus. Although Heisenberg eventually conceded to Bohr, it was not until the mid-1990s, long after the death of both scientists, that the 'thought experiment' was performed in the laboratory.[2] The Bohr-Heisenberg debate challenges the traditional conception of scientific knowledge as 'accurate representation', where the scientist seeks to discover 'objective', pre-existing facts about independently existing phenomena. The alternative, 'performative' understanding emphasises how knowledge emerges in the process of material engagements with the world of which the scientist is part. The physical-material limitations of the apparatus suggest that nature is not like 'a passive surface awaiting the mark of culture' (Barad 2007: 183). Nature and culture are entangled, as are the subject (the knower) and the object (the known): 'the knower does not stand in a relation of absolute externality to the natural world – there is no such exterior observational point . . . we know because we are *of* the world' (pp. 184–5). This account departs from claims to scientific objectivity premised on a complete detachment of the scientist from the objects of study, to argue for objectivity based on a clear communication of reproducible experiments.

Barad thus takes a step further than Kuhn, who associates a paradigmatic shift to a change in perception, by pointing out that the practice of coming to know may enact a material change in the world and not just a paradigmatic shift:

> Making knowledge is not simply about making facts but about . . . making specific worldly configurations . . . in the sense of materially engaging as part of the world in giving it specific material form.
>
> (p. 91)

An important example of ambiguity in relation to the boundaries between the scientist and the apparatus is illustrated by the Stern-Gerlach experiment (Barad 2007; Friedrich and Herschbach 1998, 2003). Stern and Gerlach sought to find out whether 'space quantisation', a theoretical aspect of Bohr's model of the atom, was achievable in laboratory conditions. The experiment involved passing a beam of silver atoms through a magnetic field to observe their traces on a glass plate. It was designed by Stern, with Gerlach tasked with preparing the apparatus. The material complexity of laboratory experimentation, often left unaccounted for by science textbooks, was compared to a 'Sisyphus-like labour' by Schütz, one of Gerlach's students, who reported unimaginable difficulties of heating up the silver used in the experiment in an oven that could not be fully heated because the seals would melt and where:

> a vacuum . . . had to be produced and maintained for several hours . . . the pumps were made of glass and quite often they broke . . . In that case the several day effort of pumping, required during the warming up and heating of the oven, was lost.
>
> (Friedrich and Herschbach 1998: 179)

The success of the experiment turned out to rely as much as on the 'Sisyphus-like labour' of Gerlach, who eventually managed to make the apparatus work, as on . . . cheap cigars that Stern smoked at the time. On removing the glass plate at the end of the experiment, expecting to see silver traces, to his disappointment, Gerlach observed none and passed the plate to Stern, who had just smoked a cigar. As Stern peered closely at the plate, to his surprise he could see a trace of the silver beam emerge and soon the two scientists realised what had happened. As Stern recounted:

> I was then the equivalent of an assistant professor. My salary was too low to afford good cigars, so I smoked bad cigars. These had a lot of sulfur in them, so my breath on the plate turned the silver into silver sulfide, which is jet black, so easily visible.
> (Friedrich and Herschbach 2003: 5–6)

For Barad, this incident is illustrative of the ambiguous boundary between the scientist and his apparatus, as well as the broader factors that affect the processes of knowledge production. As she points out, in the Stern-Gerlach experiment, the 'bad' cigar with a high sulphur content was crucial, reflecting broader social issues:

> Apparatuses are not static laboratory setups but a dynamic set of open-ended practices . . . the cigar is a . . . 'nodal point' . . . of the workings of other apparatuses, including class, nationalism, economics, and gender, all of which are a part of this Stern-Gerlach apparatus. Which is not to say that all relevant factors figure in the same way or with the same weight . . . Nor is it to suggest that social factors determine the outcome of scientific investigations.
> (p. 167)

The point here is that, in tracing the complex factors that contributed to the scientists' success, we can appreciate how they come to matter in ways that cannot be planned in advance. These broader factors are crucial in the intertwining of the ontology, epistemology and ethics of scientific practice. The developments in quantum physics accentuate the nature of scientific practice, the application of knowledge and their relation to ethics, in the light of the later efforts of Heisenberg and Gerlach to develop an atomic bomb for Germany during the Second World War. As noted by Barad, the crucial question of ethics in this context has been: 'Does one as a physicist have the moral right to work on the practical exploitation of atomic energy?' (p. 7). The question of ethics is revisited below, in the context of knowledge deployed to transforming education.

'Education revolution' and the 'science of getting things done'

The previous discussion reveals that prediction and control are central to the sciences of certainty. Applied to transforming education, the sciences of certainty contribute to comparative data-driven methodologies as well as a range of policy levers and leadership models and tools. Standardised high-stakes tests scores are elevated to 'the ultimate measure of education quality' and utilised for driving up standards through competition and (inter)national comparisons (Ravitch 2014: 19). Educational change is viewed within the certainty approaches as predictable, mechanistic, centrally designed and controlled. Accordingly, educational transformation defined quantitatively as an increase in student test scores, competitive advantage gains and economic efficiencies is emerging as a key theme in the global educational governance (Sahlberg 2011; Meyer and Benavot 2013). Nothing less than an 'education revolution' is promised by policymakers (Barber 1997; Hursh 2005; Lingard 2010), with 'miraculous' policy solutions relying on instrumentalist management tools within the paradigm of measurement and statistical 'meta-data' (Lingard *et al.* 2013: 543). However, a closer scrutiny of the 'emerging science of getting things done' (Barber *et al.* 2011: vii) reveals highly reductive thinking, contestable knowledge claims and significant exclusions.

In 1997, Professor Michael Barber emerged as one of the leading figures in the 'science of getting things done' by purporting to offer the means to achieving an 'education revolution' in England (Barber 1997; Barber and Mourshed 2007; Barber *et al.* 2011). Appointed as Head of the Prime Minister's Delivery Unit (PMDU) in Tony Blair's New Labour government, Barber was the architect of the *National Strategies* (DfEE 1998, 1999), evaluated in Chapter 5. Concerns about the apparatus of targets, standards, inspections and the command and control approach to their enactment have been raised by a number of researchers (Gunter 2008, 2010; Coffield 2011; Ball 2012; Bates 2012). What Barber claimed as 'revolutionary' in his approach to reform is based on a vision of education as an industrial production line, with centrally set targets for individual children and schools. This was the first time that the industrial practice of target setting was transferred to UK education (and other public services) and rolled out nationally (Seddon 2008), together with the National Curriculum for literacy and numeracy, prescribing both content and method (Beard 2000). Target setting was to revolutionise educational practice in a simple linear model borrowed by Barber from two American management consultants, Hammer and Champy (1993). Their re-engineering model for transforming corporations is based on a radical break with tradition to introduce entirely 'new' ways of working. Barber (1997: 249–51) maintained that successful re-engineering relies on overturning assumptions that 'had governed the way [the corporations] worked for generations'. The re-engineering model shows similarities to other change models that gained popularity in the 1990s, at the time when management literature was beginning to notice the complexity sciences and develop 'new' approaches to managing organisations. In contrast to older management approaches, the 'new' models sought to 'de-stabilise' traditional ways of working in a mistaken understanding of the concept of the emergence of novelty at the 'edge of chaos'. According to their proponents, a 'new breed' of 'quantum leaders' thrived on chaos and designed blueprints for 'spontaneous' change, analogous to self-organising change in natural systems (Youngblood 1997). This fundamental misunderstanding of 'designed' emergence still persists in much of mainstream management literature (Stacey 2010).

Barber's approach to 'education revolution' was premised on godlike expertise in 'disentangling elements' in order to 'separate them out' from tradition and 'bind' them into new, policy-dictated commitments. As pointed out by Gunter (2010: 114), his reforms had little consideration for their effects on children's educational experience, which became fully standardised:

> with specifications about what is to be learned, when, and with what required outcomes. The official rationale is that . . . reform must take place with neither debate nor interpretation or, in the words of Michael Barber . . . what is in the mind of the minister must be delivered to the child.

Barber's blueprint for an 'education revolution' was subsequently developed into a 'science' of 'deliverology', with a 'delivery chain' linking ministerial decisions to the everyday experience of a child:

> Supposing that a minister promises . . . to improve standards of reading and writing among eleven-year-olds . . . What happens inside of that eleven-year-old's head is influenced chiefly by her teacher – the first link in the chain; the teacher is influenced by the school's literacy co-ordinator, who in turn is influenced by the headteacher – the second and third links in the chain. The headteacher is influenced by the governors and the local authority, who are influenced by the regional director of the National Literacy Strategy, who answers to the national director of the strategy. He in turn answers to the head of the Standards and Effectiveness Unit in the Department for Education, who answers to the secretary of state. And thus we have established the delivery chain.
>
> (Barber 2008: 85–86)

The apparently simple cause-effect link in the 'delivery chain' between the ministerial intent and what happens 'inside a child's head' is highly reductive and seems to be designed in order to facilitate control, through an 'upwards process of accountability, and a downwards process of direction' (Gunter 2008: 165). Seddon (2008) notes that, as Barber's 'deliverology' evolved, the 'trademark' management consulting tool of the two-by-two grid was added to his toolbox. Labelled as the 'Map of Delivery' (Barber 2008: 82–83), the map consists of a vertical axis denoting 'Boldness of reform' and a horizontal axis denoting 'Quality of execution'. The axes map the following four categories of educational change:

- not bold, low quality ('Status quo')
- not bold, good quality ('Improved outcomes')
- bold reform, low quality ('Controversy without impact')
- bold reform of high quality ('Transformation')

The 'boldness' of reform is linked here to quick results and quality defined as incremental increase in test scores, narrowing 'transformation' to the delivery of targets. As we have seen in Barad's (2007) analysis, measurement processes play a constitutive role in the construction of knowledge and measurement is where meaning and matter meet in a literal sense. As student test scores become the legitimate measure of educational quality, valued as the only important 'facts', traditional educational values are obscured from view. As pointed out by Samier (2006: 126), this approach loses the complexities of power, politics and ethics as well as the richness of human character and, consequently, it is not:

> equipped to deal with questions of freedom, authenticity, responsibility and individual action. An understanding of the human condition ... is suppressed by the very assumptions and methods employed in constructing large scale theories about human behaviour, efficient organisational design and effective management techniques

Based on Barad's analysis of the constitutive role of the scientific apparatus, the 'cut'[3] made in Barber's science of 'deliverology' excludes what happens in the mind of the child or her teacher, turning them into objects of observation or experimentation and elevating the policymaker to the role of the expert who defines, controls and monitors the delivery of the goals. The network of activity pursued by Barber following his work as the Head of Delivery Unit, makes him one of the most successful of the so-called modern 'policy entrepreneurs' (Ball 2007, 2012). Through their involvement in government and private consultancy, international lecture circuits, promotion and sale of 'transferrable' policy packages, 'policy entrepreneurs' treat education as '*edu-business*' (Mahony et al. 2004). In the process, they also propagate corporate management techniques in the form of the TLP (Thomson *et al.* 2014). For example, having moved from the PMDU to work as head of McKinsey's Global Education Practice, Barber co-authored two major education reports (Barber and Mourshed 2007; Mourshed *et al.* 2010), as well as a guide to systemic reform titled *Deliverology 101* (Barber *et al.* 2011). He also advised governments in over forty countries on issues of policy delivery. He currently works as Chief Education Advisor at Pearson, leading Pearson's strategy for education in developing economies.

One of his recent projects has been 'getting kids into school' in the Punjab education system and a continued advocacy of the 'science of delivery' (World Bank Group 2013).

Apart from individual 'policy entrepreneurs' such as Michael Barber,[4] supranational organisations such as the OECD, World Bank and Pearson have also been actively involved in the area of 'global educational governance' (Sahlberg 2011; Ball 2012; Sellar and Lingard 2013: 185). As pointed out by Meyer and Benavot (2013: 9), the OECD has recently assumed a prominent role as 'diagnostician, judge and policy advisor to the world's school systems'. The influence of the OECD's PISA has potential to 'change how nations and states organise public education, to what ends, and in what spirit' (ibid. 2013: 11). The PISA programme promotes technocratic rationality, despite doubts about the tests' reliability and validity (Bracey 2004; Smithers 2004). The conceptual framework designed for PISA and TALIS is based on an input-process-output model first developed in the 1980s by the International Association for the Evaluation of Educational Achievement (IEA) (Purves 1987). The framework identifies 'inputs', 'processes' and 'outputs' at four levels: students, teachers/classrooms, schools and countries/systems. According to some commentators, there is a fundamental contradiction in this design, which makes the surveys ineffective in measuring 'process' variables (Creemers and Scheerens 1994; Bechger et al. 1998). For example, whereas 'processes' at the classroom level are believed to be important predictors of differences in student 'outcomes', the paper-and-pencil tests used in PISA are not likely to provide valid measurements of the actual 'process', such as the behaviour of the teacher. This shortcoming seems to be addressed by the TALIS survey, which focuses on measuring such 'malleable' factors as quality of instruction; student assessment, teacher-student relationships, shared norms and values, leadership, teacher motivation and professional development (OECD 2013). These factors fall under the 'process' category and are measured in order to enable practitioners and policymakers to enact change. The TALIS categorisation of socio-economic status as 'input' that is 'fairly stable' provides an important conceptual 'cut' (Barad 2007). It separates the 'malleable', predominantly personal factors from 'fairly stable' socio-economic factors, marking the former as a policy lever and pushing the latter to the periphery of research and policymaking.

As explained by Purves (1987: 15), the original input-process-outcome model was developed in response to an increasing concern of nations around the world with the quality of their educational systems, based on the perception that 'school performance predicts the economic well-being of society'. Meyer and Benavot (2013: 10) note that such measurements recast the meaning of public education 'from a project aimed at forming national citizens and nurturing social solidarity to a project driven by economic demand and labor market orientations'. Like any scientific apparatus, therefore, the 'cutting-edge methods' (OECD 2013: 15) used by PISA and TALIS scientists institute significant exclusions, making their claim to be 'groundbreaking' problematic. As pointed out by Kuhn (1996: 126), methods and data are often selected within normal science 'only because they promise opportunity for the fruitful elaboration of an accepted paradigm'. The sciences of international comparisons and 'deliverology' appear to be practised in the 'spirit' of capitalising on the 'the variation among countries' and using the 'world as an educational laboratory' (Purves 1987: 15). The ethical question of 'using' the world as a laboratory does not seem to be commensurate with the paradigm of certainty.

Transforming education and complexity

In contrast to the sciences of certainty and in keeping with its etymological roots in the Latin *com* – 'together' – and *plectere* – 'to braid' (Davis *et al*. 2010: 113), complexity thinking acknowledges the inherent 'weaving together' or entanglement of entities, phenomena and processes that have been 'disentangled' since Ovid's times. The complexity sciences reveal that Newtonian reductionism is an exception rather than a set of universal laws and, consequently, it has a relatively limited set of applications (Barad 2007: 24).[5] The implications of complexity for transforming education relate to three key problems with the sciences of certainty discussed above. First, the normal science of 'getting things done' promises what it may be unable to deliver by claiming that causal links within 'delivery chains' are universally binding (Barber 2008), whereas they may be precarious. In contrast, the complexity sciences emphasise that such links can be 'co-configured', 'dissolved' or 'transformed into unanticipated directions', so that:

> what may appear to be an immutable system of performance measurement is in fact held together very provisionally by myriad connections that can be identified and reopened.
>
> (Fenwick *et al*. 2011: 5)

Second, the 'complexity reduction' (Osberg and Biesta 2010) – characteristic of 'deliverology' and the science of international comparisons – focuses on the outcome, simultaneously obscuring the process. As argued by Kuhn (1996) and Barad (2007), however, the evaluation of knowledge needs to be based on consideration of both the outcomes and the processes of knowledge production, as well as the consequences of its use. Importantly, the complexity sciences suggest that we cannot have knowledge 'once and for all', but rather that knowledge is:

> something we have to actively feel our way around and through, unendingly. Why unendingly? Because in acting, we create knowledge; and in creating knowledge, we learn to act in different ways; and in acting in

different ways, we bring about new knowledge that changes our world, that causes us to act differently, and so on, unendingly.

(Osberg *et al.* 2008: 213)

That 'complexity reduction' is difficult to resist is illustrated by Michael Fullan's work (2001, 2003). Fullan emphasises the complexities of educational change and advocates change in culture, which goes deeper than superficial attempts at raising standards. He also highlights a potential gap between planned and realised change:

> the crux of change involves the development of meaning in relation to a new idea, program, reform, or a set of activities. But it is individuals who have to develop new meaning, and these individuals are ... parts of a gigantic, loosely organized, complex, messy social system that contains myriad different subjective worlds.
>
> (Fullan 2001: 92)

While he thus ventures into the paradigm of complexity, he also tends to finish his argument with 'lessons' that reduce complexity into prescriptions, such as 'the only thing that works are virtuous circles' (Fullan 2003: 46) and 'rather than pushing an old lever beyond its natural limits, policymakers would be wise to search for new levers' (p. 6). Thinking of 'policy levers', 'cutting-edge methods' or 'groundbreaking' blueprints for an 'education revolution' may, in effect, limit the generative potential of the idea of transforming education to versions of the input-process-output model (Purves 1987) which merely add to the established normal science.

By contrast, the complexity approach to transforming education is premised on a radical re-orientation of enquiry from questions about solutions to educational 'crises' to questions about the open-ended, performative nature of knowledge, such as 'what would schooling look like if knowledge were truly appreciated as unfolding in processes of action that brings forth new worlds?' (Fenwick *et al.* 2011: 34). Such questions open the possibilities for transforming educational practice in genuinely novel ways.

Third, what makes the sciences of certainty models for engineering social change 'analytical, concrete, logical, convincing and wrong' (Mowles 2011: 16) is the attempt to hide political motives behind a benign mask of scientific objectivity. 'Wrong' can be understood here as inaccurate and morally questionable. As pointed out by Cilliers (2010: viii), hiding the 'inevitable politics involved in all forms of education behind a pretence of neutrality and objectivity is an unacceptable form of violence, a violence partly responsible for the state the world is in'. As we have seen in the previous discussion, ethical questions are at the very core of knowledge (Barad 2007). By disentangling subject/object, matter/meaning, knower/known, nature/culture and fact/value, the sciences of certainty limit ethics to codified guidelines and norms.

As suggested by the uses and misuses of knowledge within the Newtonian clockwork world, transgressing this limit may contribute to serious 'breakdowns of civilisation' (Elias 1996). In contrast, the ethical questions within the complexity sciences are premised on entanglement, calling for a radical reconceptualisation of ethics and responsibility. This reconceptualisation is based on the departure from the 'disentangled' modes of being encouraged by the Cartesian subject/object dualism, discussed further in Chapter 8. To be entangled, as Barad (2007: ix) emphasises, does not mean to be intertwined 'as in the joining of separate entities, but to lack an independent, self-contained existence'. To be entangled, therefore, is to lose the self-assured sense of control over a predetermined future, gaining, in return, uncertainty but also a future that is genuinely different and new.

In summary, ethical problems arising out of the application of the sciences of certainty to educational transformation stem not just from the essential unpredictability of the long-term consequences of education policies, but also from the will to control and engineer social change that pervades the 'new orthodoxy'. The reasons for the enduring appeal of the myth of control are explored further in Chapter 3.

Conclusion

In discussing the differences between the sciences of certainty and the complexity sciences, this chapter has focused on their main ontological and epistemological assumptions and implications for the meaning(s) of educational transformation. The sciences of certainty view educational development as leveraged in mechanistic ways and delivered through the simple causal links of Barber's 'delivery chain'. On this view, the greater the policy lever, the more certain the desired outcome. The 'new orthodoxy' is thus premised on an assumption that the outcomes of reform can be predicted and controlled. The outcomes are defined mainly in terms of literacy and numeracy skills, with the role of education in the twenty-first century narrowed down to the overarching economic goal of developing a competitive workforce. The 'complexity reduction' underlying these reforms is puzzling in the context of the increasingly complex and sophisticated nature of knowledge outlined above.

By contrast, the complexity sciences view educational change as emergent and sensitive both to complex local conditions and the possibility that a small difference in initial conditions, iterated over time, may lead to unpredicted or undesirable consequences. These complex processes of educational change will be explored in more detail in the following chapters. One of the key insights of complexity is that the meaning of 'transforming education' cannot be predetermined in advance and projected into the future, but is best understood with the benefit of hindsight. Consequently, a 'more conscious control' of the processes of educational (and social) change would start from a recognition that, just as our 'less civilised' ancestors were affected by difficulties or fears which we no longer experience, future generations may look at our current predicaments and entanglements with a clearer understanding than the one we have now (Elias 1991: xiv). As we shall see in Chapter 3, the theory of complex responsive processes turns the myth of control 'on its head' (Stacey 2010: 160). This leads to an understanding of educational transformation as emergent from many ordinary local interactions, the precise consequences of which cannot be predicted in advance.

Notes

1 The objective of the present chapter is to introduce the reader to the basic distinctions and key assumptions within the 'complexity sciences' and their implications for understanding approaches to education reform. Consequently, my focus is on the connections and commonalities within the 'complexity sciences'. This is not to imply, however, that the 'complexity sciences' are a homogenous discipline, or 'one theory with a common set of characteristics' Mowles (2014: 162).
2 The complexity of the experiment is beyond the scope of this book. A detailed explanation can be found in Chapter 7 of Karen Barad's book (Barad 2007).
3 As explained in the section *In dialogue with nature and the 'quantum revolution'*, 'the cut' is a distinction or categorisation enacted (rather than given or pre-existing) within scientific practice. For example, scientific measurement involves specific choices of apparatus, making particular sets of variables meaningful (and significant for the study of a phenomenon) at the exclusion of others. Difference is thus made, rather than given, and inclusions/exclusions constitutive in the sense of affecting our assumptions about how the world is.
4 More detailed accounts of the networks of activity of Michael Barber and other 'policy entrepreneurs' are offered by Stephen Ball (2007, 2012).
5 In explaining the relationship between quantum and classical mechanics, Barad (2007) points out that Newtonian physics serves as a helpful computational tool, because its equations are easier to solve than those of quantum theory. Newtonian approximations 'work' in the macroscopic domain, for relatively 'large' objects. Limitations of the 'computational efficacy' of Newtonian equations are revealed by laboratory equipment of high accuracy, able to measure numbers with many decimal places (p. 423).

References

Ball, S.J. 2007. *Education Plc: Understanding Private Sector Participation in Public Sector Education.* Abingdon: Routledge.

Ball, S.J. 2012. *Global Education Inc.: New Policy Networks and the Neo-Liberal Imaginary.* London and New York: Routledge.

Barad, K. 2003. Posthumanist performativity: Toward and understanding of how matter comes to matter, *Signs*, 28(3): 801–831.

Barad, K. 2007. *Meeting the Universe Halfway: Quantum Physics and the Entanglement of Matter and Meaning.* Durham, NC and London: Duke University Press.

Barad, K. 2014. Diffracting diffraction: Cutting together-apart, *Parallax*, 20(3): 168–187.

Barber, M. 1997. *The Learning Game: Arguments for an Education Revolution.* London: Indigo.

Barber, M. 2008. *Instruction to Deliver: Fighting to Transform Britain's Public Services* (2nd edn). London: Methuen Publishing.

Barber, M. and Mourshed, M. 2007. *How the World's Best Education Systems Stay on Top*. Available at: www.smhc-cpre.org/wp-content/uploads/2008/07/how-the-worlds-best-performing-school-systems-come-out-on-top-sept-072.pdf (accessed 15 February 2012).

Barber, M., Moffit, A. and Kihn, P. 2011. *Deliverology 101: A Field Guide for Educational Leaders*. London: Sage.

Bates, A. 2012. Transformation, trust and the 'importance of teaching': Continuities and discontinuities in the coalition government's discourse of education reform, *London Review of Education*, 10(1): 87–100.

Bates, A. 2013. (Mis)Understanding strategy as a 'spectacular intervention': A phenomenological reflection on the strategy orientations underpinning education reform in England, *Studies in Philosophy and Education*, 33(4): 353–367.

Beard, R. 2000. *National Literacy Strategy: Review of Research and Other Related Evidence*. Sudbury: DfEE Publications.

Bechger, T.M., van Schooten, E., De Glopper, C. and Hex, J.J. 1998. The validity of international surveys of reading literacy: The case of the IEA reading literacy study, *Studies in Educational Evaluation*, 24(2): 99–125.

Bracey, G.W. 2004. International comparisons: Less than meets the eye, *Phi Delta Kappan*, 8(6): 477–478.

Braidotti, R. 2013. *The Posthuman*. Cambridge: Polity Press.

Cilliers, P. 2010. 'Acknowledging Complexity: A Foreword'. In Osberg, D. and Biesta, G. (eds) *Complexity Theory and the Politics of Education*. Rotterdam: Sense Publishers, vii–viii.

Coffield, F. 2011. Why the McKinsey reports will not improve school systems, *Journal of Education Policy*, 27(1): 131–149.

Creemers, B.P.M. and Scheerens, J. 1994. Developments in the educational effectiveness research programme, *International Journal of Educational Research*, 21(2): 125–140.

Davis, B. and Sumara, D.J. 2006. *Complexity and Education: Inquiries into Learning, Teaching, and Research*. Mahwah: Lawrence Erlbaum Associates Inc.

Davis, B., Sumara, D. and Iftody, T. 2010. 'Complexity, Consciousness and Curriculum'. In Osberg, D. and Biesta, G. (eds) *Complexity Theory and the Politics of Education*. Rotterdam: Sense Publishers, 107–120.

Descartes, R. 2005. *Discourse on Method and Meditations on First Philosophy*. (E.S. Haldane, Trans.). Stilwell, OK: Digireads.com Publishing.

DfEE. 1998. *The National Literacy Strategy: Framework for Teaching*. London: DfEE.

DfEE. 1999. *The National Numeracy Strategy: Framework for Teaching Mathematics*. London: DfEE.

Elias, N. 1978. *What Is Sociology?* New York: Columbia University Press.

Elias, N. 1991. *The Symbol Theory*. London: Sage.

Elias, N. 1994. *The Civilizing Process: Sociogenetic and Psychogenetic Investigations*. Malden, MA and Abingdon: Blackwell Publishing.

Elias, N. 1996. *The Germans: Power Struggles and the Development of Habitus in the Nineteenth and Twentieth Centuries*. Cambridge: Polity Press.

Fenwick, T., Edwards, R. and P. Sawchuk. 2011. *Emerging Approaches to Educational Research: Tracing the Sociomaterial*. London and New York: Routledge.

Friedman, J. 2009. The crisis of politics, not economics: Complexity, ignorance, and policy failure, *Critical Review*, 21(2–3): 127–183.
Friedrich, B. and Herschbach, D. 1998. Space quantization: Otto Stern's lucky star. *Daedalus*, 127(1): 165–191.
Friedrich, B. and Herschbach, D. 2003. Stern and gerlach: How a bad cigar helped reorient atomic physics, *Physics Today*, (56): 1–11.
Fullan, M. 2001. *The New Meaning of Educational Change* (3rd edn). London: RoutledgeFalmer.
Fullan, M. 2003. *Change Forces with a Vengeance*. London: RoutledgeFalmer.
Gunter, H.M. 2008. Modernisation and the field of educational administration, *Journal of Educational Administration and History*, 40(2): 161–172.
Gunter, H.M. 2010. The standards challenge: A comment on Karsten *et al.*, *Public Administration*, 88(1): 113–117.
Hammer, M. and Champy, J. 1993. *Reengineering the Corporation: A Manifesto for a Business Revolution*. New York: HarperBusiness.
Heisenberg, W. 1958. *Physics and Philosophy: The Revolution in Modern Science*. London: Penguin Books.
Hursh, D. 2005. The growth of high-stakes testing in the USA: Accountability, markets and the decline of educational equity, *British Educational Research Journal*, 31(5): 605–622.
Jordan, C. and Jain, A. 2009. *Diversity and Resilience: Lessons from the Financial Crisis*. Available at: http://law.unimelb.edu.au/files/dmfile/Diversity_and_Resilience__14_September_2009_1.pdf (accessed 14 April 2015).
Kauffman, S. 1993. *The Origins of Order: Self-Organization and Selection in Evolution*. New York: Oxford University Press.
Kuhn, T.S. 1970. *The Structure of Scientific Revolutions* (2nd edn). Chicago, IL: University of Chicago Press.
Kuhn, T.S. 1996. *The Structure of Scientific Revolutions* (3rd edn). Chicago, IL and London: The University of Chicago Press.
Lingard, B. 2010. Policy borrowing, policy learning: Testing times in Australian schooling, *Critical Studies in Education*, 51(2): 129–147.
Lingard, B., Martino, W. and Rezai-Rashti, G. 2013. Testing regimes, accountabilities and education policy: Commensurate global and national developments, *Journal of Education Policy*, 28(5): 539–556.
MacIntyre, A. 1985. *After Virtue: A Study in Moral Theory* (2nd edn). London: Bloomsbury.
MacKenzie, D. 2011. The credit crisis as a problem in the sociology of knowledge, *American Journal of Sociology*, 116(6): 1778–1841.
Mahony, P., Menter, I. and Hextall, I. 2004. Building dams in Jordan, assessing teachers in England: A case study in edu-business, *Globalisation, Societies and Education*, 2(2): 277–296.
Mason, M. 2008. 'What Is Complexity Theory and What Are Its Implications for Educational Change?' In Mason, M. (ed.) *Complexity Theory and the Philosophy of Education*. Chichester: Wiley-Blackwell, 32–45.
Maturana, H.R. and Varela, F.J. 1998. *The Tree of Knowledge: The Biological Roots of Human Understanding*. Boston, MA and London: Shambala.
Meyer, H.D. and Benavot, A. (eds). 2013. *PISA, Power, and Policy: The Emergence of Global Educational Governance*. Oxford: Symposium Books.

Mourshed, M., Chijoke, C. and Barber, M. 2010. *How the World's Most Improved School Systems Keep Getting Better.* Available at: http://mckinseyonsociety.com/downloads/reports/Education/How-the-Worlds-Most-Improved-School-Systems-Keep-Getting-Better_Download-version_Final.pdf (accessed 10 April 2015).

Mowles, C. 2011. *Rethinking Management: Radical Insights from the Complexity Sciences.* Farnham: Gower.

Mowles, C. 2014. Complex, but not quite complex enough: The turn to the complexity sciences in evaluation scholarship, *Evaluation,* 20(2): 160–175.

Nelson, R.A. and Olsson, M.G. 1985. The pendulum – rich physics from a simple system, *American Journal of Physics,* 54(2): 112–121.

OECD. 2009. *Creating Effective Teaching and Learning Environments: First Results from TALIS,* TALIS, OECD Publishing. Available at: http://dx.doi.org/10.1787/9789264068780-en (accessed 28 April 2014).

OECD. 2013. *Teaching and Learning International Survey TALIS 2013: Conceptual Framework.* Available at: www.oecd.org/edu/school/TALIS%20Conceptual%20Framework_FINAL.pdf (accessed 7 May 2015).

Osberg, D. and Biesta, G. (eds). 2010. *Complexity Theory and the Politics of Education.* Rotterdam: Sense Publishers.

Osberg, D., Biesta, G. and Cilliers, P. 2008. 'From Representation to Emergence: Complexity's Challenge to the Epistemology of Schooling'. In Mason, M. (ed.). *Complexity Theory and the Philosophy of Education.* Chichester: Wiley-Blackwell, 182–204.

Ovid. AD8/2004. *Metamorphoses: A New Verse Translation.* (C. Martin, Trans. and ed.). New York and London: W.W. Norton & Company.

Prigogine, I. 1996. *The End of Certainty: Time, Chaos and the New Laws of Nature.* New York: The Free Press.

Purves, A. 1987. IEA: An agenda for the future, *International Review of Education* (33): 103–107.

Ravitch, D. 2014. *Reign of Error: The Hoax of the Privatization Movement and the Danger to America's Public Schools.* New York: Vintage Books.

Rorty, R. 1979. *Philosophy and the Mirror of Nature.* Princeton, NJ: Princeton University Press.

Sahlberg, P. 2011. *Finnish Lessons: What Can the World Learn from Educational Change in Finland?* New York and London: Teachers College.

Samier, E. 2006. Educational administration as a historical discipline: An apologia pro vita historia, *Journal of Educational Administration and History,* 38(2): 125–139.

Seddon, J. 2008. *Systems Thinking in the Public Sector.* Axminster: Triarchy Press.

Sellar, S. and Lingard, B. 2013. 'PISA and the Expanding Role of the OECD in Global Educational Governance'. In Meyer, H.D. and Benavot, A. (eds) *PISA, Power, and Policy: The Emergence of Global Educational Governance.* Oxford: Symposium Books, 195–206.

Smith, J. and Jenks, C. 2006. *Qualitative Complexity: Ecology, Cognitive Processes and the Re-Emergence of Structures in Post-Humanist Social Theory.* Abingdon: Routledge.

Smithers, A. 2004. *England's Education: What Can Be Learned by Comparing Countries?* Available at: www.alansmithers.com/reports/EnglandsEducation2May2004.pdf (accessed 13 April 2015).

Stacey, R.D. 2007. *Strategic Management and Organisational Dynamics: The Challenge of Complexity* (5th edn). Harlow: Pearson Education Limited.

Stacey, R.D. 2010. *Complexity and Organisational Reality: Uncertainty and the Need to Rethink Management after the Collapse of Investment Capitalism* (2nd edn). London: Routledge.

Stewart, I. 1997. *Does God Play Dice? The New Mathematics of Chaos* (2nd edn). London: Penguin Books.

Thomson, P., Gunter, H, and Blackmore, J. 2014. 'Series Foreword'. In Gunter, H.M. *Educational Leadership and Hannah Arendt*. London and New York: Routledge, vi–xii.

World Bank Group. 2013. *Delivering Results – A Conversation with Jim Yong Kim, Tony Blair, and Michael Barber*. (10 April). Available at: www.worldbank.org/en/news/speech/2013/04/10/delivering-results-conversation-jim-yong-kim-tony-blair-michael-barber (accessed 13 April 2015).

Youngblood, M. 1997. *Life at the Edge of Chaos: Creating the Quantum Organization*. Dallas, TX: Perceval Press.

Chapter 3

Complex responsive processes theory

> The world is not an object such that I would have in my possession the law of its making; it is the natural setting of, and field for, all my thoughts and all my explicit perceptions.
>
> (Merleau-Ponty 2002: xi–xii)

As discussed in Chapter 2, the 'new orthodoxy' in global education reform rests on knowledge developed within the sciences of certainty. It relies on centrally designed policy levers consisting of national curricula, standards, targets and testing regimes, as well as sophisticated data systems (Sahlberg 2011; Meyer and Benavot 2013). In order to direct the enactment of these policies in schools, generic techniques are promoted, often imported from the corporate world. An example of this is the TLP, which provides normative solutions for improving schools largely conceptualised as business enterprises (Thomson *et al.* 2014). By assuming simple causal links between improvement schemes and their desired effects, these approaches appear to overlook the possibility that, while policymakers can design policies for educational transformation, they may be unable to choose the responses of teachers. It also follows that it may be difficult, if not impossible, to predict the precise long-term consequences of such policies. Mowles (2011: 9) contends that mainstream approaches to managing change in organisations:

> promise what they cannot deliver because they are predicated on ideas of predictability and control and imply powers of intervention on the part of managers and consultants which they cannot possess. People in organisations do not fit into two-by-two-grids, and are not parts of wholes. The interweaving of intentions, hopes, aspirations and behaviour of people . . . will bring about outcomes which no one has predicted and which no one has planned.

This argument turns the myth of control 'on its head' by challenging the assumption that managers choose a future for their organisation and are able to control the implementation of their plans or strategies through the use of targets and other employee performance indicators (Stacey 2012). Strategies are mediated by the myriad local responses of the employees and this means that their enactment will 'always also produce surprises' (p. 178).

This chapter explores these and other insights into organisational and social change by drawing on the work of complex responsive processes scholars (Griffin 2002; Shaw 2002; Stacey 2007, 2010, 2012; Mowles 2011, 2015). To explain processes of human organising, they turn to the complexity sciences as a source of analogies such as the concept of self-organisation developed in the field of evolutionary biology (Kauffman 1995). One of the main insights offered by complex responsive processes theory is that organisations and systems are not abstract, idealised wholes, but ensembles of people engaging in ordinary everyday activities and communications, or 'local interactions'. Local interactions are made up of deliberate and spontaneous actions, planned and emergent activities, power relations, values and personal agendas. On this account, whatever one's role in the education system, they interact locally and no one is able to assume the privileged, exterior vantage point of an 'objective', omniscient observer. As we have seen in Chapter 2, there is no such exterior observational point (Barad 2007). Just as scientists grapple with uncertainty, ambiguity and the material limitations of their apparatus, policymakers and practitioners in schools are also enabled or constrained by material resources, social contexts and limits to their knowledge and power. Consequently, paying attention to the complex realities of the school and the classroom is more critical than designing centralised plans and expecting them to be mechanically deployed, independently of the local context. It is the school and the classroom that are the key sites for educational transformation to emerge from local interactions rather than generic, decontextualised policies.

The conceptual framework of complex responsive processes theory used for the analysis of the empirical data (Chapters 5–8) is summarised in Figure 3.1. The key concepts explored below include emergence; local and global patterns of conversation; power, compliance and resistance; the paradox of enabling constraints; values and leadership 'tools'. Before examining how these concepts define the meaning of educational transformation as profound, progressive change, let us first consider the '*complex*' in complex responsive processes theory, which signals its linkage to the complexity sciences.

Complex adaptive systems and the emergence of system-wide change

As mentioned in Chapter 2, analogies from the complexity sciences can be helpful in understanding the nature of social change. The primary analogy is that of complex adaptive systems, such as ecosystems, climate and weather, humans and other living organisms. A complex adaptive system is defined in biology as consisting of a large number ('population') of entities ('agents') each of which behaves according to a small set of rules (Stacey 2007). Each agent is required by these rules to adjust its actions to those of other agents. Each agent's interaction is local in the sense that the agent interacts with a very small proportion of the whole population, with no centrally determined rules for the agents to follow. A population-wide pattern emerges out of these local interactions rather than from a predetermined blueprint. For example, a colony of ants is able to collectively perform a wide range of functions, such as patrolling and harvesting, based on individual ants continually adjusting their behaviour to their immediate surroundings and the ants nearby. Each ant responds to the pattern of its encounters with other ants and the conditions of their environment. A population-wide pattern emerges out of countless self-organising local interactions, without central control (Gordon 1999). A key point here is that emergence and self-organisation can lead to fundamental structural development, or novelty, which is:

> 'spontaneous' or 'autonomous', arising from the intrinsic iterative nonlinear structure of the system. Some external designer does not impose it, rather, widespread orderly behaviour emerges from simple, reflex-like rules.
> (Stacey 2007: 196)

As mentioned in Chapter 2, evolutionary biology explains the emergence of the great diversity of species and ecosystems based on natural selection and self-organisation, rather than a universal 'Plan of Creation' (Kauffman 1993: 6). By analogy, understanding education as a complex adaptive system challenges the policy levers and 'deliverology' approaches to education reform. This paradigm ignores the gap between policy and the enactment of local practices in which educational transformation can be lost or found. As Stacey (2007) argues, population-wide patterns within a complex adaptive system cannot be predicted in advance:

> no one can know what that evolutionary experience will be until it occurs. In certain conditions, agents interacting in a system can produce . . . creative new outcomes that none of them was ever programmed to produce . . . even if no one can know the outcomes of their actions and even if no one can be 'in control', we are not doomed to anarchy. On the contrary, these may be the very conditions required for creativity, for the evolutionary journey with no fixed, predetermined destination.
> (p. 197)

This insight reveals how the generative potential for novelty and creativity may be lost in local interactions when standards, competition and centralised control become a hegemonic formula for transforming education. In order to enact this formula, it is necessary to reduce the concept of education to a closed system, like the Newtonian clockwork or the input-process-outcome model (Purves 1987; OECD 2013) discussed in Chapter 2. Such mechanistic models of education systems may be used to justify the dependence on policy levers and 'delivery chains', but they also bring about a multitude of unintended consequences. These consequences range from 'legislated conformity' on the part of the teaching profession, which inhibits the achievement of broader educational goals (Alexander *et al.* 2010; Rizvi and Lingard 2010), to an erosion of pedagogical quality (Ball 2004; Ball *et al.* 2012; Polesel *et al.* 2014) and placing 'potentially damaging expectations on children' (Bates 2013: 38). Critically, standards-based policies constrain local interactions within a reductive definition of educational transformation as incremental increase in high-stakes tests scores. This may inhibit the emergence of 'local' approaches to improvement, which would enable the necessary local adjustments to be made and novel meanings of transformation created. It is emergence that 'makes an almost indefinite organization possible' (Mead 1956: 36), opening up new possibilities, where 'the possible is richer than the real' (Prigogine 1996: 72).

By linking analogies from the complexity sciences to sociological and philosophical theories, complex responsive processes theory develops nuanced understandings of the processes of human organising. For example, in order to explain the reasons for the enduring popularity of the myth of control, Stacey *et al.* turn to Mead's philosophical account of evolution and social progress as emergent phenomena. Mead (1932: 46) argues that emergence may be difficult to accept within the prevailing paradigm of prediction and control:

> the emergent has no sooner appeared than we set about rationalizing it, that is, we undertake to show that it . . . can be found in the past that lay behind it . . . in such a restatement of the past as conditioning of the future that we may control its reappearance.

The tendency to 'rationalise' the emergent stems from a desire to control and, as suggested by the popularity of simplistic, linear models and tools, may lead to the 'complexity reduction' characteristic of mainstream approaches to education reform (Osberg and Biesta 2010). The complex politics underlying the global spread of the 'new orthodoxy' for achieving educational transformation is explored in the penultimate section of this chapter.

Transdisciplinary understandings of change (and continuity)

Complex responsive processes theory offers transdisciplinary understandings of change, aimed at developing an entire 'spectrum of theories of human organization' (Griffin 2002: x). This transdisciplinary approach is also demonstrated by Barad's (2007: 25) methodology discussed in Chapter 2, when she draws on diverse disciplines of knowledge paying attention to 'important details of specialised arguments within a given field' in order to 'foster constructive engagements' across disciplinary boundaries. In other words, she seeks to connect understandings generated by different disciplinary practices in dialogue with one another. This is unlike the more common interdisciplinary approaches that simply aim to 'bridge' the social and natural sciences, for example by exploring 'unilaterally' the implications of physics for social theories and 'exploiting what is seen as the greater epistemological value of the natural sciences over the human sciences', or vice versa (pp. 92–3).

The notion of time as the 'living present' (Griffin 2002; Shaw 2002; Stacey 2010) represents an important example of a transdisciplinary approach in complex responsive processes theory. The 'living present' embraces the past and the future. Our present frame of reference provides us with a foundation for understanding and interpreting the past, as well as determining the future. This means that it is impossible to claim that the past 'is over' and the future 'not yet', but rather that, in 'the now', the past and future coexist. It follows that we are always in the midst of the processes of continuity and change (Shaw 2002) and the blueprints for 'education revolution' (Barber 1997), which rely on a complete break with tradition, may be unrealistic. On the contrary, change, or evolution, is possible only because the habitual patterns of relating between people in organisations are iterated, but 'never reproduced exactly' (Stacey 2007: 435). Human interactions over time are non-linear due to the imperfect reproduction of our habits, our inherent spontaneity and the unpredictability of the responses of others.

Similarly, in order to account for emergence, evolution and instability, time is conceptualised not as a parameter (independent variable), as in Newtonian science, but as irreversible (Prigogine 1996). Given the appropriate initial conditions, Newtonian equations can be used to predict the future or 'retrodict' the past (p. 4). As explained in Chapter 2, however, an essential condition for prediction (or 'retrodiction') is that important features of the environment are ignored, as in the formula for the pendulum swing. A simple systems view is thus able to provide certitudes that 'correspond only to idealizations, or approximations' (Prigogine 1996: 55). Importantly, the deterministic, time-reversible theories of classical physics have been critiqued as 'the most solid and serious obstacle to our understanding and justifying the nature of human freedom, creativity, and responsibility' (Popper 1982, as quoted in Prigogine p. 14). These contrasting notions of time mean that educational transformation can be understood either as a 'spectacular' event, cracked 'once and for all' (Arnold 2004: i), or as an evolutionary process that is never complete.

At this juncture, it is important to consider two issues that arise from the transdisciplinary pursuits discussed in this section. First, a question may be asked about the reasons why the descriptions of the physical world should provide the basis for 'prescriptions for social life' (Gough 2010: 52). Gough advocates caution in modelling education on the complex, self-organising, 'natural' systems studied by scientists. As we have seen in Chapter 2, viewed within the timeframe of humanity (Elias 1991), the natural and social sciences are interrelated, or entangled. The generative possibilities of the 'new metaphors'

52 The universe of complexity thinking

and 'new forms of social imagination' (Gough 2010: 52) offered by the complexity sciences may be helpful in resisting simplistic 'spectacular' solutions for enduring educational problems. However, caution is important in using 'new metaphors'. For example, applying the concept of a complex adaptive system as a metaphor for an education system or a school may give policymakers and leaders an illusion of 'observing' the system from an external vantage point and obfuscate their entanglement in local interactions. The complexity sciences challenge this notion of a privileged, 'divine' point of view (Prigogine 1996: 38). Second, the complexity sciences have been applied in social research in diverse ways, often without regard for the connections between complexity concepts and established social theory (Tsoukas 2005; Mowles 2014). Consequently, in an attempt to understand the implications of the complexity sciences with greater precision, complex responsive processes theory takes up complexity concepts by analogy, linking them to similar ideas from the social sciences. The remainder of this chapter provides an exposition of the conceptual framework of complex responsive processes theory (Figure 3.1) and considers how it may illuminate the complex realities of everyday educational practice.

Conceptual framework

Figure 3.1 provides a summary of the key concepts of complex responsive processes theory, which inform the discussions of 'transforming education' in this book. As mentioned above, organisational change is equivalent to changes

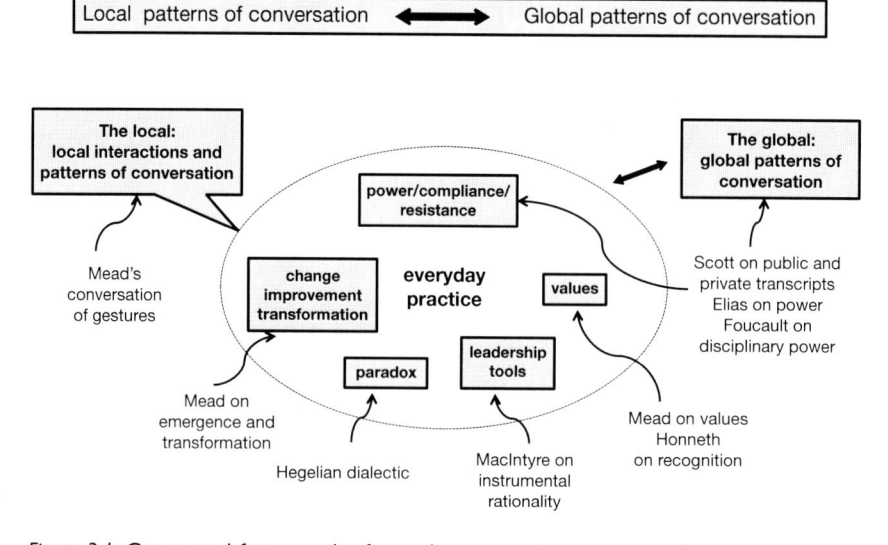

Figure 3.1 Conceptual framework of complex responsive processes theory

in patterns of local interactions, which are articulated and enacted as patterns of conversation. Local interactions are underpinned by a complex interplay of values, power relations and intentions of interdependent people engaging in everyday practice. Organisation-wide (global) patterns emerge from many local interactions, iterated over time.

The processes of designing and enacting education policy emerge from local interactions in the domain of government policymaking and the enactment of policies in the domain of schools through a myriad of local interactions. Complex responsive processes theory emphasises that local interactions within both domains are characterised by an interplay of power relations, values, intentions and rational as well as ideological choices. Although a centrally designed government policy may introduce new patterns of conversation (and, over time, new local interactions), the way it is taken up, interpreted, complied with or resisted in schools is complex and unpredictable in advance.

Because policies are generalisations and their meanings arise in specific situations involving individuals engaging in everyday practice, reciprocal communication between the two domains (of government policy making and schools) is of vital importance. As discussed below, however, the tendency among policymakers is to rely on generic, abstract models of education reform. These find their expressions as top-down communications and the apparatus of targets and inspections to ensure practitioner compliance with policy. For example, the Office for Standards in Education (Ofsted) and the National College for School Leadership (NCSL)[1] were deployed to standardise practice in schools. Ofsted inspectors were cast in the role of omniscient observers, capable of providing an impartial evaluation of improvement enacted in schools (Chapter 5). The NCSL was elevated to a pivotal role in leadership knowledge production and the training of a new cadre of headteachers and senior leaders who, as noted by Gunter and Forrester (2009: 497), would act as 'direct agents' of government reform (Chapter 7).

From the complex responsive processes perspective, transforming education is thus an inherently political process involving a complex interplay of intentions and conflicting interests. In order to account for the emergence of the GERM (Sahlberg 2011), supranational influences on education policy will also need to be considered (Rizvi and Lingard 2010). However, we will first explore the concepts summarised in Figure 3.1 to consider the complex and often contradictory processes of change and transformation.

Local interactions, a conversation of gestures and the emergence of meaning

Complex responsive processes theory explains local interactions among people working in organisations by drawing on Mead's (1934) 'conversation of gestures'. A conversation of gestures involves one body making a gesture to another body and simultaneously evoking a response in the other body.

The response is a gesture back, evoking another response. The conversation of gestures is an ongoing responsive process in which meaning:

> arises in the responsive interaction between actors; gesture and response can never be separated but must be understood as moments of one act. Meaning does not arise first in each individual . . . nor is it transmitted from one individual to another but, rather, it arises in the interaction between them.
>
> (Stacey 2007: 271)

Mead (1934) emphasises that we are unable to precisely predict or control how others respond to our gestures; we cannot, therefore, encode our meaning and transmit it through gestures to be decoded by others. Rather the function of a gesture is to make adjustments possible by entering into the attitude of the actors implicated in the social act. This highlights both the mutuality of relations and the vital importance of the response of the other in the emergence of meaning.

Understanding local interactions as communication between the actual 'embodied' people brings the human factor back to abstract models of transformation, such as Barber's two-by-two grid discussed in Chapter 2. The grid defines educational transformation in terms of abstract measures of the 'boldness' and 'quality' of reform, suggesting that these measures will be taken up in schools in a uniform way. Chapter 5 will emphasise that this may not be the case based on the empirical data on the enactment of the *National Literacy* and *Numeracy Strategies* for primary education. The refusal of the strategy designers to enter into the attitude of the teachers and school leaders tasked with their enactment appear to have profoundly affected practitioners' 'ownership' of the *National Strategies*, suggesting that the opportunity to transform education was lost in the process.

The interplay between the local and the global

As mentioned above, complex responsive processes theory views continuity and change in terms of changes to patterns of conversation. Wherever one is in the organisational hierarchy, she is always interacting locally, with a relatively small number of others. This local communication is guided by patterns, habits and routines that may be spontaneously adapted to the contingencies of the situation. At the same time, local interactions are also constrained by population-wide patterns, which are termed by Stacey (2010: 160–161) as 'global':

> no matter who we are, we are constrained in what we do together by what may feel like major *external forces* beyond our control, widespread, overall *structures* we have to take as given, *institutionalized instruments of power* which we have no option but to submit to, pre-existing *technologies* that shape what we do, and *allocation of resources* about which we can do little.

The relationship between the local and the global can be explained by using Mead's (1934) distinction between generalising and particularising. Generalising is about individuals acting in accordance with what is common, for example, social norms and values, whereas particularising is about responding to these differently in different circumstances. Centrally designed policy is a generalisation and its meaning can only be experienced through particularisation, or its enactment in everyday practice. Because particularising involves a complex interplay of many intentions and values, this interplay cannot be designed 'except temporarily in fascist power structures' (Stacey 2010: 167). What this entails in the context of educational transformation is that, rather than seeking closure and certainty, an effective policymaker or school leader would be open to not knowing in advance. He would respect and encourage local conversations as vital in providing conditions in which novel meanings of educational transformation can be found.

Articulating power, compliance and resistance: public and private transcripts

In explaining power relations, complex responsive processes theory turns to the work of Elias (1978) and his understanding of power as premised on interdependence. As explained by Stacey (2012: 28–29):

> Since I need others, I cannot do whatever I please, and since they need me, neither can they. We constrain each other at the same time as enabling each other and it is this paradoxical activity that constitutes power. Furthermore, since need is rarely equal, the pattern of power relations will always be skewed more to one than to another.

Power relations and the resulting dynamic of inclusion and exclusion mean that our everyday interactions have to be negotiated and are, therefore, essentially political. The mutuality of power relations leads to an understanding of power as 'enabling constraint'. While organisational hierarchies and norms constrain individual behaviour, they are also affected and changed by individuals engaging in the ongoing processes of local interaction. Issues related to power are often discarded by mainstream management theories in favour of models and 'tools' that codify patterns of organisational interaction. The use of such 'tools' maintains an impression of managers being in control, even though it cannot be claimed that the tools cause stability or change. The core reason for their utilisation appears, therefore, to be aimed not as much at improvement in organisational outcomes, but the maintenance of disciplinary power (Foucault 1979). Disciplinary power operates through the use of simple techniques of hierarchical surveillance, judgement and examination. Modern leaders seem to be 'prime agents administering the techniques of discipline', who are simultaneously also subject to disciplinary constraints themselves (Stacey 2012: 66–67).

Power relations, domination, compliance and resistance are expressed and enacted through language. Scott's (1990) distinction between 'public' and 'private transcripts' is helpful here in gaining a deeper understanding of organisational patterns of conversation. From the position of a subordinate group, such as practitioners enacting education policy, the 'public transcript' is the language that articulates compliance with official themes imposed by powerful elites, whereas the 'private transcript' is the 'discourse that takes place "offstage", beyond direct observation by powerholders' (p. 4). This 'backstage discourse' takes the form of anecdotes, jokes and euphemisms, which can signal resistance to the public transcript. While powerful elites consciously perform in public the rituals of domination, subordinate groups rarely speak the truth 'directly and publicly in the teeth of power' (p. xiii). As a result:

> the public transcript will typically, by its accommodationist tone, provide convincing evidence for the hegemony of . . . dominant discourse. It is in precisely this public domain where the effects of power relations are most manifest, and any analysis based exclusively on the public transcript is likely to conclude that subordinate groups endorse the terms of their subordination and are willing, even enthusiastic partners in that subordination.
>
> (p. 4)

Such publicly expressed compliance has important implications for understanding the concept of values, discussed below.

Management by values

Mead's (1923) examination of values has been utilised by complex responsive processes scholars in developing a critique of organisational culture change programmes and '*management by values*' (Mowles 2011). Mowles contends that *management by values* has replaced '*management by objectives*' in much of mainstream management literature. As a management tool, values can be audited, measured and 'used' to legitimate management interventions and 'align' the people in the organisation in pursuing one common purpose or vision. Once managers have identified values that could bring about a desired behaviour change, they use an appeal to these values to reward or discipline employees through inclusion or exclusion from the dominant group. According to mainstream management literature, the culture of 'positivity' is instrumental in achieving organisational outcomes. This culture operates at the level of discourse as a 'can do' approach, suggesting that all our human pursuits can be managed. In private corporations, the culture of 'positivity' appears to borrow from sales techniques (ibid.: 21), whereas in educational contexts, vision and values are part of a 'toolkit' used by strategic leaders to 'align' their staff to strategic ends. For example, according to Davies and Davies (2009: 16), the function of strategy is to combine 'moral purpose and values' with 'vision' in the process of 'operational planning'. Vision and values thus interpreted are embedded in the sciences of certainty and based on an assumption that people's behaviour and beliefs can be moulded by charismatic leaders, through their expertise in using motivational techniques.

In discussing an alternative approach, Mowles (2011) emphasises that organisational value statements are idealisations, 'which by their very nature are unachievable in any direct manner' (p. 152). On the contrary, they require an interpretation of what they might mean in the contingencies of everyday practice. The paradox of values, Mowles explains, is that they are 'voluntary compulsions'; they are simultaneously voluntary and compelling or, in other words, we choose to be compelled by our values (p. 156). Strong emotions are attached to values, because they imbue our lives with meaning and give us a sense of identity. In organisational contexts, shared values can also give people a sense of a 'we', of a community connected in a pursuit of common goals. Consequently, it is not surprising that values may be approached by managers as:

> a legitimate object of management manipulation and moulding. People's values could be bent to the utility of the organisation.
>
> (p. 169)

When values are used as a management tool for creating universal group norms, they may become a form of 'coercive persuasion' and lead to resistance and conflict. Critically, it is not adherence to universal, standardised values, but diversity that leads to novelty. Conversely, the 'suppression of difference is likely to lead to stuck and potentially destructive patterns of organising' (p. 165). In education, the totalising logic of performativity may lead to an erosion of pedagogical and collegial relationships whereby children and colleagues are no longer recognised for their inherent value, but rather treated instrumentally as 'implementers' of a particular notion of educational transformation.

Leadership 'tools' and instrumental rationality

Just as values can become means to organisational ends, other leadership 'tools' can also be utilised in the belief that they will enable leaders to 'choose an improved future' and to 'control movement towards that future' (Stacey 2012: 5). They range from tools for strategic planning, such as the Strengths, Weaknesses, Opportunities and Threats (SWOT) analysis or the Boston Consulting Group (BCG) Matrix (Davies and Ellison 2003), to decision making and motivational tools aimed at enhancing 'organisational development' (Mullins 2007). As pointed out by Stacey (2012), these tools are characterised by efficient causality, rules and steps to follow, and high levels of abstraction.[2] Efficient causality underlying mainstream conceptualisations of change is referred to as 'if . . . then . . .' causality. This approach is derived from the sciences of certainty and premised on an assumption that '*if* action A is taken, *then* outcome B will occur' (p. 13). For example, in the field of education policy, the 'if . . . then . . .' causality underpins the claim that setting and monitoring targets will lead to improved performance. The role of school leaders is to mediate government policy by controlling and being accountable for its enactment. To this end, they need to follow rules and steps, such as the fifteen-step model for delivering 'ambitious' targets (Barber 2008). However, the high level of abstraction inherent in targets and other monitoring tools encourages a disconnection from the everyday organisational experience. This, in turn, leads to targets and other abstractions becoming accepted as universally valid, analogous to the laws of the sciences of certainty. The preoccupation with the use of these tools may distract attention from teaching and learning. For example, as suggested by Harris (2007), terms such as 'policy' and 'strategy' seem to have pushed the concept of curriculum planning to the periphery of educational practice.

Leadership tools are underpinned by instrumental rationality in the sense that each is meant to be used for realising a particular goal or intention for an organisation. However, the scientific evidence for the efficacy of these tools is frequently sparse, contradictory or inconclusive. For example, research on strategy is often based on case studies of successful companies captured at the peak of their success, often short lived and narrowly focused on recipes for successful growth (Chia and Holt 2009; Mowles 2011). Leadership tools cannot be used in a purely rational, 'objective' way, because:

> their use can only ever occur in the ordinary politics of daily organizational life. This means that the use of the tools . . . cannot be rational in an objective, instrumental sense. Their use will arouse emotions, threaten or sustain existing power relations, provoke resistance and conflict between different ideologies. Instrumental rationality turns out to be a fiction in ordinary everyday life in organizations.
>
> (Stacey 2012: 51)

A similar logic of simplification, abstraction and standardisation is also employed in the domain of policymaking, despite its limitations, fictions and undesirable consequences. In trying to explain why simplifications and abstractions are attractive to policymakers, Stacey (2010: 112) notes that modern governance would be impossible without the activity of mapping, standardising, abstracting and replacing 'real' people with simplified averages. As elaborated by James Scott (1998: 11), the contemporary state utilises simplified designs for social organisation, because they enable a 'high degree of schematic knowledge, control and manipulation'. Scott illustrates the dangers of a hegemonic planning mentality with historical examples such the Soviet collectivisation post 1929. As an extreme example of authoritarian planning, the forced collectivisation of agriculture utilised a public transcript of modernisation to disguise the mass appropriation of land, grain and other agricultural products. The vision of collectivisation was described in a highly rational, scientific language of planning, statistics, projections and commands. The centralised plans for Soviet collective farms were, however, based on unrealistic estimates of the harvest, which ignored the complexities of the context, both social and physical. As noted by Scott, a farm, unlike its plan, is not:

> a hypothecated, generic, abstract farm but an unpredictable, complex, and particular farm, with its own unique combination of soils, social structure, administrative culture, weather, political structure, machinery, roads, and the work skills and habits of its employees.
>
> (p. 201)

Soviet collectivisation resulted in disastrous social and economic consequences: food shortages, famine and serfdom of the collective farm workers. The key danger with the hegemonic planning mentality is that a 'facade or a small, easily managed zone of order and conformity may come to be an end in itself' or, in other words, 'the representation may usurp reality' (p. 196). Detrimental, if not disastrous, effects arise when the planning mentality becomes 'so fixed on isolating simple elements of instrumental value that it dismisses complexity, diversity, tradition, local knowledge and resistance' (Bates 2013: 43). Similarly to the 'master builders of Soviet society' (Scott 1998: 193; Amann 2011), English policymakers also tend to dismiss the vital importance of local diversity. The persistent policy focus on standards, targets and other abstractions seems to be changing the patterns of conversation about everyday practice as well as the conditions defining children's educational experience. Their unpredicted, undesirable consequences are explored in Chapters 5 and 6, through the empirical data on the case study schools.

Transformation and the priority of recognition

As noted in Chapter 1, the meaning of educational transformation explored in this book provides an alternative to the standards-based mainstream approaches, which define transformation as quantitative improvement in student test scores and other abstract measures. This alternative meaning originates in Mead's (1956) insights into social change and his definition of transformation as a profound, progressive change in the minds of individuals and the quality of social relations. Improvement in the quality of social relations is 'progressive' to the extent that individuals are willing and able to 'enter into the attitude of others' (Mead 1956: 40). The recognition of the perspectives of others provides the conditions for the emergence of greater social integration. Analogous to the two processes that led to the evolution of biological species, self-organisation and natural selection (Kauffman 1993), the evolution of human consciousness is emergent rather than engineered. The assumption of the independence and autonomy of the Cartesian *homo clausus* (Elias 1994) needs to be, therefore, replaced with a recognition of our interdependence. As Mead (1956: 269) puts it, transformation:

> presupposes a basis of common social interests . . . shared by all the individuals whose minds must participate in, or whose minds bring about, that construction . . . the changes that we make in the social order in which we are implicated necessarily involve our also making changes in ourselves.

Mead (1956) emphasises genuinely democratic relations, based on sharing common interests, as leading to self-change as well as social change. In contrast to the instrumental 'if . . . then . . .' causality characteristic of leadership tools and policy levers, such a change is underpinned by transformative causality whereby individuals transform and are simultaneously transformed through social relations. The complexity of transformation conceived in this way is predicated on far-reaching changes to our perceptions and assumptions about ourselves and others, as well as democratic social relations and organisational value systems that embrace diversity. This requires a kind of reason or consciousness that transcends the instrumental reason and is open to contradiction, ambiguity and paradox.

The way in which we approach paradox aligns our thinking either with the sciences of certainty or complexity. When a paradox is understood as an apparent contradiction, a simultaneous existence of two conflicting elements, the dualism can be removed by privileging one element over the other or by reframing the problem to remove the contradiction. This approach to paradox is rooted in Aristotelian logic that eliminates contradictions because 'they are a sign of faulty thinking' (Stacey 2007: 14). Conversely, the recognition that opposing elements, forces or ideas cannot be eliminated is rooted in Hegelian dialectic logic. As pointed out by Mowles (2015: 16), embracing this logic may help us to understand paradox in a 'richer, more dynamic way' than approaching it as a case of static binary opposites. Hegelian logic is of vital importance to complex responsive processes theory, particularly in relation to the paradox of 'enabling constraints' and values as 'voluntary compulsions', discussed above.

The concept of interdependence may require a particularly far-reaching shift in understanding, on the scale of the quantum 'revolution' in physics discussed in the previous chapter. Mead's (1956) insights into interdependence have been elaborated by Axel Honneth (1995, 2006), who argues that, because of interdependence, 'our everyday activity is not characterised by a self-centred, egocentric stance but by the effort to involve ourselves with given circumstances in the most frictionless, harmonious way possible' (Honneth 2006: 111). This fluent interaction with others depends on forms of relating underpinned by recognition. Honneth explains that recognition involves:

empathetic engagement in the world, arising from the experience of the world's significance and value . . . [which] is prior to our acts of detached cognition. A recognitional stance therefore embodies our active and constant assessment of the value that persons or things have in themselves.

(p. 111)

Honneth's (2006) argument for the priority of recognition over cognition, based on inherent as opposed to instrumental value of others, challenges the Cartesian 'cogito ergo sum' and its unshaken faith in the primacy of detached, 'objective' reasoning.

The vital role of recognition in the psychologically and socially healthy development of children and young people means that recognition should be given primacy over instrumentalist, performance-driven approaches to educational transformation. Recognition, however, may be difficult if not impossible to realise in an education system that prioritises the aspirations of national governments and is designed as performance 'data flows' (Lawn 2011: 279). Prioritising abstraction over reality and cognition over recognition may lead to a tendency to perceive children as 'mere insensate objects' (Honneth 2006: 129). Conversely, recognising a child as a person does not involve an application of general standards or norms, but rather 'the graduated appraisal of concrete traits and abilities' (Honneth 1995: 113). An alternative approach to 'transforming education' would, therefore, begin with a consideration of what it means in relation to the (mis)recognition of the essential needs of *this* child, rather than the generic child (Chapter 8).

Rethinking the myth of control

From the complex responsive processes perspective, the myth of control can be understood as a conversational pattern that uses a high level of abstraction in order to justify particular policy levers and leadership tools on ideological grounds. Just as in the leadership tools discussed above, 'real' people are replaced in myth with 'types' and complex everyday realities get simplified in order to convey a specific message. This interpretation resonates with the explication of myth by Roland Barthes (2000). As signalled in Chapter 1, Barthes posits that myth is a type of communication. The myth of control reduces the complexities of transforming education to simplistic models, so that the control over their 'delivery' appears natural and, therefore, beyond contestation.

The reason for its enduring presence in highly scientific Western culture could be because it is myth, rather than science, that makes our lives intelligible. As noted by Leszek Kołakowski (1989), the ultimate goal of the sciences of certainty[3] is technological application, which does not satisfy our essential human need to make our empirical realities meaningful. Kołakowski emphasises that the 'purposeful order of the world cannot be deduced from what may validly be regarded as the experimental material of scientific thought' (p. 2). The presence of myth originates in three kinds of human needs that science is unable to address: the need for purpose, a faith in the permanence of human values and the desire to see the world as continuous (pp. 2–4). It is no wonder, therefore, that mythology is 'at the heart of things' (MacIntyre 1985: 251). As noted by MacIntyre, myth is an important expression of human life lived as a narrative, addressing both uncertainty and our yearning to live purposeful lives. Consequently, man (or woman):

> becomes through his [her] history, a teller of stories that aspire to truth ... I can only answer the question 'What am I to do?' if I can answer the prior question 'Of what story or stories do I find myself a part?'
>
> (p. 250)

The rise of the complexity sciences suggests that we are part of a different story to that projected by the sciences of certainty, a narrative of possibility, rather than control. For Stuart Kauffman (1995: 4), the sciences of complexity may help us 'find our place in the universe', lost during the 'age of reason'. A similar optimism about the complexity sciences is shared by Prigogine (1996: 7), who sees them within the narrative of humanity 'at a turning point in which science is no longer identified with certitude and probability with ignorance'. In exploring these narrative themes in organisational contexts, complex responsive processes theory offers a promising alternative perspective on the complexities of transforming education.

Limitations of complex responsive processes theory

As signalled in the introduction to this chapter, complex responsive processes theory has been developed through bringing together analogies from the complexity sciences and social science theories that illuminate the processes of human interaction. This methodology enables Stacey and colleagues to explain diverse aspects of organisational change. For example, Douglas Griffin (2002) focuses on 'linking self-organisation and ethics', Patricia Shaw (2002) develops approaches to 'changing conversations in organisations', while Chris Mowles (2011) challenges dominant management thinking by drawing on more 'radical insights from the complexity sciences'. Complex responsive processes theory itself could be viewed as an interactive process of researchers conversing together, responding to previous publications and contributing new insights based on a widening range of theorists. Although such an 'eclectic' approach could be critiqued as lacking theoretical or methodological 'purity', its generative potential is rooted in the 'we-centredness of knowledge' (Elias 1991: 113). Elias challenges the traditional view of knowledge as a product of an individual, 'I-centred' activity. Knowledge creation as a 'we-centred' process has 'the character of messages from person to person' and draws on the 'humankind's social fund of knowledge' and not just contributions by single individuals (p. 113).

This book aims to make a contribution to complex responsive processes theory by taking it to a relatively unexplored level of analysis of the patterns of conversation articulated in two case study schools. Because the theory has been developed mainly at the conceptual level, the analyses it offers are focused mainly on theoretical explanations. For example, Shaw (2002: 171) poses the question 'How do we participate in the way things change over time?' In her answer, she refers to the concepts of narrative sense-making and power figurations. However, her analysis remains at the level of abstractions, as illustrated by the following:

> We met several times together to talk about this and, as we did so, we both developed the personal resources to draw attention differently, to point to and sustain different possibilities in the conversational life of the Borough. We developed together a shift in the way we could speak of our organizational practice.
>
> (p. 98)

Without detailed empirical data,[4] the references to 'personal resources to draw attention differently' and 'shift' [in patterns of conversation] appear to be abstractions from the actual conversational patterns.

In order to address this limitation and analyse empirical data, I have also utilised Fairclough's (2003) critical discourse analysis (CDA) (Chapter 4). The links between complex responsive processes theory and Fairclough's CDA are as follows. From the complex responsive processes perspective, the policy discourse of educational transformation is a generalisation, a global pattern of conversation, which is simultaneously expressive and enactive. As it is particularised and iterated in schools, over time, it may profoundly change education 'through its tireless continuity and pervasiveness' (Chia and Holt 2009: 192). Fairclough (2003: 12) explains such a transformation by highlighting the constitutive and enactive nature of discourse:

> Discourses not only represent the world as it is (or rather is seen to be), they are also projective, imaginaries, representing possible worlds which are different from the actual world, and tied into projects to change the world in particular directions.

Fairclough's position is thus based on the premise that, as a salient and potent element of social life, discourse may have transformative effects on other elements with which it is interconnected. Because processes of social change appear to be influenced by changes in discourse, discourse analysis is helpful in developing understandings of how discourse positions various social agents in the processes of continuity and change. For example, at the level of linguistic markers of agency, the use of nominalisation is a typical feature of policymakers' discourse. Nominalisation is defined by Fairclough (2003: 220) as a grammatical metaphor that represents processes (usually represented as clauses containing the subject/agent) as entities (by using nouns). The use of nominalisation signals an elision of agency (and obfuscation of responsibility). For example, in the following assertion, the noun 'world' represents the process of someone in authority (an agent) making an assumption (unsupported by 'evidence') about desirable and undesirable values:

> The world is indifferent to tradition and past reputations, unforgiving of frailty and ignorant of custom or practice.
> (Barber and Mourshed 2007: 6)

The above use of nominalisation obfuscates agency, as well as political interests underpinning the above assertion. As explained further below, nominalisation is frequently deployed in education policy discourse in order to hide political intentions and interests behind the facade of necessity.

The politics of global educational transformation

That the core argument for the 'new orthodoxy' in transforming education is often presented as necessity and therefore beyond debate can be exemplified by the following assertions by the Department for Education under the New Labour and Coalition governments respectively:

> To prosper in the 21st century competitive global economy, Britain must transform the knowledge and skills of its population. Every child, whatever their circumstances, requires an education that equips them for work and prepares them to succeed in the wider economy and society . . .
> (DfES 2001: 5)

> But now, shifts in technology and the global economy make the education of every child and young person more important than ever . . . the position is radically changed: many of the industries which once required these forms of labour have declined sharply in this country; and even in higher technology industries, much lower level work is now carried out overseas . . . This is the new economic reality.
> (DfE 2010: 3)

These statements by policymakers from different political parties articulate the recurring theme of the necessity to respond to the demands of globalised, knowledge-based economy. In a similar vein, the US Secretary of Education

Arne Duncan (2010) also rehearsed the familiar argument about the knowledge economy and the resulting imperative for education to become 'the new currency by which nations maintain economic competitiveness'. The use of nominalisation in the above statements ('Britain must transform'; 'shifts in technology'; 'many of the industries . . . have declined') conveys a sense that globalisation is an abstract necessity to be addressed, rather than complex processes created and sustained through the decisions of 'real' people engaging in local interactions. As noted by Mulderigg (2003: 101):

> to call education policy solely a *response* seems to endorse the . . . legitimatory rhetoric, which constructs globalization as an inexorable force of change to which nations and individuals must be prepared to adapt; it obfuscates the realities of the capitalist system whose intrinsic instability demands adaptability and flexibility from its workforce.

Such policy arguments align education with the needs of the economy. From the complex responsive processes perspective, they promote global patterns of conversation supporting and spreading the neoliberal project. As pointed out by Rizvi and Lingard (2010: 14), such global education reform discourses are no longer located within the national space, but 'increasingly emanate from international and supranational organizations'. The idea of 'transforming education' may, therefore, be integral to sustaining the neoliberal themes of free markets, economic competition and other requirements of the global economy by organisations such as the OECD, European Union and the World Bank.

A serious consideration of political interests that shape the rhetoric of globalisation demonstrates the moral problems that can arise from the promotion of 'strategic and cold-calculating activity' within the modern capitalist society (Honneth 2006: 96). Honneth writes about an increasing commoditisation of social relations in modern capitalism, stemming from an egocentric calculation of particular situations and relationships solely on the basis of their utility value in achieving specific goals. The discourse of necessity within the global education reform may thus be obscuring from view the moral cost of reducing the value of education to purely economic considerations. As Honneth explains:

> Subjects in a commodity exchange are mutually urged (a) to perceive given objects solely as 'things' that one can potentially make a profit on, (b) to regard each other solely as 'objects' of profitable transactions, and finally (c) to regard their own abilities as nothing but supplemental 'resources' in the calculation of profit opportunities.
>
> (p. 97)

What the rising pattern of such calculative transactional relations means for the 'local' school is explored further in Chapter 8.

Conclusion

As we have seen in this chapter, in the world of complex responsive processes, social change is articulated and enacted through countless ordinary everyday interactions. Analogous to self-organising interactions among agents in complex adaptive systems, people in organisations interact locally, following local self-organising influences such as power, choice and local patterns of conversation. Although a government policy may introduce new patterns of conversation, the way it is taken up in schools depends on these self-organising influences, making it difficult, if not impossible, to control the outcomes of its enactment. The assumption of the individual as interdependent means that, in making our choices, we need to constantly engage with the actions and intentions of others. This applies equally to policymakers who design education policies and practitioners in schools who are accountable for their enactment.

The theory thus offers an understanding of transformation that arises from *within* educational practice and involves profound changes in our 'selves'. In contrast to the mainstream meaning of 'transforming education' as quantitative improvement in pupil performance and other outcomes, transformation denotes a qualitative change in our relations with others. While the 'cold-calculating' demands of performativity, characteristic of the 'new orthodoxy', compel school practitioners to perform to a pre-prepared script, or public transcript, it is an empathetic engagement with others that has a genuinely transformative potential. In upholding the myth of control, the public transcript of education reform retains the idea of determinism, with economic necessity as a dominant theme in the discourse of the global education reform. Although useful in legitimating particular policies, the language of necessity also obfuscates the agency (and responsibility) of 'policy entrepreneurs', power elites and, as explored further in Chapter 8, presents practitioners working in schools with serious ethical problems. In the world that is interconnected through complex networks of interdependence, avoiding responsibility may 'come back to haunt' us, through a 'vast array' of undesirable consequences (Scott 1998: 21).

Complex responsive processes theory emphasises both the *responsive*ness in the processes of communication and the *respons*ibility each one of us holds for our participation in local interactions. While challenging mainstream views, the theory does not aim to negate the role of policymakers or leaders in transforming systems and organisations. This critique does not imply that the policy or managerial interventions are not required, but is an invitation for the policymakers and leaders to engage in the realities of everyday local interactions in more reflective and reflexive ways. As we shall see in Chapter 4, this reflective-reflexive approach is an enabling constraint: it enables insight because it 'slackens the intentional threads which attach us to the world and thus brings them to our notice' (Merleau-Ponty 2002: xiv), at the same time locating us more firmly within the world. The epigraph to this chapter is evocative of how this approach pays attention to the world experienced not as an 'object' for some 'divine' intervention, but as our natural environment to which we belong.

Notes

1 The NCTL is a government-funded agency, opened in 2000 by New Labour under the name of the National College for School Leadership (NCSL). The original vision for the NCSL was aligned with the policy of decentralisation in the public sector services. However, the actual devolution of power to school leaders turned out to be constrained by policies that increasingly constructed 'leadership knowledge' in terms of compliance with the government agendas and efficient implementation of policy (Gunter 2004).
2 Stacey (2010) distinguishes between 'first-order' and 'second-order' abstractions analogous to first- and second-order systems thinking. First-order systems thinking refers to a system viewed as a 'closed', 'mechanical' model, such as a clockwork mechanism. In mainstream management theory, first-order systems thinking positions the manager or a system designer as a detached observer able to control the system by manipulating it *as if* from an external vantage point. Second-order systems thinking emphasises multiple realities of people in organisations conceived as 'open' (complex adaptive) systems. The focus here is on organisational learning, collaborative construction of meaning and participative forms of management. Second-order systems thinking, however, also maintains an idealised, normative conception of organisations as systems and focuses on an idealised future ('what should be') rather than a 'messy' reality of the here-and-now ('what is').
3 Although Kołakowski (1989: 1) does not distinguish between the sciences of certainty and the complexity sciences, approaches characteristic of the former are implicit in his point that science is 'the extension of civilization's technological core'.
4 The research approach used by complex responsive processes researchers is framed as reflexive narrative enquiry, premised on the researcher's positioning as a participant and as a narrator (Stacey 2010, 2012). This researcher position is consistent with Stacey *et al.*'s critique of mainstream management knowledge created from a detached, 'objective' observer vantage point. The task of the researcher-as-participant is to make explicit her assumptions, ideology and power relations intertwined in the everyday organisational interactions of which she is a participant. Research 'data' consist of accounts of practice which are critically and reflexively analysed within the conceptual framework of complex responsive processes theory, by the researcher-as-narrator. Detailed examples of the application of the reflexive narrative enquiry can be found in Shaw (2002), Stacey (2007) and Mowles (2011).

References

Alexander, R., Armstrong, M., Flutter, J., Hargreaves, L., Harlen, W., Harrison, D., Hartley-Brewer, E., Kershner, R., MacBeath, J., Mayall, B., Northen, S., Pugh, G., Richards, C. and Utting, D. 2010. *Children, Their World, Their Education: Final Report and Recommendations of the Cambridge Primary Review*. Abingdon: Routledge and the University of Cambridge.

Amann, R. 2011. A Sovietological view of modern Britain, *The Political Quarterly*, 74(4): 287–301. Malden, MA: Blackwell.

Arnold, R. 2004. *Transforming Secondary Education: The Beacon Council Scheme: Round 4*. Slough: National Foundation for Educational Research.

Ball, S.J. 2004. *The Sera Lecture 2004: Education Reform as Social Barberism: Economism and the End of Authenticity*. Available at: www.scotedreview.org.uk/media/scottish-educational-review/articles/251.pdf (accessed 12 April 2015).

Ball, S.J., Maguire, M. and Braun, A. 2012. *How Schools Do Policy: Policy Enactments in Secondary Schools*. London and New York: Routledge.

Barad, K. 2007. *Meeting the Universe Halfway: Quantum Physics and the Entanglement of Matter and Meaning.* Durham, NC and London: Duke University Press.

Barber, M. 1997. *The Learning Game: Arguments for an Education Revolution.* London: Indigo.

Barber, M. 2008. *Instruction to Deliver: Fighting to Transform Britain's Public Services* (2nd edn). London: Methuen Publishing.

Barber, M. and Mourshed, M. 2007. *How the World's Best Education Systems Stay on Top.* Available at: www.smhc-cpre.org/wp-content/uploads/2008/07/how-the-worlds-best-performing-school-systems-come-out-on-top-sept-072.pdf (accessed 15 February 2012).

Barthes, R. 2000. *Mythologies.* (A. Levers, Trans.). London: Vintage Books.

Bates, A. 2013. Transcending systems thinking in education reform: Implications for policy-makers and school leaders, *Journal of Education Policy*, 28(1): 38–54.

Chia, C.H. and Holt, R. 2009. *Strategy without Design: The Silent Efficacy of Indirect Action.* Cambridge: Cambridge University Press.

Davies, B. and Davies, B.J. 2009. 'Strategic Leadership'. In Davies, B. (ed.) *The Essentials of School Leadership.* London: Sage, 13–36.

Davies, B. and Ellison, L. 2003. 'Strategic Analysis: Obtaining the Data and Building a Strategic View'. In Preedy, M., Bennett, N. and Wise, C. (eds) *Strategic Leadership and Educational Improvement.* London: Sage, 157–184.

DfE. 2010. *The Case for Change.* London: Crown Copyright.

DfES. 2001. *Schools Achieving Success.* Annesley: DfES Publications.

Duncan, A. 2010. *The Vision of Education Reform in the United States: Secretary Arne Duncan's Remarks to United Nations Educational, Scientific and Cultural Organization (UNESCO)*, Paris, France (November 4). Available at: www.ed.gov/news/speeches/vision-education-reform-united-states-secretary-arne-duncans-remarks-united-nations-ed (accessed 13 April 2015).

Elias, N. 1978. *What Is Sociology?* New York: Columbia University Press.

Elias, N. 1991. *The Symbol Theory.* London: Sage.

Elias, N. 1994. *The Civilizing Process: Sociogenetic and Psychogenetic Investigations.* Malden, MA and Abingdon: Blackwell Publishing.

Fairclough, N. 2003. *Analysing Discourse: Textual Analysis for Social Research.* Abingdon: Routledge.

Foucault, M. 1979. *Discipline & Punish: The Birth of the Prison.* New York: Vintage Books.

Gordon, D.M. 1999. *Ants at Work: How an Insect Society Is Organized.* New York: W.W. Norton & Company.

Gough, N. 2010. 'Lost Children and Anxious Adults: Responding to Complexity in Australian Education and Society'. In Osberg D. and Biesta, G. (eds) *Complexity Theory and the Politics of Education.* Rotterdam: Sense Publishers, 39–56.

Griffin, D. 2002. *The Emergence of Leadership: Linking Self-Organisation and Ethics.* London and New York: Routledge.

Gunter, H. 2004. Labels and labelling in the field of educational leadership, *Discourse: Studies in the Cultural Politics of Education*, 25(1): 21–41.

Gunter, H. and Forrester, G. 2009. School leadership and education policy-making in England, *Policy Studies*, 30(5): 495–511.

Harris, S. 2007. *The Governance of Education: How Neo-Liberalism is Transforming Policy and Practice.* London: Continuum.

Honneth, A. 1995. *The Struggle for Recognition: The Moral Grammar of Social Conflicts.* (J. Anderson, Trans.). Cambridge: Polity Press.

Honneth, A. 2006. *Reification: A Recognition-Theoretical View.* Available at: http://tannerlectures.utah.edu/lecture-library.php#h (accessed 14 March 2014).

Kauffman, S. 1993. *The Origins of Order: Self-Organization and Selection in Evolution.* New York: Oxford University Press.

Kauffman, S. 1995. *At Home in the Universe: The Search for the Laws of Self-Organization and Complexity.* New York: Oxford University Press.

Kołakowski, L. 1989. *The Presence of Myth.* Chicago, IL: The University of Chicago Press.

Lawn, M. 2011. Governing through data in English education, *Education Enquiry*, 2(2): 277–288.

MacIntyre, A. 1985. *After Virtue: A Study in Moral Theory* (2nd edn). London: Bloomsbury.

Mead, G.H. 1923. Scientific method and the moral sciences, *International Journal of Ethics*, 23: 229–247. Available at: www.brocku.ca/MeadProject/Mead/pubs/Mead_1923.html (accessed 10 April 2015).

Mead, G.H. 1932. *The Philosophy of the Present.* New York: Prometheus Books.

Mead, G.H. 1934. *Mind, Self, and Society from the Standpoint of a Social Behaviourist.* Chicago, IL and London: The University of Chicago Press.

Mead, G.H. 1956. *On Social Psychology.* Chicago, IL: Chicago University Press.

Merleau-Ponty, M. 2002. *Phenomenology of Perception.* (C. Smith, Trans.). Abingdon: Routledge Classics.

Meyer, H.D. and Benavot, A. (eds). 2013. *PISA, Power, and Policy: The Emergence of Global Educational Governance.* Oxford: Symposium Books.

Mowles, C. 2011. *Rethinking Management: Radical Insights from the Complexity Sciences.* Farnham: Gower.

Mowles, C. 2014. Complex, but not quite complex enough: The turn to the complexity sciences in evaluation scholarship, *Evaluation*, 20(2): 160–175.

Mowles, C. 2015. *Managing in Uncertainty: Complexity and the Paradoxes of Everyday Organizational Life.* London and New York: Routledge.

Mulderigg, J. 2003. Consuming education: A critical discourse analysis of social actors in New Labour's education policy, *Journal for Critical Education Policy Studies*, 1(1): 96–123.

Mullins, L.J. 2007. *Management and Organisational Behaviour* (8th edn). Harlow: Pearson Education.

OECD. 2013. *Teaching and Learning International Survey TALIS 2013: Conceptual Framework.* Available at: www.oecd.org/edu/school/TALIS%20Conceptual%20Framework_FINAL.pdf (accessed 7 May 2015).

Osberg, D. and Biesta, G. (eds). 2010. *Complexity Theory and the Politics of Education.* Rotterdam: Sense.

Polesel, J., Rice, S. and N. Dulfer. 2014. The impact of high-stakes testing on curriculum and pedagogy: A teacher perspective from Australia, *Journal of Education Policy*, 29(5): 640–657.

Popper, K. 1982. *The Open Universe: An Argument for Indeterminism.* London and New York: Routledge.

Prigogine, I. 1996. *The End of Certainty: Time, Chaos and the New Laws of Nature.* New York: The Free Press.

Purves, A. 1987. IEA: An agenda for the future, *International Review of Education* 33(1): 103–107.
Rizvi, F. and Lingard, B. 2010. *Globalizing Education Policy*. Abingdon: Routledge.
Sahlberg, P. 2011. *Finnish Lessons: What Can the World Learn from Educational Change in Finland?* New York and London: Teachers College.
Scott, J.C. 1990. *Domination and the Arts of Resistance: Hidden Transcripts*. New Haven, CT: Yale University Press.
Scott, J.C. 1998. *Seeing Like a State: How Certain Schemes to Improve the Human Condition Have Failed*. New Haven, CT and London: Yale University Press.
Shaw, P. 2002. *Changing Conversations in Organizations: A Complexity Approach to Change*. London: Routledge.
Stacey, R.D. 2007. *Strategic Management and Organisational Dynamics: The Challenge of Complexity* (5th edn). Harlow: Pearson Education.
Stacey, R.D. 2010. *Complexity and Organisational Reality: Uncertainty and the Need to Rethink Management after the Collapse of Investment Capitalism* (2nd edn). London: Routledge.
Stacey, R. 2012. *Tools and Techniques of Leadership and Management*. Abingdon: Routledge.
Thomson, P., Gunter, H, and Blackmore, J. 2014. 'Series Foreword'. In Gunter, H.M. *Educational Leadership and Hannah Arendt*. London and New York: Routledge, vi–xii.
Tsoukas, H. 2005. *Complex Knowledge: Studies in Organizational Epistemology*. Oxford: Oxford University Press.

Chapter 4

Researching complexity

> The world is not what I think, but what I live through.
> (Merleau-Ponty 2002: xviii)

As we have seen in Chapter 3, complex responsive processes theory is aligned with the complexity sciences (Kauffman 1995; Prigogine 1996), which recognise the provisional nature of knowledge and are located in the complexity paradigm. Applied to educational transformation, complex responsive processes theory challenges abstractions and idealisations of school improvement policies designed from a distance in favour of understanding the complexities of everyday practice in 'all its uncertainty, emotion and messiness' (Stacey 2010: 224). This understanding resonates with Merleau-Ponty's statement in the epigraph to this chapter. Merleau-Ponty emphasises our experience of the world as 'lived through' rather than 'thought' and made sense of from a position of a detached observer. It is in the 'lived experience' of working with *this* child, in *this* school, in *this* locality that deeper understandings of the nature and meaning of education arise. Everyday practice is a rich source of local knowledge, generated from '*within*' (Tsoukas 2005). Local knowledge emerges in unique contexts; it is subjective, rich in descriptive detail and nuanced meaning, at the expense of generalisation.

By contrast, much of mainstream research on educational improvement is oriented towards objectivity, precise measurement, reliability, prediction and 'evidence'. In alignment with the sciences of certainty, mainstream research seeks to achieve these goals by reducing or simplifying complexity. Evidence-based policy in England relies on predominantly positivist research methodologies that provide policymakers and school leaders with a 'factual' base of 'what works' (Hammersley 2013). Knowledge of 'what works' is then used for leveraging and measuring policy 'delivery' independently of the local context, in a similar way to the policies driven by international comparisons (Meyer and Benavot 2013; Sellar and Lingard 2014) and the generic toolkit provided by the TLP (Thomson *et al.* 2014). Chapters 5–8 will illustrate how strategies for 'delivering' school improvement are narrowly focused on pupil performance data. There are limits to the validity of such strategies, as well as to what school leaders and teachers can do in order to continuously improve pupil test scores. Therefore, both the production and application of knowledge are more complex than is typically assumed within these mainstream approaches.

The focus of this chapter is on the methodological implications of a commitment to complexity and in particular more practical concerns in relation to research designs consistent with complex responsive processes theory. We will return to the distinction between the sciences of certainty and the complexity sciences discussed in Chapter 2 to draw connections between their key assumptions (Table 2.1 in Chapter 2) and research paradigms within the social sciences (Figure 4.1). The following section offers an overview of the orientations of complexity research in the social sciences. It also explains how complexity has been positioned as an 'emerging' paradigm in educational research (Cohen *et al.* 2011: 28) and how it challenges knowledge underpinning evidence-informed policy, international comparisons and the TLP. I then move on to discuss how a research study consistent with complex responsive processes theory was designed to explore the enactment of government policies for transforming education in two schools. The emphasis in this chapter is on how the paradigm of complexity challenges the epistemology of the reductive mainstream approaches and the associated 'politics of complexity reduction' (Biesta 2010: 7).

Complexity and research paradigms in the social sciences

This section focuses on the relationships between research paradigms in the social sciences and the sciences of certainty or the complexity sciences. As explained in Chapter 2, the sciences of certainty view the world as made up of objects with predetermined properties that are measurable and divisible into smaller units. Universal laws about the workings of the Newtonian clockwork world are presented in the form of linear equations and simple cause and effect, or 'if . . . then . . .' causality (Stacey 2012). By contrast, the sciences of complexity pay attention to the dynamic, evolving 'nature of nature' and, consequently, view knowledge as provisional, interconnected and essentially complex. The sciences of complexity also challenge the view of knowledge as entirely objective and pay attention to the processes of knowledge generation as inseparable from the socio-political context (Table 2.1). Consequently, a commitment to complexity in researching the social locates the researcher in paradigms that assume a degree of subjectivity as well as uncertainty (Figure 4.1).

The concept of 'paradigm' was introduced by Kuhn (1996) to denote a distinctive epistemological-methodological framework shared by a given scientific community (Chapter 2). Through his historical analysis of paradigmatic shifts, for example from the pre-Copernican to Copernican worldviews, Kuhn (1996: 103) arrived at the notion of 'incommensurability' of scientific paradigms, concluding that the 'differences between the successive paradigms are both necessary and irreconcilable'. However, as suggested by recent developments within the complexity sciences, the issue may be not as much about whether distinctive paradigms are commensurable, but about the conceptions of knowledge generation and application they uphold. For example, quantum physics does not contradict but supersedes its Newtonian predecessor (Barad 2007).[1] Similarly, an approach to research in the social sciences that is consistent with complexity may need to accept the uncertainty arising from non-linear patterns of interaction in social life as 'the norm, rather than the exception' (Mowles 2014: 161). As pointed out by a number of commentators, however, many applications of complexity to researching the social world are based on a direct transfer of models from the natural sciences (Chia 1998; Callaghan 2008; Mowles 2014). This simplistic application of complexity can be illustrated by the way Michael Barber (1997: 160) turns to chaos theory, stating that:

> The fact is that wherever we look – science, history, management, politics – systems are giving way to chaos . . . It is time to recognise that reforming structures alone will not bring about real change, least of all in education, where quality depends so heavily on a chaotic myriad of personal interactions.

The above offers a simplistic interpretation of 'facts' about chaos, since non-linear ('chaotic') patterns of interaction emphasise uncertainty rather than possibilities of 'bringing about real change'. As noted by Byrne and Callaghan (2014: 256), applying complexity concepts to understanding the social needs to be 'mediated' through a careful, systematic consideration of issues 'raised in social theory'.

Similar complex considerations are implicit in Guba and Lincoln's (1998) definition of paradigms. A 'paradigm' in the social sciences may be understood as a framework of three questions pertaining to ontology (the nature of reality, or a worldview), epistemology (the relationship between the knower and the known) and methodology (a way to establish the validity of a particular worldview):

> A paradigm may be viewed as a set of *basic beliefs* (or metaphysics) that deals with ultimates or first principles. It represents a *worldview* that defines for its holder, the nature of the 'world', the individual's place in it, and the range of possible relationships to that world and its parts . . . The beliefs are basic in the sense that they must be accepted simply on faith (however well argued); there is no way to establish their ultimate truthfulness. If there were, the philosophical debates . . . would have been resolved millennia ago.
> (p. 200)

Two points are important here. First, no methodology can establish the 'ultimate truthfulness' of a worldview framed within a particular paradigm.

74 The universe of complexity thinking

Second, a paradigm is a 'human construction', representing the most informed view 'that its proponents have been able to devise', given the methods chosen for finding the answers to the three questions above (pp. 201–202). It follows that knowledge is subject to error and paradigmatic positions may need to be justified through utility or persuasion rather than proof. Figure 4.1 illustrates, in general terms, approximate relationships between different research paradigms.[2]

The paradigm of positivism is oriented towards reductionist methodologies developed within the sciences of certainty. Research paradigms which, like complexity, approach education as a complex object of study include critical realism, interpretivism, postmodernism and social constructionism.[3] While the paradigm of complexity shares a commitment to complexity with critical realism and postmodernism, it is also distinctive in bridging the divide between the natural and social sciences.[4] As explained in Chapter 3, complex responsive processes theory is distinctive within the complexity paradigm in how it takes up complexity concepts by analogies (rather than direct transfer) and combines them with insights from philosophy and social theory to explain the complexities of human organising. Through its philosophical antecedents and interest in human interaction, complex responsive processes theory also shares some notable commonalities with social constructionism, discussed below.

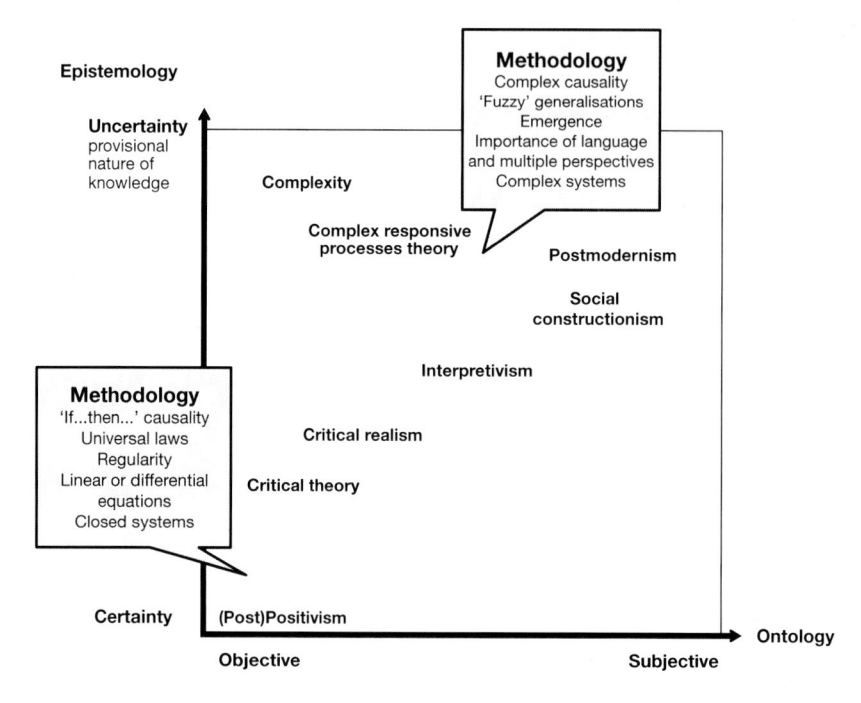

Figure 4.1 Research paradigms and their relative orientations

The argument for giving complexity the status of an 'emerging paradigm' in educational research (Cohen *et al.* 2011; Fenwick *et al.* 2011) is based on the substantive body of knowledge which the complexity sciences developed for explaining complex educational dynamics (Cohen *et al.* 2011). Cohen *et al.* emphasise the potential of complexity concepts such as complex systems, emergence and connectedness to facilitate deep understandings of educational contexts and processes. Crucially, insights from the complexity sciences into the complex nature of causality lead Cohen *et al.* to challenge positivist approaches in educational research:

> Complexity theory not only questions the values of positivist research and experimentation, but it also underlines the importance of educational research to catch the deliberate, intentional, agentic actions of participants and to adopt interactionist and constructivist perspectives.
> (p. 30)

Opportunities for more nuanced understandings of educational change within the paradigm of complexity have also been highlighted by other commentators. They include the possibilities for transforming the curriculum and pedagogy (Doll 2008; Mason 2008), changing relations within schools and beyond (Davis *et al.* 2010), and developing research approaches that create complex knowledge (Davis and Sumara 2006; Kuhn 2008; Fenwick *et al.* 2011). Theories in the complexity paradigm, such as complex responsive processes theory, expose the political bias inherent in reductive mainstream approaches. As pointed out by Biesta (2010: 11), the key question about the 'politics of complexity reduction' is who 'has the "right" and "power" to identify and define what counts as learning'. For Davis and Sumara (2006: 135), education for a complex world needs to be 'oriented toward the as-yet unimagined – indeed the currently unimaginable'. Research within the paradigm of complexity may thus provide knowledge for renewing educational practices and purposes (Fenwick *et al.* 2011).

Positivism is rooted in the conception of knowledge as 'accurate representation' (Rorty 1979). This conception can be traced back to the Enlightenment and Descartes' view of the mind as a 'mirror of nature' (Chapter 2). The key implication of this view for knowledge generation is, metaphorically speaking, that it relies on 'more accurate representations by inspecting repairing, and polishing the mirror' (p. 12). The ways of 'polishing the mirror', or discovering 'objective', pre-existing facts about independently existing phenomena, were advanced in the nineteenth century through the positivist scientific method. They include precise measurement, sophisticated apparatuses and other procedures for increasing reliability and decreasing the contamination of empirical data, in what is conceptualised as a linear, rigorous, factual enquiry (Cohen *et al.* 2011). These procedures are replicable and underpinned by an assumption that the conceptual categories and sensory experience of the scientist are fixed and neutral, as is the language of scientific observations and reports (Kuhn 1996).

In contrast to positivism, interpretivism assumes that 'there is no such thing as unmediated data or facts' and, therefore, a focus on interpretation rather than accurate representation of reality may be more helpful in understanding the complexities of social worlds (Alvesson and Sköldberg 2009: 12). Barad (2007) takes the distinction between knowledge as 'accurate representation' and interpretation further, by positing a performative conception of knowledge. She explains how the choice of the scientific apparatus may perform significant inclusions and exclusions. Similarly, data collection instruments used in social research may also define and categorise and include or exclude social phenomena in ways that are not entirely neutral. The process of knowledge creation is thus not merely about discovering 'facts' but about affecting potential change in the world. This means that researcher 'objectivity' may not just be about seeking accurate, replicable representations, but also about being accountable for that change. This, in turn, calls for a 'methodology that is attentive to, and responsive/responsible to' how coming to knowledge contributes to '*(re)configuring the world*' (Barad 2007: 91).[5] Research may contribute to transforming worldviews and explaining how social realities are socially constructed. The latter provides the focus for research in the paradigm of social constructionism (Holstein and Gubrium 2008).

One of the first systematic accounts of the 'social construction of reality', authored by Berger and Luckmann, was published in 1966. Since then, social constructionism has grown as a research paradigm in its own right, though sharing some similarities with other theoretical orientations such as postmodernism and critical realism (Burr 2003). These theoretical orientations challenge taken-for-granted ways of understanding the world and seek alternatives to (post)positivism (Figure 4.1). They acknowledge that meanings and worldviews are rooted in culture, history and social institutions. They thus 'complexify' the notion of 'truth', emphasise the provisional nature of knowledge and reject the positivist idea of language being a neutral medium for representing reality. One consequence of viewing knowledge as political acts seeking to legitimate preferred representations of the world (and invalidate others) is that researchers within the social constructionist, postmodern and interpretivist traditions face the challenge of validating their own analyses. The criteria of 'trustworthiness' or 'soundness of analysis' in research may not appear as convincing as the criteria of reliability and validity that legitimate research in the positivist paradigm (Burr 2003). For example, social constructionism can be understood as avoiding 'playing the truth game' (Gergen 2009: 160), which makes it vulnerable to attack from the more normative positions of realism and positivism. In the spirit of reflexivity discussed later in this chapter, social constructionism needs to recognise itself as a social construction, on a par with other paradigms.

The complexity researcher and 'grades of commitment'

In writing about complexity-informed research in the social sciences, Byrne and Callaghan (2014) emphasise the nature of the world as ontologically complex. They also point out the vital role of human agency in social transformation. Social change, they argue, is 'driven by individuals and institutions' and is, therefore, a manifestation of specific, often conflicting interests (p. 261). The process of knowledge production is underpinned by myriad interests, motives and objectives. This means that a commitment to complexity in research is linked to the researcher's 'grade of commitment' to the social phenomenon being investigated (Hacking 1999). While positivist researchers claim detached objectivity in their search for deterministic laws, research premised on subjective worldviews highlights the importance of the researcher's orientation towards the 'object' of study, as well as his/her approach to the dissemination and application of knowledge. Hacking's 'grades of commitment'[6] are rooted in the social constructionist orientation towards a critique of the status quo, based on the thesis that:

> X need not have existed, or need not be at all as it is. X, or X as it is at present, is not determined by the nature of things; it is not inevitable.
> (p. 6)

Recognising and articulating one's 'grade of commitment' may enhance researcher 'trustworthiness' and accountability for knowledge generated through research. Ironically, on this account, it is the claims to complete neutrality and objectivity that need to be approached with caution, since:

> No human being can step outside of their humanity and view the world from no position at all, which is what the idea of objectivity suggests, and this is just as true of scientists as of everyone else.
> (Burr 2003: 152)

Researcher orientation and complex responsive processes theory

Complex responsive processes theory shares some of its research interests and insights with the broad canon of complexity-informed social science. As explained in Chapter 3, it is also distinctive in arguing against unproblematically applying explanations generated in the natural sciences to human action. This is in contrast to complexity-informed research that uses computer modelling to map the trajectories of complex (human) systems (such as organisations, cities or public services), or focuses on 'hunting' for 'multiple interacting causes' within 'multiple interacting causal sets' to inform 'action directed towards the achievement of futures' (Byrne and Callaghan 2014: 189–190).

Complex responsive processes scholars focus instead on patterns of everyday local interactions, 'power relations expressed in the dynamics of inclusion, exclusion and identity formation, communication understood as conversation, and evaluative choices that reveal ideology' (Mowles 2014: 170). They have also taken a radical position in going beyond 'looking at' organisations as systems and expressing caution about high levels of abstraction involved in modelling social phenomena.

This has implications for research designs consistent with complex responsive processes theory. Just as making sense of our experience can be enhanced through continuous reflexive evaluation, the value of research is also in 'taking one's own experience seriously' (Stacey 2010: 226), the core purpose being:

> to develop the practitioner's skills in paying attention to the complexity of the local, micro interactions he or she is engaged in, because it is in these that wider organizational pattern emerge.
>
> (p. 222)

Two paradoxical processes of 'abstracting' and 'immersing' contribute to making sense of this experience. As explained by Stacey, 'immersing' denotes a pre-reflective state of being involved in experience (p. 110). 'Abstracting' is the opposite movement of drawing away from experience and becoming aware of what we are engaging in, as suggested by its Latin meaning 'to draw away' (the preposition '*ab*' means 'away' and the verb '*trahere*' means to 'draw'). For example, narrating is an act of abstracting: when narrating an event we detach from it and as a result cease to be immersed in experience. The opposite happens when we are so immersed in the moment that we stop abstracting or rationalising. Human thought is based on simultaneously immersing in and abstracting from experience. Narrating presents a first-order abstraction, whereby we create mental categories of experience at one remove from reality as 'lived'. Measuring, objectifying, modelling, setting targets and operating on these abstract categories is a second-level abstraction, involving a further remove from 'lived' experience. As Stacey (2010) points out, the intention behind second-order abstraction is to exert some form of control from a distance. The implication of the distinction between abstracting and immersing for researching everyday experience is that a narrative account is a first-order abstraction. It is, therefore, closer to 'lived' reality than second-order abstractions such as surveys and other statistical data framing management tools and blueprints for a 'perfect' future in evidence-based policy.[7]

Researching everyday practice

As discussed above, complex responsive processes theorists emphasise the importance of paying attention to ordinary everyday local interactions and communications. Their focus on everyday practice as *experienced*, rather than idealised in the form of abstractions, resonates with the phenomenological interest in the world as 'what I live through' (Merleau-Ponty 2002: viiii). For example, an idealised vision of English education as a 'world-class' system fails to capture how the focus on ambitious school performance targets shapes the everyday experience of working in a particular rather than an abstract school. No abstract measures can fully convey the successes and failures, compassion and frustration, togetherness and divide – the complex day-to-day 'lived experience' of practitioners. 'Lived experience' is defined by Van Manen (1990) as experience that involves our immediate, pre-theoretical consciousness of life. Writing in the phenomenological tradition,[8] Van Manen (1990: 182) argues that being-in-the-world makes us inextricably involved in the world of immediate experience. This argument, in turn, reveals strong resonances with the treatise on the sociology of knowledge by Berger and Luckmann (1966). Berger and Luckmann are interested in how subjective meanings become objective 'facts' and, to answer this question, consider 'what people "know" as "reality" in their everyday, non- or pre-theoretical lives' (p. 27). Foremost in this context is the 'I', experienced as embodied, intentional, subjective and always directed towards objects and people around. Our sense of self is possible because other selves are implicated in our everyday experience. It follows that '*Homo sapiens* is always ... *homo socius*' (p. 69), unlike the Cartesian *homo clausus* (Elias 1994).

Berger and Luckmann (1966) draw on the theories of Mead to emphasise the vital part played by the shared symbols of language in constructing what appears to be an 'objective' social reality:

> On the level of symbolism ... linguistic signification attains the maximum detachment from the 'here and now' of everyday life, and language soars into regions that are not only *de facto* but *a priori* unavailable to everyday experience. Language now constructs immense edifices of symbolic representations that appear to tower over the reality of everyday life like gigantic presences from another world. Religion, philosophy, art, and science are the historically most important symbol systems of this kind.
>
> (p. 55)

Language provides us with readymade patterns for ongoing objectification of everyday experience. The result is a paradox of humans constructing a social world that they experience as 'something other' than a social construct (p. 78). The maintenance of a particular social worldview involves an appeal to tradition, exclusion of deviant behaviour and use of power 'to determine decisive socialization processes and, therefore, the power to *produce* reality' (p. 137). Seemingly 'objective' reality is thus constructed in social practice and at the same time experienced as if the nature of this reality was fixed and predetermined.[9]

Researchers within the tradition developed by Berger and Luckmann are interested in an analysis aimed at revealing how discourses work to create particular systems of meanings and frameworks for understanding the world (Burr 2003). This partly aligns social constructionism with complex responsive processes theory, which emphasises the importance of local patterns of conversation as simultaneously expressing and enacting organisational change. The conceptual framework of complex responsive theory (Figure 3.1) may, therefore, be further refined with the help of analytical tools developed within CDA (Fairclough 2003). A closer textual analysis of discursive patterns of conversation within an organisation may provide more subtle insights into how individual and collective identities and power relations are articulated and institutionalised, or contested and changed. The relationship between the CDA and complex responsive processes theory is illustrated by Figure 4.2 below.

Research design and complex responsive processes theory

This section summarises the case study design consistent with complex responsive processes theory, which generated the empirical data discussed in Chapters 5–8. My overarching aim was to explore what 'transforming education' means to practitioners tasked with enacting government improvement policies. The research objectives focused on: (a) an analysis of the processes of improving two case study schools from complex responsive processes perspective, (b) unplanned consequences of the *National Literacy* and *Numeracy Strategies* for primary education and (c) alternatives to mainstream approaches to educational leadership and policy.

The main focus of the research on the interpretations of government improvement policies and their ordinary, 'real-life' manifestations in everyday practice is aligned with the qualitative case study approach (Stake 1995; Simons 2009). Defined as an in-depth empirical investigation of a complex phenomenon in its real-life context, the qualitative case study also accords with the conceptual framework of complex responsive processes theory (Figure 3.1). The data were collected in two schools, 'Abbey Primary' and 'Green Lanes Primary' (pseudonyms), and included semi-structured interview transcripts, observation notes and documents produced by the schools, for internal and public view. Data analysis focused on participants' understandings of school improvement (and transformation) and the enactment of school improvement policies in everyday practice. A sample of two schools in the same locality was deemed suitable, given the focus on 'local diversity', multiple perspectives of participants, depth of meaning and complexity of changes in response to government policies. An advantage of designs based on a small number of cases is the opportunity they afford for understanding the particularity and complexity (Simons 2009), as well as for preserving the wholeness of the case and the people being studied (Stake 1995). Stake's claim that it 'startles us all to find our own perplexities in the lives of others' points to the commonality that can be found in studying particular cases (p. 7).

To be human 'is to be concerned with meaning, to desire meaning' (Van Manen 1990: 78–79) and meaning 'can only be communicated textually – by way of organised narrative or prose'. As Stake (1995: 87) points out, a narrative approach that provides the reader with a vicarious experience may accentuate the meanings and insights emerging from the data. In complexity-informed organisational research, narrative-based methodologies offer potential for in-depth understanding of change processes and their intended and unintended consequences, as well as bringing together multiple perspectives of practitioners (Tsoukas and Hatch 2001; Mowles 2014). Accordingly, the case studies reported in Chapters 5–8 do not seek universal laws, but rather, by paying attention to everyday conversational patterns, may convey the experience of enacting government improvement policies in its complexity and 'average everydayness' (Heidegger 1962: 38).

Seeking complex forms of knowledge does not call for grandiose research designs or 'groundbreaking' instruments (OECD 2013) for collecting the empirical data. Of more importance is the researcher's orientation to his/her 'data sources' (e.g. research participants), ways of making sense of the data and grade of commitment to the knowledge generated in the process. Just as scientific revolutions are predicated on seeing differently when looking in familiar places with familiar instruments (Kuhn 1996), researching complexity is about replacing a tendency to simplify with a commitment to 'complex forms of knowing' (Tsoukas 2005). For example, connecting to the original meaning of 'data'/'datum' as something 'given' or 'granted' (Van Manen 1990: 54) has important implications for the researcher's orientation to 'data'. It implies that research participants are able to make a choice regarding what they are willing to 'give' and what to withhold. The power to 'give' or withhold data is therefore theirs. However, once data have been 'given', the power to interpret and make sense of them shifts towards the researcher.

Data collection instruments

A search for complex forms of knowledge about people engaged in 'their ordinary pursuits and milieus' relies on data collection instruments of observation, semi-structured interviews and documentary review (Stake 1995: 1). Interviewing is based on the assumption that conversation is central in knowledge production processes, particularly in research that seeks to explore multiple realities of diverse actors. The extent to which the interview is capable of conveying everyday experiences of social actors depends on a combination of factors: the researcher's approach to interviewing, the informant's motives as well as the contingencies of the interview situation seen as complex, socially and discursively (Alvesson 2011). For example:

> Interview talk may say more about role-playing and adapting to social standards in the name of impression management – including how to

appear authentic – than about how people really feel or what social reality is really like.

(p. 3)

From the complex responsive processes perspective, the interview interaction can be regarded as a paradox: it is simultaneously situated, emergent, dynamic – 'of a moment' – and also representative of the patterns of conversation shared in specific organisational contexts.

Observation provides the foundation of all research methods and every social scientist is an observer of activities and settings that provide a backdrop to human activities (Angrosino 2005). The strength of observation is in the opportunity for collecting ' "live" data from naturally occurring social situations . . . looking directly at what is taking place *in situ* rather than relying on second hand accounts' (p. 396). However, Angrosino cautions against assuming that researchers are able to 'see events through the eyes of the people being studied' (p. 732) and recommends being mindful of the extent to which the researcher's own perception plays a role in gathering fieldwork data:

No faith can be more misleading than an unquestioned personal conviction that the apparent testimony of one's eyes must provide a purely objective account . . . Utterly unbiased observation must rank as a primary myth.
(Gould, cited in Angrosino 2005: 743)

With regard to documentary review, official documents available to the researcher studying organisations provide a valuable source of the 'public transcript' (Scott 1990), which institutions use to make their culture and values available for view by different audiences. Documents thus 'offer a lens to interpret events in order to gain insights into the relationship between the written and unwritten, spoken and virtual, public and private, past and present' (Fitzgerald 2007: 279). Based on the assumption of the constitutive nature of language, documents produced by schools can also be read as enacting particular values. Schools do this through the production of their own policies, rules and regulations that are often presented in the form of artefacts and become displayed as part of the physical environment of the school (Maguire *et al.* 2011; Ball *et al.* 2012).

Large-scale surveys are favoured by positivist researchers because of their potential to produce 'objective' and generalisable quantitative data sets (Cohen *et al.* 2011). This potential, however, is problematic because of the complexity reduction entailed in survey research. Using surveys for researching complex phenomena such as organisations means getting the organisation into a 'countable, measurable form', at the risk of stripping it of the complexity that 'made it worth counting in the first place' (Weick 1979: 29). Similarly, from the complex responsive processes perspective, a questionnaire designer is able to control the assumptions, concepts and language of questions, but is unable to gather data on the actual patterns of conversation.

Data analysis and interpretation

As signalled above, discourse analysis may offer more nuanced insights into patterns of conversation and, consequently, Fairclough's (2003) CDA framework was also utilised to the analysis of the case study data (Figure 4.2). Although Fairclough refers to himself as a 'moderate' constructionist (p. 9), his view of language as both constructed (constituted) and constitutive resonates both with complex responsive processes theory and the paradigm of social constructionism. He emphasises that, even though it is meanings rather than texts that have social effects, 'one resource that is necessary for any account of meaning-making is the capacity to analyse texts in order to clarify their contribution to processes of meaning-making' (p. 11). Discourse analysis is thus helpful in developing a deeper understanding of how discourse positions various social agents in the processes of continuity and change. Figure 4.2 below builds on Figure 3.1 (Chapter 3) to illustrate how the conceptual framework of complex responsive processes theory was developed to include Fairclough's analytical tools, in order to gain deeper insights into what transforming education means to practitioners.

Figure 4.2 summarises the relationship between the local and global patterns of conversation, recurring conversational themes and the ways people

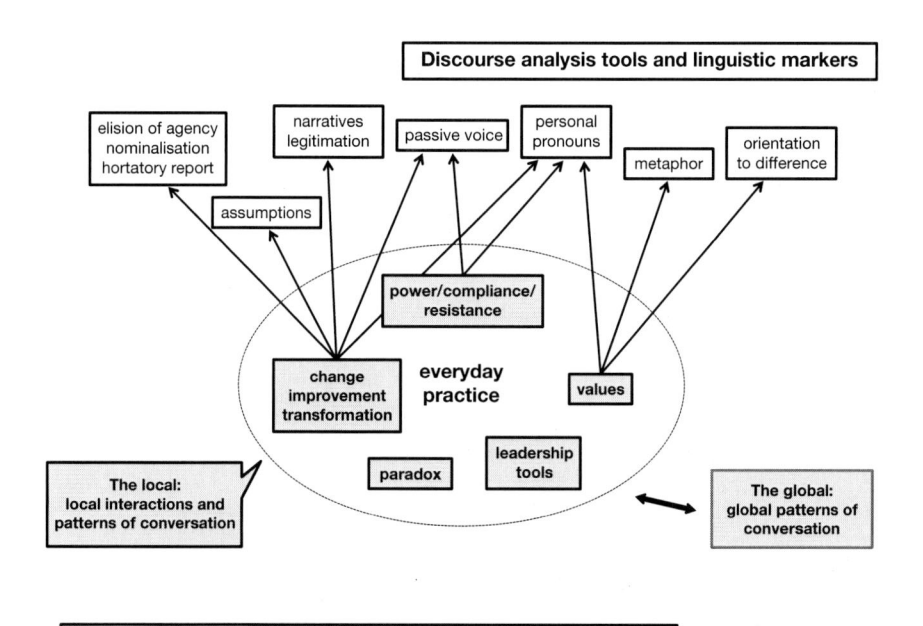

Figure 4.2 Analysis and interpretation of the empirical data

communicate them in order to affect change or maintain stability. Because researching everyday practice entails researching conversational patterns, more subtle insights into meanings conveyed through particular linguistic markers can be generated at this additional level of analysis. These markers include semantic relations between clauses and sentences (e.g. elaboration and explanation), grammatical forms (e.g. the use of personal pronouns) and syntactic choices (e.g. the use of passive or active sentences). For example, as explained in Chapter 3, government policy discourse uses nominalisation to convey a sense of necessity:

> To prosper in the 21st century competitive global economy, Britain must transform the knowledge and skills of its population.
> (DfES 2001: 5)

The modal verb 'must' is used here to further emphasise the necessity of transformation. A similar sense of inevitability and obligation to follow the testing and target-driven government policies was conveyed by practitioners in the case study schools, who talked about what 'school improvement' means for them in their everyday practice as follows:

> You can't escape the fact that there are certain measurable aspects that are easy to measure. School improvement you know, you've got to look at SATs [high-stakes tests] results, you'd be stupid not to.
> (Stephen)

> We're very driven in terms of targets, but there are different priorities, for example you know how we have a very diverse population, we've got a large percentage of children without gardens or an outdoor space to play in. Obviously, our focus will be on providing opportunities for those children.
> (Miriam)

Stephen's reference to being unable to 'escape' improvement statistics and use of the modal verb 'have to' ('you've got to') implies little or no choice in relation to school improvement. Noteworthy in Miriam's answer is the use of passive voice ('we're very driven') when talking about targets and a more active (more 'agentic') articulation of 'providing opportunities for children' when talking about the school's own improvement priorities. The use of the contrastive conjunction 'but' and an elaboration of the school's 'local' priorities imply that Miriam may not have embraced the government targets agenda as her 'own' personal meaning of 'school improvement'.

Further explanations of the use of Fairclough's discourse analysis concepts listed in Figure 4.2, and the subtle meanings they convey of the conversational patterns in the case study schools are integrated within the analysis of the empirical data in Chapters 5–8.

Generalising from case studies

A search for diverse understandings of school improvement (and transformation), combined with an endeavour to preserve the unique and the particular, inevitably affects claims to generalisability. As Bassey (1999) explains, case study research may generate knowledge and insight in the form of 'fuzzy' generalisations. While the traditional (inductive) logic leads to predictive statements of the type: 'In *this* case it *has been* found that . . .', 'fuzzy' logic leads to predictive statements such as: 'In *some* cases it *may be* found that . . .' (p. 12). In emphasising case study's usefulness for policymaking, Simons (1996: 239) notes that, paradoxically, in-depth particularisation may lead to universal understanding:

> The tension between the study of the *unique* and the need to generalise is necessary to reveal both the *unique* and the *universal* and the *unity* of that understanding.

Research ethics

Educational researchers in England are bound by the ethical guidelines of the British Educational Research Association (BERA 2011) regarding informed consent, privacy, confidentiality as well as ethics of research with children. To these guidelines, Pring (2000: 144) adds moral principles and values such as truth, trust, democracy, and Bassey (1999) adds respect for the person. Research ethics may need to also be part of broader considerations arising from the potential of knowledge to transform worldviews and enact material change in the world. It is, therefore, difficult to disentangle research ethics from the research process as a whole and this includes the production and application of knowledge as well as the consequences of its use. For example, the crucial question of ethics posed in Chapter 2, in relation to the discoveries in quantum physics, was about the moral right of a physicist to work on practical applications of atomic energy, including the atomic bomb (Barad 2007). Being explicit about one's 'grade of commitment' (Hacking 1999) in relation to the purpose of one's search for knowledge is, therefore, important for all social scientists, notwithstanding their paradigmatic positioning.

A reflexive interlude

The recognition that the process of coming to know is mediated by the researcher's understandings and epistemological influences highlights the importance of reflexivity. The premise that we are unable to 'step outside' our humanity to assume an objective, 'divine' point of view is vital in being reflexive. Reflexivity is about working with the paradox of abstracting and immersing and with tensions, ambiguities and contradictions that are inevitable in a complex world. The reflexive interlude outlined below works through of some of the tensions encountered in my research.

This qualitative case study design could be viewed as positioning me as an 'outsider researcher' and therefore in tension with the 'insider researcher' methodology favoured by other complex responsive processes scholars (Shaw 2002; Stacey 2010; Mowles 2011). However, my interest in transforming education originates in my lived experience of enacting government improvement policies as a former primary practitioner of twelve years. It is also embedded in my current experience as a leadership and management educator and researcher. These roles have absorbed most of my professional life, immersing me in the world of school improvement. The most vivid memory I have of being tasked with 'transforming education' is the pressure to make sense of the sweeping changes to the curriculum, pedagogy and professional values demanded of teachers by the *National Literacy* and *Numeracy Strategies* for primary education (DfEE 1998, 1999). Questions about the purpose of these changes in relation to the purpose of education remained unanswered, lost in the detailed prescription of the *Strategies*. We (teachers, school leaders and other practitioners working with children) were expected to meet 'ambitious' targets for pupil performance within very short timeframes, under the scrutiny of Ofsted inspectors. Although the *National Strategies* were ended by the Coalition government in 2011, the 'new orthodoxy' persisted, taking a more decisive turn towards the neoliberalisation and privatisation of the system. Initiated in the Thatcherite years (1979–1997), the gradual privatisation of English education was continued by New Labour (1997–2010) and accelerated by the Coalition government to a point that threatens the survival of education as a public good (Ball 2007; Gunter 2008). The overarching aim of this research has, therefore, been to pay attention to the complexity of local and global interactions, from the position of an educator and researcher with a commitment to education as a public good.

According to complex responsive processes theory, reflexivity entails an explicit acknowledgement of the personal and political values informing research, as well as a recognition of research as a process in which data are co-created by the researcher and participant 'selves-in-relation' (Mauthner and Doucet 2003: 422). A tension in accounts of reflexivity is inevitable, because of the abstraction inherent in the act of accounting. The very act of telling is a movement away from immersing in experience to narrating and detaching from research participants. I do, however, recall moments of being immersed and fully in the presence of each research participant, completely attentive to the other and also acutely aware of who I am in terms of my own position, history, investment and politics (Skeggs 2002). These were the moments of *being* reflexive, moments of connection to my research participants and of enormous gratitude for their time, their stories and thoughts – the gift of their 'data'. In these moments power was mutual: power to gesture as little or as much of ourselves to the other as we chose to, in the moment, in response to the other.

Complex knowledge and the 'politics of complexity reduction'

The discussions in this chapter point to two main orientations to complexity: an orientation towards complex forms of knowledge and complexity reduction. Complex forms of knowledge understand the world as 'being full of possibilities' that are 'enacted by purposeful agents', engaging in practice that knows itself from *within* (Tsoukas 2005: 5). Complex forms of knowledge are aligned with research paradigms that value the uniqueness of particular contexts and people and multiple meanings of individual and collective endeavours that arise *within* everyday experience. The processes of knowledge production, mediation and application are aimed here at capturing the 'essence' of the 'human condition or social context of the times' (Simons 2009: 167) and communicating it in ways that may influence educational practice through deeper understandings.

This is in contrast to epistemologies oriented towards complexity reduction, such as those found in positivist approaches. These epistemologies tend to reduce the process of knowledge production to 'outcomes', objects of study to numerical values and disparate phenomena to abstract categories that can be compared. Their overarching aim is the discovery of relationships between quantifiable variables, causal links, prediction and generalisation. Based on their universal applicability, positivist knowledge claims may then be utilised to control and engineer educational change, analogous to controlling technology.

These two orientations have been and remain in tension in the education policy field in England. Since the 1990s, the proponents of positivist approaches have sought to elevate randomised controlled trials (RCT) to the 'gold standard' of research-based policy and practice (Hammersley 2007, 2013; Cohen *et al.* 2011; Byrne and Callaghan 2014). In evidence-based medicine, RCTs are used in conjunction with 'systematic reviews' involving statistical meta-analyses of all relevant research about a particular treatment, the latter made possible through the rise of large online databases (Hammersley 2013: 3). The debates between proponents of the medical models in educational research, such as David Hargreaves (1997), and scholars contesting the appropriateness of these models in education, such as Martyn Hammersley, have become known as the 'paradigm wars' (Gage 2007). Evidence-based policy movement is now an important component of the 'new orthodoxy' for achieving educational transformation in England. Positivist knowledge provides policymakers with a 'factual' base of 'what works' and can, therefore, be used instrumentally for leveraging and measuring policy 'delivery' and its 'countable' outcomes. It does, however, have important shortcomings, including inflated claims to knowledge and an 'anti-professional' orientation that undermines the value of local knowledge gleaned from everyday practice (Hammersley 2013: 17). Evidence-based policy approaches seem to privilege knowledge that can be utilised for moulding schools in the shape of policymakers' idealisations and abstractions.

Similar approaches can be observed in what Sellar and Lingard (2014: 917) refer to as 'new global modes of governance in education'. The evidence informing the global policy field has increasingly been produced by supranational organisations such as the OECD. The OECD research claims neutrality, quantifies education systems and relies on 'commensurative work': using numbers to compare disparate phenomena (p. 926). As noted by Sellar and Lingard, the normative framing of policy problems and solutions, combined with generating large data samples and using data to increase the explanatory potential of international assessments, produces knowledge that has an 'explicit governance purpose' (p. 932). The growing influence of the OECD is a manifestation of the alignment:

> of policy habitus across the global and national scales of educational governance. This habitus accepts the reliability and validity, and global (or universal) applicability of 'commensurative work' in education (Espeland, 2002), seeing the globe as a commensurate space of performance measurement.
>
> (p. 932)

As noted by Alexander (2012: 10), the key problem with international comparisons is not so much the reliability of PISA and other OECD studies, but the 'disproportionate' influence they exert on policymaking. Since these studies use data selectively to present it to policymakers in a 'palatable' form, they also tend to be 'high on political rhetoric', 'low on classroom practice' and 'cleansed of problematic realities' (p. 11).

In these national and global policy contexts, the knowledge underpinning the TLP (Thomson *et al.* 2014) is also oriented towards genericism and control. Because of their role of mediating policy, school leaders are an important 'link' in the 'delivery chain'. To address the demands of evidence-informed policy, educational leaders are expected to use research on 'what works' to improve performance and increase the accountability of their 'staff' for raising standards. This conception of leadership has its antecedent in managerialism, which was introduced to public sector services through New Public Management (NPM) (Randle and Brady 1997; Deem and Brehony 2005). School leaders have an array of models and tools to use in order to deliver improvement in pupil outcomes. The tools comprising the TLP are a generic 'assemblage of ideas and activities' that 'contains a few genuinely new ideas but plenty of normative rhetoric about urgency to buy and use' (Thomson *et al.* 2014: x). From the complex responsive processes perspective, these tools are second-order abstractions that codify patterns of interaction and their usefulness is in maintaining disciplinary power rather than providing rich knowledge for illuminating the complexity of educational change.

A question, therefore, arises about how else we could understand the complexities of leading educational transformation. As discussed in this chapter, complex knowledge and understandings can be generated through reflexive narrative enquiry and case study research. In taking everyday experience seriously, these research approaches offer opportunities for developing deeper understandings of complex settings and processes. Case study methodology is particularly important in evaluating the 'soundness' of policy agendas (Simons 2009). Through their investigation of complex realities and experience, case studies provide insights that may be relevant to other contexts of a similar nature. The findings of the case studies presented in Chapters 5–8 may, therefore, be of relevance to anyone involved in education, be it at the grass roots of change, at the level of policymaking and other networks of educational practice. If some of the insights on the following pages resonate with the reader's experience then this may be because of the paradox of the universal in the unique. Implicit in this paradox is that the everyday practice at 'Abbey Primary' and 'Green Lanes Primary' is textured as events, relationships and patterns of conversation that may be local and unique and at the same time widely recognisable.

Conclusion

This chapter focused on the methodological dimensions of researching complex processes such as those involved in transforming education. A commitment to complexity in the broader sense highlights the need to challenge the complexity reduction characteristic of knowledge utilised for maintaining the 'new orthodoxy'. A commitment to complex responsive processes theory entails paying attention to the expressive and constitutive potential of language and being attuned to everyday conversational themes which, over many iterations, may sustain the status quo or lead to an emergence of a new 'universe of discourse' (Mead 1956: 36). Paying attention to how we interact and communicate is important because the way in which we articulate our understandings of the purposes of schooling constructs a world into which pupils are socialised, a constructed world that will inevitably be taken-for-granted as 'real'. The responsibility of educators, therefore, reaches beyond delivering the curriculum and transforming performance. The transformation that educators, policymakers and educational researchers are responsible for is linked to the kind(s) of world they construct for children and the modes of engagement in this world that they convey as legitimate. Through its explanations of how local interactions lead to the emergence of global patterns and, conversely, how global patterns are taken up locally, with unpredictable consequences, complex responsive processes theory provides conceptual foundations for deeper understandings of government policy enactments in the 'local' school.

The following four chapters focus on transforming education as experienced by practitioners working in two primary schools located in outer London. Like Ball *et al.* (2012: 146), I am aware of 'gaps and omissions' in my research and, therefore, of being able to 'only write . . . about the things [I] have done'. For example, conversations with different people in the two schools could have generated a different data set, possibly leading to a different set of themes. However, a systematic, iterative analysis and triangulation of the interview, documentary and observation data revealed sufficient internal consistency within participants' interview transcripts and commonalities across the participant sample in each school to warrant a number of 'fuzzy' generalisations (Bassey 1999). Before considering how government improvement policies affected local interactions in the two schools, let me first recall Mead's (1934) explanation discussed in Chapter 3, about how meaning arises in a conversation of gestures, not through encoding, transmission and decoding, but in the response to my gesture by others. When reflecting on his research findings, Mowles (2011: 85) notes that they are a gesture:

> the full meaning of which will only become apparent once the people I am working with have responded. There is no guarantee that any observation I make, or judgment that I offer will be interpreted or made use of as I intend.

The following chapters are also a gesture that can only acquire the full meaning with the response of the reader.

Notes

1. As explained by Barad (2007), the immutable Newtonian-type laws of nature are useful approximations of the sophisticated calculations of quantum physics. While the former can be applied to the macroscopic domain, the calculations of quantum physics operate both in the macroscopic and the microscopic domains.
2. The paradigms presented in Figure 4.2 reflect the classifications by Cohen *et al.* (2011), specifically in relation to educational research, and Guba and Lincoln (2005) who write more generally about paradigms in the social sciences. Cohen *et al.* (2011: 47–48) identify four paradigms in educational research: positivism, interpretivism, critical theory and complexity. They use 'interpretivism' as an overarching term to signal commonalities between the 'qualitative', subjective, hermeneutic research traditions such as ethnomethodology and symbolic interactionism, as well as to distinguish the interpretive paradigm (focused on the subjective world of human experience) from the normative paradigm (utilising methods of natural science to discover rules governing human behaviour). Guba and Lincoln (2005: 195–196) refer to five paradigms (with distinct ontological underpinnings) within the social sciences:

    - Positivism ('naïve realism' – a belief in one 'real' objective reality)
    - Postpositivism (critical realism, complex reality apprehensible probabilistically)
    - Critical Theory (historical realism, reality shaped by socio-political, cultural, economic, gender and ethnic values)
    - Constructivism (relativism underpinned by local, co-constructed realities)
    - Participatory (reality co-created through the subject-object interactions)

3. The term 'social constructionism' is used in a number of published sources, including *The Handbook of Constructionist Research* (Holstein and Gubrium 2008). Where references are made to the 'constructivist paradigm' or 'constructivism', I have adhered to authors' original terminology.

4 For example, Byrne and Callaghan (2014: 57) position themselves as critical realists researching within the 'ontological frame of reference' of complexity theory, while Paul Cilliers (1998) draws connections between complex systems such as language and postmodernism.
5 Because of space limitations, it is impossible to consider here in detail the paradigm of 'agential realism' developed by Barad (2007: 48–49) within the performative conception of knowledge, nor her argument that both social constructivists and scientific realists adhere to the conception of knowledge as accurate representation.
6 The six 'grades of commitment' identified by Hacking (1999: 19–20) define the researcher's orientation towards the phenomena investigated and include historical, ironic, reformist, unmasking, rebellious and revolutionary. They range from the historical orientation aimed at neutral reportage of events to reformist and unmasking orientations that aim at stripping ideas of a 'false appeal or authority' and 'exposing the function they serve'. The rebellious and revolutionary orientations encourage a movement from the world of ideas towards action.
7 While complex responsive theory provides foundations for challenging the complexity reductions characteristic of positivism, it does not position itself in a binary opposition to the positivist ontological, methodological and epistemological frameworks. As explained in Chapter 2, it is the sciences of certainty (and positivist methodologies derived from these sciences) that emphasise binary distinctions (such as mind/matter, nature/culture, fact/value, etc.) and atomise complex phenomena into a restricted set of variables, ignoring their dynamic relationships. The overarching aim of complex responsive processes scholars is to avoid binary oppositions in favour of the logic of the paradox, understood as a simultaneous occurrence of opposing phenomena or tendencies. This does not mean that complex responsive processes theory precludes statistics or other quantitative data, but rather that, because of their high level of abstraction (and remove from the dynamics of everyday interactions), it does not place them at the centre of its investigations.
8 Van Manen draws on philosophers such as Merleau-Ponty (2002), Heidegger (1962) and Gadamer (1975).
9 As pointed out by Ian Hacking (1999: 24–25), social constructionism is often critiqued from a premise that 'everything is a social construct', which is a misinterpretation of the position of many social constructionists. Berger and Luckman's book, argues Hacking, is about 'the social construction of our sense of, feel for, experience of, and confidence in, commonsense reality. Or rather ... of various realities that arise in the complex social worlds we inhabit'.

References

Alexander, R. 2012. Moral panic, miracle cures and educational policy: What can we really learn from international comparisons? *Scottish Educational Review*, 44(1): 4–21.
Alvesson, M. 2011. *Interpreting Interviews*. London: Sage.
Alvesson, M. and Sköldberg, K. 2009. *Reflexive Methodology: New Vistas for Qualitative Research* (2nd edn). London: Sage.
Angrosino, M.V. 2005. 'Recontextualizing Observation: Ethnography, Pedagogy, and the Prospects for a Progressive Political Agenda'. In Denzin, N.K. and Lincoln, I.S. (eds) *The Sage Handbook of Qualitative Research* (3rd edn). Thousand Oaks, CA: Sage Publications, 729–746.
Ball, S.J. 2007. *Education Plc: Understanding Private Sector Participation in Public Sector Education*. Abingdon: Routledge.
Ball, S.J., Maguire, M. and Braun, A. 2012. *How Schools Do Policy: Policy Enactments in Secondary Schools*. London and New York: Routledge.

Barad, K. 2007. *Meeting the Universe Halfway: Quantum Physics and the Entanglement of Matter and Meaning*. Durham, NC and London: Duke University Press.

Barber, M. 1997. *The Learning Game: Arguments for an Education Revolution*. London: Indigo.

Bassey, M. 1999. *Case Study Research in Educational Settings*. Buckingham: Open University Press.

BERA. 2011. *Ethical Guidelines for Educational Research*. Available at: www.bera.ac.uk/guidelines (accessed 15 December 2012).

Berger, P. and Luckmann, T. 1966. *The Social Construction of Reality: A Treatise in the Sociology of Knowledge*. London: Penguin Books.

Biesta, G. 2010. 'Five Theses on Complexity Reduction and Its Politics'. In Osberg, D. and Biesta, G. (eds) *Complexity Theory and the Politics of Education*. Rotterdam: Sense, 5–14.

Burr, V. 2003. *Social Constructionism* (2nd edn). Hove: Routledge.

Byrne, D. and Callaghan, G. 2014. *Complexity Theory and the Social Sciences: The State of the Art*. Abingdon: Routledge.

Callaghan, G. 2008. Evaluation and negotiated order: Developing the application of complexity theory, *Evaluation*, 14(4): 399–411.

Chia, R. 1998. From complexity science to complex thinking: Organization as simple location, *Organization*, 5(3): 341–370.

Cilliers, P. 1998. *Complexity and Postmodernism: Understanding Complex Systems*. London and New York: Routledge.

Cohen, L., Manion, L. and Morrison, K. 2011. *Research Methods in Education* (7th edn). Abingdon: Routledge.

Davis, B. and Sumara, D.J. 2006. *Complexity and Education: Inquiries into Learning, Teaching, and Research*. Mahwah, NJ: Lawrence Erlbaum Associates.

Davis, B., Sumara, D. and Iftody, T. 2010. 'Complexity, Consciousness and Curriculum'. In Osberg, D. and Biesta, G. (eds) *Complexity Theory and the Politics of Education*. Rotterdam: Sense, 107–120.

Deem, R. and Brehony, K.J. 2005. Management as ideology: The case of 'new managerialism' in higher education, *Oxford Review of Education*, 31(2): 217–235.

DfEE. 1998. *The National Literacy Strategy: Framework for Teaching*. London: DfEE.

DfEE. 1999. *The National Numeracy Strategy: Framework for Teaching Mathematics*. London: DfEE.

DfES. 2001. *Schools Achieving Success*. Annesley: DfES.

Doll, W. 2008. 'Complexity and the Culture of Curriculum'. In Mason, M. (ed.) *Complexity Theory and the Philosophy of Education*. Chichester: Wiley-Blackwell, 181–203.

Elias, N. 1994. *The Civilizing Process: Sociogenetic and Psychogenetic Investigations*. Malden, MA and Abingdon: Blackwell.

Espeland, W.N. 2002. 'Commensuration and Cognition'. In Cerulo, K.A. (ed.) *Culture in Mind: Toward a Sociology of Culture and Cognition*. London and New York: Routledge, 63–88.

Fairclough, N. 2003. *Analysing Discourse: Textual Analysis for Social Research*. Abingdon: Routledge.

Fenwick, T., Edwards, R. and P. Sawchuk. 2011. *Emerging Approaches to Educational Research: Tracing the Sociomaterial*. London and New York: Routledge.

Fitzgerald, T. 2007. 'Reading between the Lines: Documents and Documentary Analysis'. In Coleman, M. and Briggs, A. (eds) *Research Methods for Educational Leadership and Management*. London: Sage, 278–294.
Gadamer, H.G. 1975. *Truth and Method*. (J. Weinsheimer and D.G. Marshall, Trans.). London and New York: Continuum.
Gage, N. 2007. 'The Paradigm Wars and Their Aftermath: A 'Historical' Sketch of Research on Teaching since 1989'. In Hammersley, M. (ed.) *Educational Research and Evidence-based Practice*. London: Sage, 151–167.
Gergen, K.J. 2009. *An Invitation to Social Construction* (2nd edn). London: Sage.
Guba, E.G. and Lincoln, Y.S. 1998. 'Competing Paradigms in Qualitative Research'. In Denzin, N.K. and Lincoln, Y.S. (eds) *The Landscape of Qualitative Research: Theories and Issues*. Thousand Oaks, CA: Sage, 105–117.
Guba, E.G. and Lincoln, Y.S. 2005. 'Paradigmatic Controversies, Contradictions and Emerging Confluences'. In Denzin, N.K. and Lincoln, I.S. (eds) *The Sage Handbook of Qualitative Research* (3rd edn). Thousand Oaks, CA: Sage, 191–216.
Gunter, H.M. 2008. Modernisation and the field of educational administration, *Journal of Educational Administration and History*, 40(2): 161–172.
Hacking, I. 1999. *The Social Construction of What?* Cambridge: Harvard University Press.
Hammersley, M. (ed.) 2007. *Educational Research and Evidence-Based Practice*. London: Sage.
Hammersley, M. 2013. *The Myth of Research-Based Policy & Practice*. London: Sage.
Hargreaves, D.H. 1997. In defence of research for evidence-based teaching: A rejoinder to Martyn Hammersley, *British Educational Research Journal*, 23(4): 405–419.
Heidegger, M. 1962. *Being and Time*. (J. Macquarrie and E. Robinson, Trans.). Malden, MA and Oxford: Blackwell.
Holstein, J.A. and Gubrium, J.F. 2008. *Handbook of Constructionist Research*. New York: The Guildford Press.
Kauffman, S. 1995. *At Home in the Universe: The Search for the Laws of Self-Organization and Complexity*. New York: Oxford University Press.
Kuhn, L. 2008. 'Complexity and Educational Research: A Critical Reflection'. In Mason, M. (ed.) *Complexity Theory and the Philosophy of Education*. Chichester: Wiley-Blackwell, 169–180.
Kuhn, T.S. 1996. *The Structure of Scientific Revolutions* (3rd edn). Chicago, IL and London: The University of Chicago Press.
Maguire, M., Hoskins, K., Ball, S. and Braun, A. 2011. Policy discourses in school texts, *Discourse: Studies in the Cultural Politics of Education*, 32(4): 597–609.
Mason, M. 2008. 'What Is Complexity Theory and What Are Its Implications for Educational Change?' In Mason, M. (ed.) *Complexity Theory and the Philosophy of Education*. Chichester: Wiley-Blackwell, 32–45.
Mauthner, N.S. and Doucet, A. 2003. Reflexive accounts and accounts of reflexivity in qualitative data analysis, *Sociology*, 37(3): 413–431.
Mead, G.H. 1934. *Mind, Self, and Society from the Standpoint of a Social Behaviourist*. Chicago, IL and London: The University of Chicago Press.
Mead, G.H. 1956. *On Social Psychology*. Chicago, IL: Chicago University Press.
Merleau-Ponty, M. 2002. *Phenomenology of Perception*. (C. Smith, Trans.). Abingdon: Routledge Classics.
Meyer, H.D. and Benavot, A. (eds). 2013. *PISA, Power, and Policy: The Emergence of Global Educational Governance*. Oxford: Symposium Books.

Mowles, C. 2011. *Rethinking Management: Radical Insights from the Complexity Sciences*. Farnham: Gower.

Mowles, C. 2014. Complex, but not quite complex enough: The turn to the complexity sciences in evaluation scholarship, *Evaluation*, 20(2): 160–175.

OECD. 2013. *Teaching and Learning International Survey TALIS 2013: Conceptual Framework*. Available at: www.oecd.org/edu/school/TALIS%20Conceptual%20 Framework_FINAL.pdf (accessed 7 May 2015).

Prigogine, I. 1996. *The End of Certainty: Time, Chaos and the New Laws of Nature*. New York: The Free Press.

Pring, R. 2000. *Philosophy of Educational Research*. London: Continuum.

Randle, K. and Brady, N. 1997. Managerialism and professionalism in the 'cinderella service', *Journal of Vocational Education and Training*, 49(1): 121–139.

Rorty, R. 1979. *Philosophy and the Mirror of Nature*. Princeton, NJ: Princeton University Press.

Scott, J.C. 1990 *Domination and the Arts of Resistance: Hidden Transcripts*. New Haven, CT: Yale University Press.

Sellar, S. and Lingard, B. 2014.The OECD and the expansion of PISA: New global modes of governance in education, *British Educational Research Journal*, 40(6): 917–936.

Shaw, P. 2002. *Changing Conversations in Organizations: A Complexity Approach to Change*. London: Routledge.

Simons, H. 1996. The paradox of case study, *Cambridge Journal of Education*, 26(2): 225–240.

Simons, H. 2009. *Case Study Research in Practice*. London: Sage.

Skeggs, B. 2002. 'Techniques for Telling the Reflexive Self'. In May, T. (ed.) *Qualitative Research in Action*. London: Sage, 349–375.

Stacey, R.D. 2010. *Complexity and Organisational Reality: Uncertainty and the Need to Rethink Management after the Collapse of Investment Capitalism* (2nd edn). London: Routledge.

Stacey, R.D. 2012. *Tools and Techniques of Leadership and Management*. Abingdon: Routledge.

Stake, R.E. 1995. *The Art of Case Study Research*. Thousand Oaks, CA: Sage.

Thomson, P., Gunter, H, and Blackmore, J. 2014. 'Series Foreword'. In Gunter, H.M. *Educational Leadership and Hannah Arendt*. London and New York: Routledge, vi–xii.

Tsoukas, H. 2005. *Complex Knowledge: Studies in Organizational Epistemology*. Oxford: Oxford University Press.

Tsoukas, H. and Hatch, M.J. 2001. Complex thinking, complex practice: The case for a narrative approach to organizational complexity, *Human Relations*, 54(8): 879–1013.

Van Manen, M. 1990. *Researching Lived Experience: Human Science for an Action Sensitive Pedagogy*. New York: SUNY.

Weick, K. 1979. *The Social Psychology of Organizing*. New York: McGraw-Hill.

Part II

'Global' policies and local interactions

Chapter 5

The myth of 'spectacular' solutions

The *Literacy* and *Numeracy Strategies* and their (un)desirable consequences

> How helpful they were? Variable, I think. They were starting points where we needed to have starting points, but they then became the masters and the effect was to take away teachers' confidence in their professionalism overall.
> (Sophie, deputy head, Abbey Primary)

This chapter, together with Chapter 6, explores the empirical data collected in two case study schools, 'Abbey Primary' and 'Green Lanes Primary'. The main focus of both chapters is on the interplay between the 'global' and the 'local', where the 'global' refers to education policy and the 'local' to policy agendas being taken up and enacted in schools (Figure 3.1 in Chapter 3). A policy or strategy is 'global' in the sense that it is a generalisation that introduces new norms, objectives, values or conceptions of 'good' practice. These are enacted by being particularised, or responded to differently in different local school contexts, a process that involves a complex interplay of many individual intentions and values. Therefore, local enactments of education policy that emerge over time cannot be precisely predicted and controlled. This is illustrated by the empirical data on the 'strategies era' of English policymaking (1998–2011), which reveal how the strategies were mediated (or particularised) by practitioners who struggled to cope with their undesirable consequences.

The *National Literacy Strategy* (NLS) (DfEE 1998) and the *National Numeracy Strategy* (NNS) (DfEE 1999) were designed as 'spectacular' solutions aimed at 'cracking' (Arnold 2004) the problem of literacy and numeracy standards in one massive 'attack'. As the 'most ambitious attempt ever in this country' to improve teaching approaches 'across the entire education service' (DfEE 1997: 19), the *Strategies* were expected to deliver ambitious targets for pupil performance in literacy and numeracy tests by the year 2002.[1] According to Michael Barber, Chief Adviser to the Secretary of State for Education on School Standards, their effective delivery relied on a policy apparatus of school performance targets, resourcing, monitoring infrastructure and Ofsted inspections to check that schools were adopting the prescribed 'better practices' (Mead 2006). The empirical data on practitioners' experiences of enacting the

NLS and NNS[2] point to a significant disjuncture between the certainty about their transformative potential reported by policymakers and the 'variable' consequences conveyed by practitioners, as emphasised by Sophie in the epigraph to this chapter. For example, Stephen Anwyll, an NLS director, noted how 'fantastically exciting' it was for him to be 'doing something that affects eighteen and a half thousand schools and two hundred thousand primary teachers' (Hall 2004: 125). While Sophie noted teachers' loss of confidence, the DfE emphasised the contribution of the *Strategies* to 'building teacher confidence' (DfE 2011a: 3). According to Sophie, the opportunity to improve practice offered by the *Strategies* as 'starting points' was lost when they became 'the masters'. The command and control dynamic between policymakers and schools established by the *Strategies* was a recurring theme in practitioner accounts of the 'strategies era'.

It is important to emphasise here that this chapter seeks to approach the themes that emerged from the empirical data as 'knots in the webs of our experiences, around which certain lived experiences are spun and thus lived through as meaningful wholes' (Van Manen 1990: 90). For example, the notion of 'command and control' is an abstraction that emphasises asymmetrical power relations. As a 'knot' in a web of lived experience, the meanings arising from command and control interactions may be manifested as a range of practitioner perceptions and responses. Such interactions may undermine their identity and purpose as educators and as interdependent individuals entangled in complex webs of interactions with colleagues and the children they teach. Themes thus understood are conveyed through the textual data collected in the case studies: observation notes, interview transcripts and documentary data. Fairclough's (2003) discourse analysis tools, combined with complex responsive processes concepts, enabled more nuanced insights into how the *Strategies* affected participants' understandings and interactions (Figure 4.2 in Chapter 4). For example, this chapter will consider how the myth of 'spectacular' solutions has been sustained through 'hortatory' reporting. A 'hortatory report' lists often disconnected 'facts' to promote a particular position (Fairclough 2003). Policy texts produced during the 'strategies era' often resorted to hortatory reporting to persuade the public that the *Strategies* were a great success (DfES 2003a). However, their highly prescriptive nature and the command and control approach to their delivery led to a range of undesirable consequences in schools, despite adjustments made to the *Strategies*. For example, the deployment of an elaborate policy apparatus to increase compliance and standardisation diminished the capacity of practitioners to exercise their own professional judgement.

Literacy, numeracy and large-scale reform: New Labour's *National Strategies*

The 'strategies era' started in 1998 with the introduction of the *National Literacy Strategy* by the New Labour government (1997–2010) (Table 5.1).

Table 5.1 Key events in the development of the *National Strategies* for primary education

Year	Key event
1998	Within a year of New Labour coming to power in 1997, the *National Literacy Strategy* (DfES 1998) is introduced and ambitious targets for literacy set for 2002
1999	The *National Numeracy Strategy* (DfES 1999) is introduced and targets for numeracy are set for 2002
2000	The National Curriculum is slimmed down, but the *Literacy* and *Numeracy Strategies* remain unchanged
2002	The literacy and numeracy targets set in 1998 are not achieved
2003	*Excellence and Enjoyment: A strategy for primary schools* (DfES, 2003a) is published, consolidating the *Literacy* and *Numeracy Strategies*
	Every Child Matters (DfES 2003b: 7) introduces five 'outcomes' across the primary curriculum (being healthy, staying safe, enjoying and achieving, making a positive contribution, economic well-being) as well as joined-up education and care services
2004	*Five Year Strategy for Children and Learners* (DfES 2004) introduces the concept of 'transformation' and reconstructs the role of the policy apparatus (Local Authority consultants and school leaders)
2005	Education Act 2005 sets the aim of raising standards in all schools through more efficient inspections, budgetary reform and profiles of every school's performance
2006	*Primary Framework for literacy and mathematics* (DfES 2006) consolidates the *Literacy* and *Numeracy Strategies* and makes teaching materials available on the *National Strategies* website
	Rose Report (Rose 2006) sets recommendations for teaching phonics as key approach to learning to decode (read) and encode (write/spell)
2007	*The Children's Plan* is published (DCSF 2007: 1) as a ten-year strategy aimed at making England 'the best place in the world for our children and young people to grow up'
2008	The 1998 literacy and numeracy targets are finally met
	Williams Review (2008) of mathematics teaching recommends developing a mathematics specialist in every primary school
2009	Primary curriculum review (Rose 2009) recommends integrating curriculum subjects into six 'areas of learning' to be implemented in 2011
2010	Following general election, the Coalition Government sets out their education policy in the *Schools White Paper 2010* (DfE 2010a) promising more 'freedoms' to schools and announcing a replacement of many of the New Labour's policies with 'simple' solutions
	After six years of research and regular interim reports published from 2007, the final report of the independent *Cambridge Primary Review* (Alexander et al. 2010) sets 75 recommendations for improving primary policy and practice
2011	The *National Strategies* are terminated. None of the recommendations of the *Cambridge Primary Review* are referred to in the key publications setting out the Coalition education policy (DfE 2010a, 2010b, 2011b)

The NLS and the NNS were followed by two more strategies consolidating primary literacy and numeracy (DfES 2003a; DfES 2004), as well as strategies for secondary English, mathematics and science and for 'Behaviour and Attendance', 'Narrowing the Gap' and 'Gifted and Talented' (DfE 2011a).[3] The *Strategies* established a '*businessification*' (Cummings 2015) of educational purposes as a key theme. Their measures for maximising pupil outcomes resembled those deployed in industrial settings, such as performance management, accountability, workforce training and external consultancy. Despite the paucity of extant data on targets in education, the NLS and the NNS introduced targets for pupils and schools, on the basis of the 'long-standing use' of targets in industrial management and 'its increasing use in improving public services' (Beard 2000: 10).

Their design made the NLS and the NNS 'the most ambitious large-scale reform initiative anywhere is the world' (Fullan 2003:1). The policy apparatus for the 'delivery' of the *Numeracy* and *Literacy Strategies* consisted of performance targets, resourcing, infrastructure for the monitoring of implementation at the national, Local Authority and school levels and Ofsted inspections. The *Strategies* consisted of centrally prescribed curriculum as well as standardised lesson plans and other materials to be used by teachers in their daily literacy and numeracy hours. The literacy model was based on teaching at word, sentence and text levels, fitted into parts of an accurately timed literacy hour. The hour was to be divided as follows:

- 15 minutes: whole class text level, reading and writing
- 15 minutes: whole class word level, spelling and vocabulary
- 20 minute task time: one group working with the teacher and the rest independently
- 10 minute plenary: round up of lesson

(DfEE 1998: 8)

The numeracy hour also followed a prescribed, three-part lesson structure, with clear 'lesson objectives' and 'success criteria' to be displayed in every classroom and detailed in lesson plans (DfEE 1999). The *Strategies* displayed characteristics of an aims-and-objectives curriculum (Ross 2000; Kelly 2009). Teachers were expected to focus their energies on delivering 'off the shelf' materials instead of having to 'reinvent the wheel' by designing their own curriculum (Beard 2000: 12). The standardised notion of 'good practice', disconnected from educational theory and limited to delivering the prescribed lesson content, was reinforced by Ofsted inspections. This technicist approach to pedagogy was justified by policymakers on the basis of research evidence suggesting that 'schools which build on an externally developed programme (using an "off the shelf" approach) experience greater success than schools which implement locally developed school-wide projects' (Beard 2000: 13). The 'off the shelf' literacy curriculum was, however, extremely fragmented, making it difficult to draw meaningful links between the word, sentence and text work and combine discrete lessons and units of study into a coherent whole (Moss 2004). Both literacy and numeracy teaching were constrained by the stop-start lesson structure and a tendency to prioritise curriculum coverage over children's learning. Target setting was meant to motivate both children and teachers and measure the efficacy of the *Strategies*. As a means of managing policy, target setting appeared to act as a public guarantee that the policy is working: '[t]he closer the target gets to being met, the greater the policy success' (Moss 2009: 159).

The NLS made a double promise: 'to raise standards' and to improve 'the life chances of many children' (DfEE 1998: 4). High standards of literacy were seen to bring both individual and economic benefits. The former included 'valuable ways of thinking about and understanding the world and ourselves' (Beard 2000: 7), while the latter were linked to developing an efficient workforce:

> Weaknesses in processing written information can make a workforce less efficient and the companies which employ them less competitive in world markets ... 60% of all jobs now require reasonable reading skills e.g. being able to understand and act on written instructions, obtain simple information and understand a price list.
>
> (pp. 8–9)

Importantly, the teaching methods prescribed by the NLS were originally developed to meet specific needs of disadvantaged pupils and were at the time piloted in a number of intervention programmes in different countries (Beard 2000; Bryan 2004).[4] These intervention programmes were still subject to completion and evaluation **before** the *Literacy Strategy* was rolled out in England. This was, however, dismissed because of a trend in international thinking:

> While none of these programmes have yet run their full course, their overlaps with the NLS indicate the general direction of global thinking.
>
> (Beard 2000:12)

A large-scale roll-out of such programmes prior to their completion and review gives the *National Literacy Strategy* an air of a large-scale experiment. Indeed, as argued by Barber (2008: 27), 'the need to transform the way governments work requires experimentation'.

Despite mixed initial evaluations of the effectiveness of the NLS and NNS (Fisher *et al.* 2000; Brown *et al.* 2001; Earl *et al.* 2003) and concerns about their prescriptive, technicist approaches (Dadds 1999), two further strategies followed, consolidating and 'renewing' the literacy and numeracy agendas (Table 5.1). The first one of these, *Excellence and Enjoyment: A strategy for primary schools* (DfES, 2003a), was published following the failure to reach the literacy and numeracy targets in 2002. Although the targets were missed, *Excellence and Enjoyment* repeatedly refers to the success of the NNS and NLS:

> Our primary schools are a success story. The best are the best in the world. They are a joy to visit and a credit to our nation.
>
> (DfES 2003a: 2)

> Ofsted have also celebrated the success of schools that make a broad and rich offering to their students.
>
> (p. 11)

> Literacy and numeracy consultants have been key to the success of the National Literacy and Numeracy Strategies.
>
> (p. 63)

The discourse of *Excellence and Enjoyment* displays the characteristics of a hortatory report, a text that is framed as a list of 'unordered lists of appearances ... or evidences' (Fairclough 2003: 95):

> Our leading primary schools ... are characterised by high standards in literacy and numeracy; a rich, broad and balanced curriculum; a happy, safe and supportive atmosphere, with a strong commitment to helping all children succeed whatever their background or abilities; and they have strong relationships with parents and the community.
>
> (DfES 2003a: 9)

The above text constructs a list of unrelated characteristics of 'leading schools' to demonstrate the success of the NLS and NNS. The problem here is that by simply listing the characteristics of 'leading schools', the underlying processes explaining how or why the specific items on the list contribute to the raising of standards are not addressed. The function of such discourse and its underpinning 'logic of appearances' is to promote and legitimate existing systems of meaning. Fairclough's alternative to the 'logic of appearances' is 'explanatory logic'. By focusing on the underlying processes, explanatory logic reveals complexity, tensions and alternative possibilities. A key objective of *Excellence and Enjoyment* was to challenge schools to continue to raise standards by encouraging the children to develop 'ownership' of their targets:

> We want every primary school to review its performance and to set targets for Level 4 and Level 5 up to 2006 which are ... owned: understood by the school, including governors and pupils, and having a visible life and meaning in the classroom.
>
> (p. 19)

As signalled in Chapter 1, the *Five Year Strategy for Children and Learners* (DfES 2004: 9), introduced the notion of 'transformation', defined as 'real change', made 'quickly'. The document repeatedly referred to 'transformation' in the context of 'transforming standards', 'transforming life chances ... aspirations and opportunities' and 'transforming skills'. School leadership was also constructed in terms of transformation, as the 'ability to manage people and money with the creativity, imagination and inspiration to lead transformation' (p. 109). Published at a 'low' point in the 'strategies era', when pupil test results plateaued after an initial gain, casting doubt on the 'magic bullet' of the literacy and numeracy hours (Moss 2009:165), the *Five Year Strategy for Children and Learners* signalled a turn towards new policy drivers and levers: 'spectacular' school leaders, strategy consultants and quasi-markets in education.

Reconstructing the policy apparatus

From 2004, direct intervention through command and control began to be replaced by a more decentralised approach. As noted by Moss (2009), highly centralised reforms are politically risky when they fail to produce a quick success and, consequently, the New Labour government redefined their role as 'purchasers' rather than 'providers' of policy, showing an increasing reluctance to embrace solutions that promise uncertain outcomes. More power and responsibility for 'transforming education' was now devolved to school leaders, Local Authority and private strategy consultants, with education reconceptualised as a 'quasi-market' (PSR 2006). A new policy discourse emerged, referring to consumer 'choice and voice', market incentives as quality levers and capacity building through leadership and workforce remodelling. 'Devolution and transparency', 'quasi-markets' and 'command and control' were now presented as three distinct 'Twenty-First-Century Solutions' for large-scale reform in education (Barber 2009: 263). This new approach, which viewed education as a 'self-improving system' (PSR 2006; Mead 2006; Ball 2013; Bates 2013; Hargreaves 2010), was taken up post 2010 by the Coalition government and, in the guise of creating a more diverse school system, led to the opening of more academies and new 'free schools' (Chapter 6).

An increasing reliance on 'spectacular' school leaders was facilitated by the opening of the NCSL in 2000. The actual devolution of power to school leaders was, however, limited because leadership knowledge tended to be constructed as compliance with the reform agenda and efficient implementation of policy (Gunter 2004). More power was devolved to strategy consultants, who now became leading 'policy drivers' (Bryan 2004). As a result, the second phase of the 'strategies era' saw an increase in contracting the NLS out to external consultants (Mills 2011). A large-scale deployment of private consultancy firms, as well as consultant headteachers and Local Authority personnel is symptomatic of the now widespread phenomenon of 'consultocracy' in education policymaking in England (Gunter *et al.* 2014). By the time the *Strategies* were terminated by the Coalition government in 2011 (to introduce a new wave of reforms), the services of 2,000 strategy consultants had been purchased (DfE 2011a), with millions of pounds spent on IT and management consultancy (Gunter *et al.* 2014). The legacy of the *Strategies* includes several disjunctures: between policy abstractions and complexities of policy enactment, between the knowledge of 'expert outsiders' and knowledge gained 'within' practice, between what standards mean for the policymaker and the meanings of standards that emerge in the lived experience of *this* child and *this* teacher in *this* school. From the policymakers' perspective, the beginning of the 'strategies era' in 1998 marked a radical break with traditional approaches to pedagogy and a beginning of a large-scale 're-engineering' (Barber 1997) of the English education system (Chapter 2). Schools, however, have their own contexts and trajectories and they are always in the midst of the processes of continuity and change. It is to these unique contexts and trajectories that we now turn.

Local diversity: real places and real people

Abbey Primary (AP) and Green Lanes Primary (GLP) are located on the outskirts of the same social housing (council) estate in outer London. AP is a 'three-form-entry' school, with three classes ('forms') in each year group and 700 pupils in total. GLP is 'two-form-entry', with two classes in each year group and a total of 420 pupils. Both schools educate 'Infants', children aged between 4 and 6 years, and 'Juniors', aged 7–11. Infants attend the 'Reception', 'Year 1' and 'Year 2' classes, while Juniors attend Years 3–6. Both schools serve children and families of a broad 'socio-economic mix'. This includes children eligible for 'free school meals (whose parents are in receipt of welfare benefits) and well-off middle class families. The proportion of pupils on free school meals is at the national average in GLP and lower than average in AP. Both schools have a high proportion of pupils of different ethnic backgrounds who speak English as an additional language (40 per cent in AP and 50 per cent in GLP). During the data collection period (March 2011–July 2012), an Ofsted inspection was held at GLP and the school was re-graded from 'satisfactory' to 'good'. AP was inspected in 2013 and re-graded from 'good' to 'outstanding'.[5]

Abbey Primary: the trajectory to an 'outstanding' school

AP is located in ample grounds in a residential part of the Borough.[6] It has three large playing fields and light, airy, one-storey buildings. The school is very popular in the local community and unable to accept all families applying for a place. This popularity is based on a strong position of the school in national league tables, its ethos of ambition and hard work, as well as a rich range of after-school activities for the children. The school's league table performance improved steadily since the appointment of a new headteacher (Jenny) and deputy head (Sophie) in 2000 and 2001, respectively.

At the time of Jenny's arrival, AP was a 'coasting' school, previously led by a headteacher nearing his retirement and absent a lot because of ill health. This resulted in more ambitious parents moving their children to other schools. Jenny's key priorities were, therefore, first, to improve relationships with parents, and second, to 'battle' for a better school ethos, which, at the time, was characterised by a 'lack of teacher expectation', especially in relation to children from the local council estate:

> When I came here, the attitude was: 'if the children are from the estate, they are not going to do anything' ... And I said: 'That's not good enough!' ... It's hard, because a lot of teachers who've been here for a long time were entrenched. And I had to face battles with some of them and then they moved ... I don't care if I win, but I want to be the best that I can be.
>
> (Jenny, H, AP)

The big exodus of teachers by the end of the first year enabled Jenny to employ new, young staff who shared Jenny's ambition to 'be the best that I can be'. It also provided an opportunity for building a more cohesive team, because 'the school was very divided at that point, there were the Juniors and then the Infants and they didn't talk to each other and they fell out over the pencil stock' (Sophie). The 'battle' with parents took even longer and involved both Jenny and Sophie, who joined the school as a new deputy head a year later:

> I thought that the best way, because I know what they're like out there, yakking (*laughs*) ... so I thought 'bring them in' ... so we introduced coffee mornings, every week. I would sit there, usually with Sophie, and we'd just get this **barrage** of abuse, week after week after week.
>
> (Sophie, DH, AP)

Jenny believes that 'battling' with parental and teacher attitudes requires headteachers to be 'thick skinned', 'determined' and 'relentless':

> And it took us, oh, over a year to start turning it round and getting positive. And then it got to the stage where, if somebody came and said something negative, other parents said 'well no actually, that's not true'. If they were unhappy about something, I would get them in and discuss it. I'd then follow it up and make a little card saying: 'Have we resolved your problem? Or would you like to come in and discuss it further?' And one mum was in nearly every week, we had six months before I finally wore her down ... (*laughs*) And we still get it and they still moan, that's what they do, that's what school gates are for.
>
> (Jenny, H, AP)

Jenny's sense of humour seems to deflect from talking about the difficult choices she made in her first year at AP, which resulted in an exodus of staff. During the eleven years of Jenny's leadership, AP changed radically. In terms of pupil test results, the percentage of children achieving Level 4 in literacy and numeracy rose from 70 per cent in 2001 to 98 per cent in 2012, placing the school in the top band in the national league tables.

The transformation of Green Lanes Primary

Stephen, the headteacher of GLP, compares a primary school to a 'complex organism' where change is a 'two-way process' involving school leaders sharing their values and absorbing 'a lot of the school culture as well'. When he took up his first headship post at GLP four years ago:

> What surprised me was how quickly people picked up on the way that I said things, that people learned very quickly what was important to me, even though I wasn't standing on a pedestal and saying: 'This is what's important to me' . . . And I think I connected and I think that I'd made the right choice with regard to feeling comfortable at the school and having a team of staff that I think I would hopefully be able to mould and also from whom I could learn a lot as well.
>
> (Stephen, H, GLP)

The last twenty years of the school's history are closely interlinked with the changes in its immediate locality, as well as broader educational and social change. As Stephen points out:

> A lot of people get the wrong impression of the school; the façade, the local roads tell a story of middle class aspiration, high achievement. That's added to by the mature trees in the ground, a kind of countryside look to it . . . There are enormous pockets of hardship around here, a very, very needy local estate.
>
> (Stephen, H, GLP)

Thirty years ago, the school was attended by middle-class children living in the big houses in the school's vicinity. As Jeanne, the Receptionist, states, 'it was almost like a private school. We had bowler hats for girls, blazers for boys'. With time, the big houses were converted into flats, and the 'very needy' council estate was built nearby. These changes in the neighbourhood affected the socio-economic mix of the school. The more recent effects of globalisation brought large numbers of ethnic families into the local area and the school.

On becoming headteacher in 2007, Stephen had an idealised view of education, central to which was 'giving children who might come from a less privileged background every opportunity to succeed'. His key priority was to improve the outside play space, because most GLP children do not have their own back garden. A small environmental project snowballed into a building site. New first-floor classrooms were built to enable the school to take on an extra Reception class and alleviate the predicted shortage of primary places in the Local Authority because of a demographic peak. Prior to extending, the school had two separate staffrooms for Infant and Junior teachers; one of the newly built spaces is now being used as a joint staffroom. Spacious, light and airy, well furnished and decorated, with skylights and ecological lighting, it is a big improvement on two small staffrooms used before, cluttered with bookshelves and folders. Stephen hopes that this new addition will help create a more cohesive team, with everybody meeting in the common space where:

> it's not Infants and Juniors, where it's not teachers and ancillary staff and teaching assistants, but where we hopefully share common values and we recognise that we are all trying to move in the same direction together.
> (Stephen, H, GLP)

Stephen finds his greatest support in Miriam, the deputy head, who also started at GLP in 2007 and is 'an absolute godsend, somebody who is very good at the things that I'm not very good at, so I hope that we complement each other well'.

One of the key themes in the 'story' of GLP is that a focus on creating and sustaining a caring, inclusive environment could be as important as academic success. For example, an important yearly event in the school's calendar is 'International Evening', when all families are invited in to cook and taste traditional food. Stephen recalls 'International Evening 2010' as follows:

> To get communities working together it was **just brilliant**! We've got a lot of Asian families who historically haven't engaged much with the school and with other parents. I mean it was just fantastic; a whole group of them got together in the school's kitchen and were just cooking up a storm! And when they turned up with their *pecoras*, and their *bhajis*, it was just brilliant!
> (Stephen, H, GLP)

Over the years, GLP 'evolved' from a 'little cosy middle class enclave' (Jeanne) to a community school. This transformation has been a complex process that emerged as a result of changes within the school and its immediate environment, rather than direct government policy. More than a central blueprint, the process of community building involved goodwill and sensitivity to the needs of the community that the school serves and opportunities to celebrate together.

The people

The majority of AP teachers are in their twenties or early thirties and were employed by Jenny within a year of taking up a headship position. Conversely, most of the teaching assistants (TAs) and administrative staff (AS) are the parents of former Abbey pupils, who have worked their way 'up' to their current positions through volunteering to read with children or doing ancillary part-time work. The TAs and AS at GLP followed routes to their current positions similar to those at AP. Most of the teachers, however, have worked in the school for many years and are in their late thirties to late forties (see Appendix).

The staff at GLP are 'extraordinarily loyal' and, consequently, Stephen made just three new appointments during his four years at GLP. Stephen admits that the low turnover of staff ensures stability and continuity, but it is also 'a real privilege for new headteachers to be able to appoint their own staff, that share their values'. Susan (T) shares Stephen's view: 'the staff have **all** been here quite a long time, so it's been difficult trying to introduce new things'. However, Stephen appreciates 'organic' growth and, as a 'reflective democrat', acknowledges the importance of mutuality in leader–followers interactions: 'The way forward can't just come from one person, and you've got to listen to the voices outside of your own head'.

At the time of data collection, Jenny was just about to retire. On joining AP in January 2000, she had thirteen years' headship experience in three schools in deprived areas. She had also taught for fifteen years in deprived areas, in Salford, 'by the docks in Manchester' and later in East Ham in London. Jenny's understanding of education originates from 'life', 'intuition' and is premised on expectation:

> So it's about teacher expectation, that's the biggest thing. Expect a child to fail, they'll fail. You cannot make a school in a deprived area as successful as here, because you've got all those other things you've got to battle against, but you can still make a huge difference.
>
> (Jenny, H, AP)

The *Strategies* and their (un)desirable consequences

As discussed above, the *Strategies* were expected to deliver a significant rise in pupil tests results by 2002. The determination of Michael Barber to drive his agenda to the exclusion of other considerations was a powerful gesture expressing an unwillingness of Barber and officials working in his Delivery Unit to enter into the attitude of teachers tasked with delivering the *Strategies*. Interpreted as a conversation of gestures (Mead 1934), this approach lacked the reciprocity that would make the enactment of the *Strategies* more meaningful, both to practitioners and the policymakers themselves. As we have seen in Chapter 3, in Mead's account, meaning does not arise in an individual nor is transmitted in a gesture, but arises in the response of the other. It is this response that makes mutual adjustments possible, as participants enter into the attitude of the other. However, rather than waiting for a response from practitioners, Barber's Delivery Unit introduced 'accountability' and 'checking' systems to 'get buy-in' (Mead 2006). As reported in earlier research studies, typical practitioner responses to this gesture ranged from an exodus of a whole generation of teachers who refused to 'buy into' the *Strategies*, to 'severe identity crises', 'strategic' adjustment and 'game playing' of those who remained in the profession (Woods and Jeffrey 2002). As conveyed in Abbey and Green Lanes accounts, despite the 'structure' and 'progression' provided by the *Strategies*, their over-prescription adversely affected teachers' confidence and ability to do their own planning (Sophie, AP). Alison and Susan (GLP) emphasised that the *National Literacy Strategy* resulted in a generation of children who were turned off reading books. After several years of adjustments made by practitioners, the *Strategies* 'began working' (Alison). The story ended with the Coalition government's decision to 'scrap them' and 'close the websites down' in 2011 (Stephen). What seems to continue, however, is the command and control communication that demands compliance with reform even if it fails to 'meet the needs of our children' (Pete, AP) and therefore may not make much sense to teachers (Chapter 6).

Two generations of practitioners making sense of . . . 'lots of folders'

The accounts of the *Strategies* related by the participants varied between 'generations' (Appendix), demarcated by the introduction of the first *Literacy* and *Numeracy Strategies* in 1998 and 1999, respectively. Teachers from the 'older' generation, who had taught before 1998, vividly remember being 'exposed to this idea of the literacy hour and the numeracy hour' (Stephen). The 'younger' generation comprises teachers who received induction into the *Strategies* during Initial Teacher Training, as well as teachers newer to the profession, whose knowledge was limited mainly to using the government website resources for the *Literacy* and *Numeracy Strategies*.

The initial response to the highly prescriptive *Strategy* materials distributed to schools as 'lots of folders' (Miriam) was that of 'teaching for the sake of it':

> When it first came in everybody felt really tied to it, and I think we went through a period where we were teaching for the sake of it. We had to cover this, this and this, it didn't matter whether children enjoyed it, we had to say we'd cover it. And what's more, I don't think the children were getting much from it, because we couldn't adapt it, or we **felt** we couldn't adapt it.
>
> (Alison, ST, GLP)

The accounts of the *Strategies* told by the 'older' generation recur in the accounts of the 'younger' teachers, albeit as less detailed explanation. For example, Jenny recalled the stage of adapting the *Strategies* thus:

> Like many schools, we went along with it to begin with. And then we thought, that doesn't suit us that bit, so we'll keep that but we're ditching that. Because in some things we were finding that our children were not doing well in things, because we were doing it in that prescribed way, so we changed it.
>
> (Jenny, H, AP)

This was echoed by her 'younger' staff:

> When I then became literacy co-ordinator and I was teaching in year 6, I didn't feel that that was right for our children here.
>
> (Alice, DH)

> Obviously, we follow them as we're meant to, and we make them work for us and for the children, we may have to adapt things slightly but we do cover it.
>
> (Fiona, SLT)

> We then took on the literacy and we kind of tweaked a little bit, we didn't use it as religiously as we did the numeracy one.
>
> (Maggie, SLT)

The frameworks and materials for the *Literacy Strategy* in particular were criticised for being 'deadly dull' (Caroline), 'a bit wishy-washy' (Mark), 'quite blurry' (Stephen), 'regimented' (Angelika), 'limiting and ... just boring' (Susan). Practitioners soon realised that using them 'religiously' de-motivated children and started turning teachers into 'robots' (Alison). 'Ditching', 'tweaking', 'adapting', making them 'more up to date and modern and exciting for the children' were practitioners' ways of making the *Strategies* meaningful for them and their children. This suggests that the claims about the quality of the *Strategies* as 'off the shelf' resources (Beard 2000) made by their designers may have been over-inflated. The situation was also exacerbated by the sheer volume of strategies and policies schools were tasked with implementing during the 'strategies era' (Table 5.1). As signalled in Chapter 1, according to one estimate, 459 policy documents on teaching literacy were issued between 1996 and 2005, with the average of more than one document every week (Hofkins and Northen 2009). Consequently, the processes of sense-making and adjusting professionals' responses to the *Literacy Strategy* took time while, in the meantime, adversely affecting children's 'love of reading' (Susan). Alison's reflection articulates tension between being obliged to deliver the literacy curriculum despite children not learning from it:

> I remember going through a period, only a couple of years ago, saying 'Ah, I can't get it done, and the children aren't learning from it. I was thinking, 'don't tie yourself, do what you do well'.
>
> (Alison, SLT, GLP)

These accounts of practitioners' responses to the *Strategies* resonate with Mead's (1934) point about the impossibility to predict or control how others respond to our gestures. The function of a gesture, therefore, is not to transmit our meanings to others, but to make adjustments possible by entering the attitude of the other. The unbending will of a policymaker who refuses to consider the attitude of others makes an impact, 'for good or for ill' (Stephen) and it is this impact that is discussed next.

The Strategies as a 'double-edged sword'

In contrast to the policymakers' hortatory reports promoting the success of the *Strategies*, practitioners' evaluations are more complex, especially when analysed from a long-term perspective. As suggested by Fairclough (2003), 'real' understanding of events is predicated on 'time depth', or taking a long-term view. Without a long-term perspective, we are in danger of losing the sense of the contingency of events and stop thinking about 'how changing things at one level could produce different possibilities' (p. 95). In the case of the *Strategies*, the long-term effect of policymakers' command and control communication was loss of confidence and dependency on the part of teachers, especially the 'younger' generation. As noted by Sophie, the *Strategies* provided:

> starting points where we needed to have starting points, but they then became the masters and the effect was to take away teachers' confidence in their professionalism overall. And when we made the decision here that we would not continue with the *Literacy Strategy* because we felt we could do a much better job, we went to our staff and said 'Alright, you don't have to stick to the *Strategy* any more. We'll look at the planning together but you don't have to stick to the *Strategy*'. And we thought everyone was going to be happy. But actually, it was only the teachers over a certain age who said: 'We can be teachers again'. But the young ones were so engrained, so trained and dependent upon the *Strategy*, that at that point, they didn't know what they were going to do without it.
>
> (Sophie, DH, AP)

Stephen is aware of the time depth needed for a full evaluation of the impact of the *Strategies*. As he points out, 'enough water has passed under the bridge' to realise that:

> a lot of good came out of that. First of all, it raised the profile of literacy and numeracy. And it kind of boosted this idea of entitlement, you know

that these were very important subjects. And it did send out a strong message to the world that we need to raise standards in numeracy, and in literacy, OK? That's the positives. Because there were schools that were ... selling their children short by not providing a rigorous diet of two key subjects.

(Stephen, H, GLP)

The rigour of the *Strategies*, however, turned them into a 'double-edged sword':

Obviously the rigour, which on one hand was a good thing, became a problem as well. Some of the texts were so dry and inaccessible and inappropriate for certain children, I can't explain it anymore than that. There's a fear that some children got turned off the written word by the way of: 'oh it's another literacy lesson, another printed sheet for me to look at'. And it became so kind of stylised, you know 'this is the way we did it', that even children who were talented readers and talented writers could get switched off.

(Stephen, H, GLP)

In his evaluation, Stephen enters the attitude of the children, teachers and, as apparent below, policymakers:

You can understand why a government might want to do that, sort of almost moving towards a French model of 'on this day of the week, we're all going to be studying this at a certain time', and what have you, so that everybody gets the same experiences across the country.

(Stephen, H, GLP)

Despite official claims that the *Strategies* transformed children's 'life-chances' (DfES 2004:14), practitioners' evaluations suggest that they were 'not always plain sailing' (Mark, AP). As Mark admitted, the contingencies of everyday practice made the frameworks 'fall by the wayside a bit'.

The 'black cloud' of Ofsted and the element of chance

This section discusses the impact of Ofsted inspections on teachers. As explained above, school inspections are an important part of the policy apparatus. For Barber, the function of Ofsted was simple: to 'check that people were adopting better practices' (Mead 2006). As suggested by the case study data, however, the role of Ofsted is more complex than providing an 'objective' judgement of a school's performance and policy enactment. An Ofsted report on a school is a powerful gesture made available for public view on the Ofsted website. Schools judged as 'requiring improvement' or 'inadequate' are put under 'special measures' and risk closure or conversion to academies.[7] Much is, therefore, at stake for schools and, consequently, the pressure of an impending inspection may feel like . . . 'it's a black cloud that Ofsted are coming' (Miriam). Prior to the inspection visit, which lasts two to three days and is spent mainly on observing lessons and interviewing, the inspectors scrutinise pupil results in high-stakes tests ('Standard Assessment Tasks', commonly known as 'SATs'), the school's self-evaluation documents and other statistical data (Ofsted 2014). Although Year 6 pupils' performances in literacy and numeracy are pivotal to Ofsted judgement, the final grade also depends on the school's 'performance on the day', under Ofsted's intensive 'gaze' (Jeffrey and Woods 1996; Perryman 2006). As reported in the national press, pressures of inspection and a desire to make an impression at times result in 'game playing', such as 'parachuting' top teachers from neighbouring schools to teach on the day of inspection, loaning outstanding pupil artwork from other schools or even asking poorly behaved children to stay off school (Paton 2012). What, however, often goes unreported are the more 'ordinary' experiences of the 'rituals' of inspection and what they mean to practitioners. The key theme that emerged from the narratives of the inspection at GLP in November 2011 was the 'element of chance' contributing to the final Ofsted grade. The element of chance was a result of the interplay of a number factors: the Ofsted team and their 'script', the timing of the inspection, the school's performance on the day and the 'us'–'them' interaction (Table 5.2).

A key theme in the Ofsted–school conversations is statistical data and other 'objective' evidence. In accordance with official Ofsted protocols (Ofsted 2011), the ritual of interaction at GLP consisted of a pre-inspection briefing, the actual inspection visit, feedback meeting and official report published on the Ofsted website.[8] The focus on statistical data was established from the outset and entailed verifying the school's 'evidence':

> They were very good at coming back to us if they weren't hundred percent sure on something, so for example they wanted more evidence of our community cohesion and we were able to find that evidence.
>
> (Miriam, DH)

The purpose of the feedback meeting on the last day of inspection was to present preliminary findings and advice for how to move the school forward:

> The Ofsted team invited not just Stephen into the meetings but myself . . . And I found that very useful and I learnt an awful lot from that because they talked us through their decisions and then they gave us some constructive feedback, they were saying things like: 'well if we were head of this school, this is something that we would look at, this is somewhere where we'd want to go next'. . . . They give you your key targets to work on, but because we were involved in their feedback meeting, we were also

able to pick up a lot more than is written down [in the final report]. They were very good, we were allowed to make copious notes on everything that they were saying so that we made our own targets from that.

(Miriam, DH)

Table 5.2 'Element of chance' in accounts of Ofsted inspection at GLP

'Element of chance'	Participant's reflection
Ofsted team	I think we've been very lucky with the two teams that we've had. (Stephen)
	So I think it was the team . . . Yeah, it was a fair team. (Miriam)
Timing of inspection	I think we were fortunate we got it in, because we weren't expecting it until December at the earliest, but it came earlier than we were expecting, which I think is a blessing because otherwise it's there, it's a black cloud that Ofsted are coming. And we were lucky, we were told on the Thursday I think, and they came in on the Monday, so we did have a weekend. Well it wasn't really a weekend because we were all in here. But it was useful. (Miriam)
School's performance on the day	People put phenomenal effort into the visit and really put themselves forward in a very positive way. The children, everyone was fantastic. (Angelika)
	By and large though, I do think they got a good snapshot. (Stephen)
Interaction with Ofsted inspectors	But we knew that we had to perform and when a couple of lessons didn't go as well as the teacher would have hoped, very impressed with the way that the Ofsted team dealt with it. It was really sensitively done. (Stephen)
	And I found when I had the one to one interviews with them it was very useful because it wasn't just interrogation, it was very constructive advice that I got . . . I've never had a team that involved me personally as deputy head quite so much, so I do find that quite useful. And the lead inspector came down at the end of the first day and said, you know, how it had gone that day, so you feel quite informed. (Miriam)
Ofsted inspectors' 'script'	They were much hotter this year, I mean it's still the end of the old regime, late autumn 2011 before the new Ofsted kicked in, but they were very much, much tighter on the way we carried out lesson observations . . . we're all clever enough to know that the next Ofsted inspector will have a different script, a completely different script. (Stephen)

The image of Miriam and Stephen 'making copious notes' in the feedback meeting is symbolic of power relations in the Ofsted–school interaction. Only senior school leaders were invited to the meeting and the lack of mutuality in the interaction is signalled by phrases such as 'they talked us through', 'they give you your key targets to work on', and the use of passive voice in 'we were allowed to make copious notes'.

However, it is not only the schools that 'perform' for Ofsted (Perryman 2009); the inspectors themselves also perform to a 'script'. This 'script' has been subject to a number of changes in recent years, in terms of grading criteria and methodology, lowering the reliability of much of the Ofsted data on school performance (Alexander *et al.* 2010). That some of the Ofsted judgements are arbitrary and unrealistic is illustrated by Stephen's account:

> So on that first morning I was kind of put under the spotlight and how I graded the lessons that I saw. As it happened, the lead inspector . . . was a difficult guy to please, and he said to me that in something like ten years he'd only given something like six 'outstandings' in all of the lessons. And he wasn't a monster, I mean his argument was that it's so difficult to prove that all of the children in that class have made above average progress in that one hour.
>
> (Stephen, H)

The lead inspector seems to have cast himself as 'a difficult guy to please' by maintaining that it is difficult to 'prove' the progress for all children an observed lesson. He thus appears to take for granted an unrealistic (and un-measurable) criterion for an 'outstanding lesson' – 'proof' that all children in class 'have made above average progress in that one hour'. This calls into question the feasibility and 'objectivity' of lesson grades:

> If you've got this bit in the Ofsted grades descriptors that says all of the children make above average progress, I mean that's a ridiculous thing to write in there in the first place, because it's just not attainable . . . He made the point that as a headteacher you wouldn't want somebody who turned out outstanding lessons day after day, because he said you cannot sustain that.
>
> (Stephen, H)

Ofsted inspectors' claims to 'objectivity' appear to be sanctioned by the power of office and a privileged 'expert' perspective. Conducted from a purportedly superior epistemological position, Ofsted 'rituals of verification' create a gulf between 'poorly rewarded "doing" and highly rewarded "observing"' (Power 1997: 147), which can damage understandings embedded in practice. In this regard, Pete (H, AP) expressed his concern about 'the way Ofsted can damage schools just by sweeping judgments and things it doesn't know enough about'.

Conclusion

This chapter has focused on the *National Literacy* and *Numeracy Strategies* and the command and control communication institutionalised in the processes of their enactment. The discursive hierarchies established through the *Strategies* rank the knowledge and voice of practitioners as inferior to those of the policymakers, school inspectors, consultants or other 'expert' outsiders. Most practitioners who participated in the research espoused the belief that 'standards have risen' as a result of the enactment of the *Strategies*. However, their accounts also revealed some undesirable consequences of the 'strategies era', in particular a loss of confidence in their professionalism and ambiguous, often 'damaging' role of school inspections.

The *Strategies* were rolled out nationally as a 'spectacular' solution, expected to transform pupil performance in high-stakes tests. To this end, a regime of targets and an elaborate policy apparatus were deployed. In effect, the ambitious targets set in 1998 for the year 2002 were not reached until 2008, in the context of growing research evidence pointing to the limitations and undesirable consequences of the *Strategies* for children's education, in particular the narrowing of the curriculum and pedagogy (Alexander *et al.* 2010). In the meantime, however, policymakers continued responding to problems arising in the processes of enactment with 'new and more radical reforms' (DfES 2004: 9). This sequence of events illustrates how, discursively, policy often 'constructs the problem to which it is a putative solution' (Lingard and Sellar 2013: 277). The myth of 'spectacular' solutions was sustained through hortatory reports, which tended to misrepresent both the transformative potential and the undesirable consequences of the *Strategies*. In disesteeming local knowledge generated 'within' practice and privileging the knowledge of 'expert' outsiders, the myth of 'spectacular' solutions thus seems to have been used to transform education into an object for moulding and manipulation by policymakers.

This legacy suggests that the *Strategies* may have played the role of 'the most ambitious attempt' (DfEE 1997: 19) at remodelling teaching and learning into an efficient delivery of industrial-style targets. England can, therefore, be considered as 'the best (or worst?) case' illustrating problems that may arise from highly standardised, centrally controlled literacy and numeracy policies (Lingard 2010: 131). Given an increasing focus on numeracy and literacy within the GERM, much can be learned from the 'English case' by countries who may consider 'borrowing' the *National Strategies* approach to transforming education.

Notes

1   The achievement of pupils aged 11 and in the final year of primary school is assessed as 'levels' (grades based on high-stakes test scores), with 'level 3' indicating below average, 'level 4' average and 'level 5' above average performance. In 1998, performance of eleven year olds in high-stakes test was as follows:

Literacy: 63 per cent at level 4 and above
Numeracy: 60 per cent at level 4 and above

The *National Strategies* set the following targets for 2002:

Literacy: 80 per cent at level 4 and above
Numeracy: 70 per cent at level 4 and above (source: DfE 2011a)

2 To avoid unnecessary repetition, the references to the 'strategies' discussed in this chapter and throughout this book are used as follows:

- The 'NLS' refers to the first New Labour strategy, the *National Literacy Strategy* (DfEE 1998)
- The 'NNS' refers to the *National Numeracy Strategy* (DfEE 1999)
- The *Strategies*/the *National Strategies*: refer to all 'strategies' for education developed by New Labour
- Where the focus is on a specific strategy document, more detail is provided, that is, publisher and date of publication and/or the title.

3 A detailed analysis of these policy documents is beyond the scope of this book. The most comprehensive analysis of education policy for English primary schools is offered by the *Cambridge Primary Review* (Alexander et al. 2010).

4 As noted by Bryan (2004), the NLS was based on the 'National Literacy Project', inherited by New Labour from their Conservative predecessors and aimed at a minority of schools with low test scores. International studies in literacy have an even longer history of literacy 'intervention' and 'recovery' programmes, dating back to the formation of the IEA in 1959 (e.g. Binkley *et al.* 1996).

5 'Outstanding' is the top Ofsted grade. The current Ofsted (2014: 5) grades are based on standardised criteria related to the following key areas:

- achievement of pupils at the school
- quality of teaching in the school
- behaviour and safety of pupils at the school
- quality of leadership and management of the school

6 A 'borough' is a district that is under the administration of a local Council. A Local Authority represents local government, responsible for education and other local services.

7 Academies are schools that are under the direct control of the Secretary of State for Education rather than Local Authority control (Chapter 6).

8 Inspection processes and routines have undergone significant changes in recent years, from longer inspections (of 3–5 days' duration) with several months' notice given to the school, to shorter, 2–3 days' inspections announced 2–3 days in advance of the inspection. At the time of writing, further 'radical reforms' to inspections were being planned, based on 'frequent but shorter inspections of good schools', conducted every 3 years (Ofsted 2015).

References

Alexander, R., Armstrong, M., Flutter, J., Hargreaves, L., Harlen, W., Harrison, D., Hartley-Brewer, E., Kershner, R., MacBeath, J., Mayall, B., Northen, S., Pugh, G., Richards, C. and Utting, D. 2010. *Children, Their World, Their Education: Final Report and Recommendations of the Cambridge Primary Review*. Abingdon: Routledge and the University of Cambridge.

Arnold, R. 2004. *Transforming Secondary Education: The Beacon Council Scheme: Round 4*. Slough: National Foundation for Educational Research.

Ball, S.J. 2013. *The Education Debate* (2nd edn). Bristol: The Policy Press.

Barber, M. 1997. *The Learning Game: Arguments for an Education Revolution*. London: Indigo.

Barber, M. 2008. *Instruction to Deliver: Fighting to Transform Britain's Public Services* (2nd edn). London: Methuen Publishing.

Barber, M. 2009. 'How Government, Professions and Citizens Combine to Drive Successful Educational Change'. In Hargreaves, A., Lieberman, A., Fullan, M. and Hopkins, D. (eds) *Second International Handbook of Educational Change*. Dordrecht: Springer, 261–278.

Bates, A. 2013. Transcending systems thinking in education reform: Implications for policy-makers and school leaders, *Journal of Education Policy*, 28(1): 38–54.

Beard, R. 2000. *National Literacy Strategy: Review of Research and other Related Evidence*. Sudbury: DfEE Publications.

Binkley, M., Rust, K. and Williams, T. (eds). 1996. *Reading Literacy in an International Perspective: Collected Papers from the IEA Literacy Study*. Washington, DC: National Center for Education Statistics.

Brown, M., Askew, M., Rhodes, V., Denvir, H., Ranson, E. and Wiliam, D. 2001. Magic bullets or chimeras? Searching for factors characterising effective teachers and effective teaching in numeracy. Paper presented at *British Educational Research Association Annual Conference*, University of Leeds, 13–15 September. Available at: www.ncetm. org.uk/public/files/29311/Brown%25253DAskew_BERA01_chimeras.pdf (accessed 12 April 2015).

Bryan, H. 2004. Constructs of teacher professionalism within a changing literacy landscape, *Literacy*, 38(3): 141–148.

Cummings, J. 2015. The Abode of Educational Production: An Interview with Peter McLaren, *Alternate Routes: A Journal of Critical and Social Research*, 26. Available at: www.alternateroutes.ca/index.php/ar/article/view/22326 (accessed 5 April 2015).

Dadds, M. 1999. Teachers, values and the literacy hour, *Cambridge Journal of Education*, 29(1): 7–30.

DCSF. 2007. *The Children's Plan: Building Brighter Futures*. London: DCSF.

DfE. 2010a. *The Importance of Teaching: The Schools White Paper 2010*. Available at: www.ictliteracy.info/rf.pdf/Schools-White-Paper2010.pdf (accessed 15 March 2012).

DfE. 2010b. *The Case for Change*. London: Crown Copyright.

DfE. 2011a. *The National Strategies 1997–2011: A Brief Summary of the Impact and Effectiveness of the National Strategies*. London: Crown Copyright.

DfE. 2011b. *Training Our Next Generation of Outstanding Teachers: An Improvement Strategy for Discussion*. London: Crown Copyright.

DfEE. 1997. *The Implementation of the National Literacy Strategy*. London: DfEE.

DfEE. 1998. *The National Literacy Strategy: Framework for Teaching*. London: DfEE.

DfEE. 1999. *The National Numeracy Strategy: Framework for Teaching Mathematics*. London: DfEE.

DfES. 2003a. *Excellence and Enjoyment: A Strategy for Primary Schools*. London: HMSO.

DfES. 2003b. *Every Child Matters* (Green Paper). Norwich: TSO.

DfES. 2004. *Five Year Strategy for Children and Learners*. Norwich: The Stationery Office.

DfES. 2006. *Primary Framework for Literacy and Mathematics.* Norwich: Crown Copyright.

Earl, L., Watson, N., Levin, B., Leithwood, K. and Fullan, M. 2003. *Watching and Learning 3: Final Report of the External Evaluation of England's National Literacy and Numeracy Strategies.* Toronto: Ontario Institute for Studies in Education.

Education Act. 2005. Available at: www.legislation.gov.uk/ukpga/2005/18/pdfs/ukpga_20050018_en.pdf (accessed 13 April 2015).

Fairclough, N. 2003. *Analysing Discourse: Textual Analysis for Social Research.* Abingdon: Routledge.

Fisher, R., Lewis, M. and Davis, B. 2000. Progress and performance in National Literacy Strategy classrooms, *Journal of Research in Reading*, 23(3): 256–267.

Fullan, M. 2003. *Change Forces with a Vengeance.* London: RoutledgeFalmer.

Gunter, H.M. 2004. Labels and labelling in the field of educational leadership, *Discourse: Studies in the Cultural Politics of Education*, 25(1): 21–41.

Gunter, H.M., Hall, D. and Mills, C. 2014. Consultants, consultancy and consultocracy in education policymaking in England, *Journal of Education Policy*, 30(4): 518–539.

Hall, K. 2004. Reflections on six years of the National Literacy Strategy in England: An interview with Stephen Anwyll, Director of the NLS 2011–2004, *Literacy*, 38(3): 119–125.

Hargreaves, D.H. 2010. *Creating a Self-Improving School System.* Nottingham: National College for Leadership of Schools and Children's Services.

Hofkins, D. and Northen, S. (eds) 2009. *Introducing the Cambridge Primary Review.* Cambridge: University of Cambridge.

Jeffrey, B. and Woods, P. 1996. Feeling deprofessionalised: The social construction of emotions during an Ofsted inspection, *Cambridge Journal of Education*, 26(3): 325–341.

Kelly, A.V. 2009. *The Curriculum: Theory and Practice* (6th edn). London: Sage.

Lingard, B. 2010. Policy borrowing, policy learning: Testing times in Australian schooling, *Critical Studies in Education*, 51(2): 129–147.

Lingard, B. and Sellar, S. 2013. Globalization, edu-business and network governance: The policy sociology of Stephen J. Ball and rethinking education policy analysis, *London Review of Education*, 11(3): 265–280.

Mead, G.H. 1934. *Mind, Self, and Society from the Standpoint of a Social Behaviourist.* Chicago, IL and London: The University of Chicago Press.

Mead, S. 2006. *Education Reform Lessons from England: An Interview with Sir Michael Barber.* Available at: www.educationsector.org/publications/education-reform-lessons-england (accessed 12 April 2015).

Mills, C. 2011. Framing literacy policy: Power and policy drivers in primary schools, *Literacy*, 45(3): 103–110.

Moss, G. 2004. Changing practice: The National Literacy Strategy and the politics of literacy policy, *Literacy*, 38(3): 126–133.

Moss, G. 2009. The politics of literacy in the context of large-scale education reform, *Research Papers in Education*, 24(2): 155–174.

Ofsted. 2011. *Conducting School Inspections: Guidance for Inspecting Schools in England under Section 5 of the Education Act 2005, from September 2009.* Manchester: Crown Copyright.

Ofsted. 2014. *The Framework for School Inspection.* Manchester: Crown Copyright.

Ofsted. 2015. *Ofsted Confirms Radical Reforms to Education Inspection: Press Release.* Available at: www.gov.uk/government/news/ofsted-confirms-radical-reforms-to-education-inspection (accessed 9 April 2015).

Paton, G. 2012. Schools are bribing pupils into staying away when Ofsted inspectors visit, it is claimed, *The Telegraph* (6 January). Available at: www.telegraph.co.uk/education/educationnews/8995377/Schools-bribing-pupils-to-cheat-Ofsted-inspections.html (accessed 13 April 2015).

Perryman, J. 2006. Panoptic performativity and school inspection regimes: Disciplinary mechanisms and life under special measures, *Journal of Educational Policy*, 21(2): 147–161.

Perryman, J. 2009. Inspection and the fabrication of professional and performative processes, *Journal of Education Policy*, 24(5): 611–631.

Power, M. 1997. *The Audit Society: Rituals of Verification*. Oxford: Oxford University Press.

PSR. 2006. The UK Government's Approach to Public Service Reform. Available at: http://webarchive.nationalarchives.gov.uk/20070701080507/cabinetoffice.gov.uk/strategy/downloads/work_areas/public_service_reform/sj_pamphlet.pdf (accessed 13 April 2015).

Rose, J. 2006. *Independent Review of the Teaching of Early Reading: Final Report*. London: DfES.

Rose, J. 2009. *The Independent Review of the Primary Curriculum: Final Report*. London: DCSF.

Ross, A. 2000. *Curriculum: Construction and Critique*. London: Palmer Press.

Van Manen, M. 1990. *Researching Lived Experience: Human Science for an Action Sensitive Pedagogy*. New York: SUNY.

Williams, P. 2008. *Independent Review of Primary Mathematics Teaching in Early Years Setting and Primary Schools: Final Report*. London: DCSF.

Woods, P. and Jeffrey, B. 2002. The reconstruction of primary teachers' identities, *British Journal of Sociology of Education*, 23(1): 89–106.

Chapter 6

Everyday practice and the myth of perpetual crisis

> I think assessment and standards have always been very, very important which is something, being the assessment manager now, it's something I'll get my teeth into and focus on SATs and getting all the standards up.
> (Maggie, Senior Leadership Team, Abbey Primary)

> That teaching to the test ... there's far too much of this ... and an improvement here would be more rounded, perhaps, education.
> (Eve, administrative staff, Abbey Primary)

While Chapter 5 focused on how practitioners responded to (particularised) the generalised prescriptions of the *National Literacy* and *Numeracy Strategies*, the emphasis in this chapter is on how they articulated what 'school improvement' meant to them as they engaged in everyday practice. This chapter also outlines the approach to education policymaking by the Coalition government 2010–2015. Despite the rhetoric of 'greater freedoms' for schools (DfE 2010a), the Coalition continued a top-down approach to policymaking, accelerating and extending New Labour's quasi-markets in education through the Academies Programme and opening the 'school market' to new providers. Academies are removed from Local Authority control to be directly accountable to the Secretary of State for Education. The 'freedoms' offered to academies include the possibility to opt out of teaching the National Curriculum and national agreements on the conditions of work and pay for teachers. According to the Conservative Prime Minister David Cameron (2011), allowing 'new providers' to start new schools or sponsor academies, 'confronting educational failure head-on' and 'ramping up standards' were the key Coalition objectives in response to an 'urgent' need to reform education.

From the complex responsive processes perspective, the meanings of 'improving' or 'transforming education' are contingent on individuals' responses, both rational and emotional, which constantly interweave with the actions, values and intentions of others. The complex dynamics of local interactions are, therefore, not only unpredictable, but also underpinned by tensions, paradox and ambiguity. The case study findings suggest that government improvement policies frequently confine the patterns of conversation in the 'local' school to assessment and teaching to the test, as suggested by Maggie and Eve cited in the epigraph to this chapter. However, practitioners' interpretations of government conceptions of improvement were not uniform or universally compliant. Some participants appeared to hold on to their own meanings of 'improvement', for example, 'more rounded education' (Jeanne, Eve), providing 'the best for the children' (Stephen) and 'the whole child' (Sophie, Miriam). These notions existed in tension with the dominant approach to improving schools by delivering performance targets in high-stakes tests. Many participants conveyed a sense of being constrained by the performativity agenda, while others seemed to struggle for clarity when articulating alternative understandings of 'school improvement'. For example, a closer reading of Eve's point above is suggestive of being out of control in the way she hesitates and uses words such as 'perhaps', 'I would like' and 'would be' when articulating her alternative to the dominant notion of improvement. Conversely, embracing the 'new orthodoxy' of transforming education, defined in terms of pupils' results in high-stakes tests ('SATs') seemed to give practitioners a sense of certainty. This is exemplified by the confidence with which Maggie articulates her commitment to 'getting all the standards up' in her role as the school's assessment manager. This chapter engages in a closer reading of the patterns of conversation in AP and GLP using Fairclough's (2003) critical discourse analysis tools (Figure 4.2 in Chapter 4). The key emphasis here is on the experience of teachers, while the impact of the performativity agenda on children is discussed in Chapter 8.

The nuanced meanings of 'school improvement' that emerge from the data are discussed in the context of 'complexity reduction' (Biesta 2010) characteristic of the Coalition's approach to transforming education. Despite the promise of 'greater freedoms' for schools, the Coalition policies of the Conservative Education Secretary Michael Gove (2010–2014) turned out to be equally, if not more directive, than those of New Labour. Top-down policies continue to proliferate and the myth of perpetual crisis is frequently 'wheeled out' to justify the ongoing 'policy hysteria' (Stronach and MacLure 1997). As signalled in Chapter 1, crisis narratives are premised on the supposed deficiency or threat arising from the economic imperatives of the global age. In an education system conceived as the 'engine' of the economy, winning the economic race is intertwined with outperforming other countries in school performance tests such as PISA. The Coalition created a sense of crisis by invoking an image of Britain 'standing still' in the global race while 'others race past' (DfE 2010a: 3). This pressure was increased by organisations such as the Confederation of British Industry (CBI) who also warned that England 'appears to be going backwards' in international league tables of educational performance at great cost to the economy (CBI 2012: 2). The danger of losing the race is averted by devising 'spectacular' solutions, for example the *National Numeracy* and *Literacy Strategies* discussed in Chapter 5 and, post 2010, restructuring based on the Swedish 'free schools' and American charter schools models. A fundamental problem with this crisis–solution approach is a conceptualisation of educational transformation that reduces 'real' children, teachers and schools to statistics. This form of reduction may not only lead to a dehumanised education system but also to a proliferation of policies that are unworkable. As Sophie, the deputy head at AP pointed out: 'you can write policies or produce resources till you're blue in the face, but at the end it's the teachers and the teaching assistants who make it work for the children'. The myth of perpetual crisis and the resulting 'policy hysteria' may thus constrain the very processes of everyday interactions that could enable practitioners to make policy work for the children.

'Greater', 'better', 'more effective': accelerating and extending marketisation

As proclaimed by Cameron (2011), the Coalition's blueprint for 'proper' reform was simple. 'Ramping up standards' would be achieved through a relentless focus on 'the basics' of literacy and numeracy (DfE 2010a) and incentives for teachers such as performance-related pay (DfE 2011). Confronting failure to meet new ambitious performance targets would mean closing down underperforming schools or converting them to academies (DfE 2010a). Numerous references to 'greater', 'better' and 'more effective' in the *Schools White Paper 2010* suggest a continuation and extension of New Labour's market-oriented reforms. This can be illustrated by the accelerated academisation under the Coalition.

Introduced in 2000, New Labour's Academies Programme was aimed at increasing diversity in the public education system. This would enable parents to have more 'choice and voice' and schools to benefit from a 'positive' impact of private sponsors. From the outset, however, the programme raised issues of equality of opportunity, accountability to the local community and privatisation (Gunter 2011). Similar issues occurred in the development of the Swedish free school and the American charter school models. Swedish free schools receive public funding and are privately run, including some for profit. Since the rise of Swedish free schools in the early 1990s, 'small improvements' in academic achievement have been made in areas with more free schools (Allen 2010: 4), but at a greater cost and increase in social segregation (Wiborg 2010; West 2014).[1] Even greater issues of inequality, cost and educational failure emerged in the twenty years of the American charter school movement (Fabricant and Fine 2012; Ravitch 2014). As explained by Diane Ravitch (2014), the original idea was to issue a local school with a contract (charter) to work with students at high risk of failure. However, the idea was soon taken up by private companies as an opportunity to access public funding and expand by competing with local public schools. As Ravitch points out, despite policymakers' rhetoric, charter schools are, on average, 'no more innovative or successful than public schools' (p. 156). Some children have gained from being educated in charter schools, but most have not, particularly the students with special needs for whom the schools were originally designed. Many charter schools avoid offering places to such students for fear that they may lower school performance scores. According to Ravitch, the charter movement brought profound changes to educational governance across many American states and the deployment of highly authoritarian teaching methods:

> The charter movement has become a vehicle for privatization of large swaths of public education, ending democratic control of the public schools and transferring them to private management ... the most successful charters follow a formula of 'no excuses': strict discipline, eyes on the teacher, walk in a straight line, no deviation from rigid rules and routines.
> (p. 178)

Despite these controversies, Michael Gove borrowed heavily from the free school and charter school models. He also accelerated the Academies Programme, by providing financial incentives for 'outstanding' schools to convert to academies or enforcing academisation against the wishes of parents and schools (Ball 2013).[2] Within two years of coming to power in 2010, Gove claimed, on the basis of 'clear evidence', that improved 'pupil outcomes' in tests are directly linked to greater autonomy enjoyed by academies as well as the ability of private sponsors to transform schools with an entrenched 'history of educational failure' (DfE 2012: 6). Between May 2010 and November 2014, 252 free schools were established (DfE 2014) and the number of academies rose from 200 to 4,460 (DfE 2015). This means that over half of all secondary schools and over 10 per cent of primary schools in England have become academies.

However, a closer reading reveals a number of contradictions in the Coalition discourse on a diverse 'school market' as a mechanism for transforming education in England to a 'world-class' system (Hill and Matthews 2010). First, schools with the 'outstanding' grade from Ofsted can choose to 'convert' to academy status, while lowest performing schools may be forced to become academies to 'effect educational transformation' (DfE 2010a: 56). In other words, the mechanisms of a greater autonomy and private sponsorship are cited as a 'one size fits all' recipe for improvement for both outstanding and struggling schools. Second, a DfE (2013a) recommendation that '*all* schools should become academies or Free Schools [my emphasis]' in order to increase variety 'in areas where there is demand' contradicts the very notion of variety. Third, in the light of academies' and free schools' freedoms to opt out of teaching the National Curriculum, the new primary curriculum introduced in 2014 has lost the status of a *national* curriculum. As argued by Alexander (2012: 1), the projected narrow focus in the new curriculum on 'the basics' fell short of the entitlement to a broad education that the notion of a national curriculum 'minimally entails'. Alexander is particularly critical of the impoverished view of knowledge, values and culture and reduction of educational standards to basic literacy and numeracy skills underpinning the new curriculum. A preoccupation with the 3Rs ('reading', 'writing' and 'arithmetic') and memorisation of 'facts' aligns the curriculum with the Victorian approaches to mass education in the nineteenth century (ibid.) The Coalition also seem to ignore research that points to growing problems with academies competing for pupils, being run like businesses, treating exam results like 'key performance indicators' (KPIs) and spending large sums of money on marketing and branding (Gunter 2011; Hatcher 2012; Higham 2013, 2014; TUC 2014). The following claim to transformation is illustrative of a disconnection from the everyday reality of educational experience of 'real' children and their teachers:

> Now, almost three years on, England's educational landscape has been utterly transformed. All over the country, in every sort of neighbourhood, more than two million pupils are now being taught in an academy.
> (DfE 2013b: 6)

This Coalition policy discourse reveals a hegemonic planning mentality (Scott 1998: 201), myopically focused on a 'hypothecated, generic, abstract' idea of a school system motivated by a political, rather than educational, conception of improvement. In effect, English academies and free schools provide major opportunities for private organisations to access millions of pounds of DfE funding (TUC 2014) and expand their '*edu-business*' (Mahony *et al.* 2004). For example, research by the Trades Union Congress (TUC 2014) has found that, between 2010 and 2014, the DfE paid £77 million of public funds in private consultants' fees, while some academies paid millions of pounds into private businesses of their directors, trustees or relatives. Apart from questions about how public money is being spent, the key concern here is that academies and free schools allow direct and indirect privatisation of public education in England (Ball 2013; TUC 2014).

Coalition policy discourse is also characterised by 'significant absences'. As explained by Fairclough (2003: 37), significant absences, or 'relations *in absentia*', are relations between what might have been present in discursive patterns, but is not. One absence is particularly significant in the Coalition policy – the findings and recommendations of the *Cambridge Primary Review* (CPR) (Alexander *et al.* 2010). The CPR took six years to complete and was the first comprehensive review of primary education in England since the Plowden Report of 1967. Funded independently of the government, the CPR involved a team of over one hundred researchers directed by Professor Robin Alexander, thousands of research participants (including children) and fourteen authors who prepared the final report of nearly six hundred pages, setting seventy-five recommendations for policy and practice. The key recommendations in relation to the discussions presented in this book include:

- respect and support for childhood, rooted in new research on child development;
- a coherent set of aims, values and principles for primary education of the twenty-first century; ensuring that the aims 'drive rather than follow' the curriculum, teaching, assessment and policy;
- a pedagogy of evidence (rather than recipes), underpinned by the principle that 'it is not for government . . . to tell teachers how to teach';
- redefining standards in terms of the quality of learning in all curriculum domains rather than the basics of literacy and numeracy;
- reforming the policy processes by replacing top-down control and prescription with professional experience and research evidence.

(adapted from Alexander 2009: 8–9)

It is remarkable that none of the key documents setting out the Coalition policy discussed above (DfE 2010a, 2010b; DfE 2011) refer to the findings or recommendations of the CPR. This is despite regular interim reports forwarded to ministers from 2007 and the publication of the final CPR report in 2009, just before the Coalition came to power in 2010. Instead, the politicisation of education was accelerated by the Coalition, even though, according to Alexander *et al.* (2010: 501), by 2010:

> The politicisation of primary education has . . . gone too far. Discussion has been blocked by derision, truth has been supplanted by myth and spin, and alternatives to current arrangements have been reduced to crude dichotomy. It is time to advance to a discourse which exemplifies rather than negates what education should be about.

The remainder of this chapter explores how this politicisation of education is experienced in the 'local' primary school.

Patterns of transformation in everyday practice

The case study findings suggest that local conversations about 'improvement' have been constrained by the policy apparatus of performance targets, league tables and Ofsted inspections and the sheer proliferation of policies that schools were obliged to implement. These measures were deployed by the Coalition in order to 'prevent the standard of education in the UK from falling further behind that of other countries' (DfE 2014). The addition of international comparisons to the national league tables is a manifestation of a re-scaling of relations between the local, the national and the global (Fairclough 2003), whereby improving the local school becomes a national imperative ensuring global economic competitiveness. The proliferation of strategies and policies for educational 'transformation' produced by the consecutive governments since

1998 created a strong material presence in the form of numerous, bulky folders with policies that take up the shelf space in the classrooms and offices in AP and GLP. Sophie's small office, for example, was full of shelves with heavy folders, top to bottom on two walls. Many of these documents were written by the schools themselves, as 'local policies' based on the *National Strategies* and other government policies. Notably, I have not encountered a single reference to 'transformation' in school documentation or interviews in either of the two schools.[3] That the 'policy hysteria' has profoundly affected local conversations and practice at both schools is, however, apparent from the case study data to which we now turn.

Quasi-markets and the 'waiting game'

Creating quasi-markets in public services reform has been a manifestation of the neoliberal agendas of the New Labour and Conservative governments. In the words of Michael Barber, it was premised on 'exploiting the power of choice, competition, transparency and incentives' (Mead 2006). In the two case study schools, the manifestations of the 'quasi-market' ranged from competition in league tables, glossy brochures and websites with promotional messages to concerns about the Coalition policies. The conversion of schools to academies (DfE 2010a) seemed to be particularly perplexing for practitioners. Concerns about further changes announced by the Coalition meant that practitioners had to play 'the waiting game':

> Obviously the new curriculum was supposed to come out last year, but then the change of government meant that it's been held off, we're now obviously still waiting. It is very much a waiting game at the moment to see what they propose. I mean obviously they are all now suggesting that we'll become academies, very much giving us the business side ... I'm unsure of what's going to happen.
>
> (Annabel, T, AP)

In the process of legitimating their policies, the successive governments established a pattern of communication whereby teachers seem to take the 'obviousness' of 'the waiting game' for granted. The dynamic in this conversation of gestures (Mead 1934) is premised on policymakers' power to gesture and schools' response to 'wait' and 'obviously, follow them, as we're meant to' (Fiona, Senior Leadership Team [SLT], AP). Sophie was the only participant to express a concern about the consequences of the business orientation that some schools have adopted:

> We have to work to a development plan, not a business plan, and we don't want to make a profit. You know, it's not a marketplace in that sense. In some of the schools they've gone another road, and it might be terribly

efficient and they've cut their staffing bills, but the quality for the children is about what they experience at school.

(Sophie, DH, AP)

Alice referred to moral considerations shared in a governors' meeting in relation to the possibility of converting AP to an academy:

As an academy you're potentially taking money away from schools that need the money for the Local Authority support. They're going to have less.

(Alice, DH, AP)

Most concerns related to the conversion to academy status were linked to the possible changes to teachers' pay and conditions of work:

We don't know about the academies. Local Authorities will go, what will that mean? And certainly if I was a teacher thinking that the school might become and academy it would be on the terms and conditions that might change and, if they are not going to change **now**, but two years down the line.

(Jenny, H, AP)

With how things are working in the education sector, when you think of academies, schools are going to have to become businesses.

(Annabel, T, AP)

The fact that all schools are turning into academies, that's a real concern. We don't know what that means. Does that mean we lose contracts? Do we get less pay? Do our rights change? So at the moment people are talking about this school possibly turning into an academy, but we haven't been told what the benefits are, what it means for us as a staff, what's going to change. So we shall see what goes on.

(Maria, SLT, AP)

While both Jenny and Maria express uncertainty about the meaning of the academies policy, Jenny's observation that this may lead to teacher terms and conditions changing 'two years down the line' contrasts with Maria's passive expectation to 'be told' what it means for teachers. Such passivity was a recurring pattern in practitioner accounts of the Coalition policies. Notable in participants' concerns '*about*' the impending changes was the absence of questioning '*why*' these changes were being introduced and of critique.[4] For example, an obvious '*why*' question about the Academies Programme is 'why a school should perform better because you have changed its governance, and tinkered with the way it gets its money' (Beckett 2011: xxi). Instead, practitioners seemed to be preoccupied with '*how*' questions:

We have concerns about the way in which the new academies are going to work. How are the Local Authorities going to work now?

(Alice, DH, AP)

How does that then affect us, are we supposed to . . .

(Annabel, T, AP)

Government will tell you how much you'll get per pupil and you'll have to cut your cloth accordingly to that.

(Eve, AS, AP)

Maria's point that 'we shall see what goes on' is a symbolic expression of the attitude of teachers 'waiting' to see what happens. The command and control patterns of interaction discussed in Chapter 5, seem to have institutionalised teachers' role as 'policy takers' rather than 'policy makers' (Gunter and Forrester 2009). By playing 'the waiting game', practitioners may be contributing to the legitimation of these roles. As discussed later in this chapter, paradoxically, in the climate of excessive politicisation of schools (Alexander *et al.* 2010), political considerations appeared to be absent in practitioner discourse.

Practitioners' understandings of 'school improvement'

The institutionalisation of a particular notion of 'school improvement' stems from the capacity of language to provide us with ready-made patterns for the ongoing objectifications of our everyday experience. Such objectifications are a result of repetition, silencing of alternative discourses and the use of power to control behaviour and eliminate difference. Therefore, as explained in Chapter 4, discourse can be used to construct what is then perceived as the 'objective reality' (Berger and Luckmann 1966). Similarly, from the complex responsive processes perspective, when the dominant conceptions of 'school improvement' are iterated in many everyday interactions, they may over time be taken for granted as if they were 'objective' and 'real'. For example, when the assumption that grades in high-stakes tests (SATs) are accurate measures of improvement is taken for granted, it loses its character of a 'social construct' – we forget that defining improvement as SATs results need not have existed (Hacking 1999).

The findings discussed below are premised on the assumption that interview articulations of are 'of a moment' and may be shaped by the participant's desire to narrate a coherent self (Coffey and Atkinson 1996) or 'manage impressions' (Alvesson 2011). Similarly, the processes of data analysis and interpretation are influenced by the researcher's 'grade of commitment' (Chapter 4). Consequently, the analysis of the empirical data presented in this chapter aims at 'fuzzy generalisations' (Bassey 1999) rather than categorical conclusions regarding the meanings of 'school improvement' articulated by the participants. In discussing participants' understandings of 'school improvement', this section is based on the analysis of interview transcripts using Fairclough's (2003) linguistic markers of modality, evaluation and orientation to difference. Modality refers to the degree of the speaker's commitment to statements made and is signalled by modal verbs, for example, 'must', 'should' and 'might'. Evaluation is linked to value judgements of desirable/undesirable or good/bad. Orientation to difference consists of patterns of connection/disconnection or inclusion/ exclusion and is often signalled through the use of personal pronouns, for example, 'I', 'you', 'we' and 'they'. The use of these linguistic markers offers insights into how practitioners positioned themselves in relation to the dominant conception of 'improvement' and how much clarity/ambiguity and control/ disempowerment was conveyed in their answers to the question: 'What does 'school improvement' mean to you as you engage in everyday practice?' This question was answered in many different ways, for example:

> I don't think it [improvement] is just about test results, because you can improve results as long as you improve everything else about the school. So school improvement is about everything across the board. It's got to be everything. Test results are a measure and it's good, because it's a measure. But not the only one.
>
> (Jenny, H, AP)

> Some people see school improvement as a drive for standards: 'how can we get our 98% level 4 in Maths tests?' Yes, it is, because we want every child to do their absolute best and that's what we're striving for . . . So we have to make sure that we give the children every opportunity that we possibly can.
>
> (Pete, H, AP)

> Well, the bottom line for me is to have happy children, and then everything stems from there, just stems from that.
>
> (Jeanne, AS, GLP)

> Obviously, you've got high targets, but in your school your focus is to meet the needs of the children, and their needs according to their home situation.
> (Miriam, DH, GLP)

The use of personal pronouns 'I' and 'me' conveys a sense of 'ownership' of the meanings of 'improvement' articulated by Jenny and Jeanne. In contrast, Pete's reference to 'some people', the use of the collective 'we' and the modal verb 'have to' imply an elision of agency (and responsibility) for the meaning of 'school improvement' provided in his answer. Pete's answer is also underpinned by an assumption that the drive for standards is equivalent to striving to help every child to do their absolute best. Whereas Pete's articulation of 'school improvement' converges with the dominant discourse, Jenny denies its reductionism but also evaluates 'measures' of improvement as desirable. The use of repetition and categorical assertion ('It's got to be everything') implies that Jenny positions herself as an 'expert', confident enough to make herself accountable for her articulation of 'improvement', as signalled by the use of the pronoun 'I'. The absence of references to standards in Jeanne's answer reinforces her assertion that 'happy children' is the 'bottom line' in her understanding of 'school improvement'. Similarly, the use of the contrastive conjunction 'but' and an emphasis on improvement priorities 'in your school' imply that Miriam may not have embraced the targets agenda as her 'own' personal meaning of 'school improvement'. The following section presents the findings from the case study data analysed in this way.

'Leave that for the powers that be to decide'?

The majority of participants in both schools (18 out of 27) appeared to concur with the dominant conception of school improvement as the drive for standards, though 9 emphasised that SATs grades are not 'the only measure' (Jenny). Alternative conceptions of improvement could be categorised as: better teaching, improved physical environment and 'happy, confident and secure' children (Gail). Participants who expressed reservations about, or denied, the dominant construction of school improvement positioned themselves as expert in their own roles in the classroom, but not in control of improvement in their school. For example, Lynn denied what she perceives as the dominant focus of AP teachers on SATs results, but her use of modalised assertions, 'hedges' ('sort of'), and repetition of 'I suppose' implies little authority in this regard in her role as teacher assistant:

> I suppose for me personally it's different to what their [teachers'] improvement would be, obviously results and league tables, that sort of thing. I suppose our [TAs] improvement is seen purely as how children improve I suppose, you know we take it right down to that level because we're dealing with the children and are at the lowest point, so we're purely looking at making sure that those children improve. We're not interested in the jumps [in levels] that they make, but that they are improving term by term really.
>
> (Lynn, TA, AP)

The changes in pronouns from 'I' to 'we' express both the ownership of Lynn's own notion of improvement as supporting individual children in making progress irrespective of levels and belonging to a group 'at the lowest point' in the hierarchy – AP teacher assistants.

Noteworthy was the apparent ambiguity and lack of clarity in the answers by Miriam, Stephen, Alison and Angelika, who, together with Louise (AS), constitute the SLT at GLP. Surprisingly, Stephen seemed to be at loss of words and concluded with: 'This isn't a very good answer, um . . .' Angelika's lack of clarity about improving literacy in the school is implicit in the reference to 'things':

> I think you've always got that sort of pulsating going on between new ideas and the traditional ideas and it goes backwards and forwards a lot as things are tried.
>
> (Angelika, SLT, GLP)

The use of generic 'you' and the elision of agency through the passive voice in 'things are tried' recurs in Alison's discourse:

> So I think there's a lot, there's a lot of things to do, and well there will always be things to do to improve, because you can always do things differently.
>
> (Alison, SLT, GLP)

Critically, this lack of clarity and ambiguity could provide opportunities for more open-ended local conversations about the meanings of educational transformation. The condition of not knowing in advance and the absence of strong 'systems' of local control that force practice into ready-made patterns of interaction is an environment for the novel to emerge (Mead 1956). However, uncertainty, ambiguity and a sense of not being in control can be experienced as threatening, which explains the appeal of the dominant conception of school improvement. In addition to the status of the dominant discourse, standards, targets and SATs results represent the paradigm of certainty (discussed in Chapters 2 and 3) and are, therefore, less susceptible to questioning than 'difficult to measure' alternatives, such as children's well-being or happiness. That the dominant construction of school improvement has permeated Alice's, Fiona's and Maggie's leadership practice is implicit in the way they talked about improvement. School improvement is 'looking at what you do' (Fiona), 'using' the school improvement plan, 'looking at' the data on pupil progress (Maggie) and 'meeting regularly' to 'really look at the key teams and where they are going and how they are doing with their action plans' (Alice). As the deputy head and SLT members respectively, Alice, Fiona and Maggie are in charge of performance management of their teams, each is also a phase leader, assessment manager (Maggie) and Early Years leader (Fiona). They therefore have considerable power and control over the 'systems' of AP. Their discourse of improvement focused on 'doing' and making sure that all systems run smoothly, for example consultation with 'stakeholders and monitoring action plans and targets' (Fiona). For Maggie it was 'always pushing the school forward', looking at 'new strategies' or 'pulling everyone back together and saying: 'This is what you need to do, this is where we need to go, how are we getting on?' And for Alice it was about being active, 'doing':

> As a leadership team we meet regularly. We monitor the action plans of individuals, keep check of that. We performance manage quite big teams. We did the SEF altogether as a leadership team, the whole thing. Myself and Jenny went to Ofsted framework training; we came back and we sat and went through the whole framework as a leadership team. So I think as a whole it's very much a leadership team, collective decision on everything. But then the rest of the staff do get a say into all of that as well.
> (Alice, DH, AP)

The inclusive 'we' appears to bracket off difference (Fairclough 2003) among the leadership team and therefore denies the more complex notion of improvement expressed by Sophie and Jenny. As mentioned above, for Jenny, improvement 'is about everything else about the school', not just test results, while for Sophie it is about developing the child as a 'whole person':

> Although I do believe it is very, very important that we get the children to the highest possible academic standard before they go to high school, I believe that should be done alongside developing them as a whole person.
> (Sophie, DH, AP)

By contrast, children seemed to be lost in the discourse of Alice, Fiona and Maggie. Their focus on 'looking at' the key teams and action plans left little time for listening to others, reflecting on the purpose of 'doing' improvement, or thinking in more depth about what it is that the team are trying to achieve together. Alternatively, could 'impressions management' (Alvesson 2011) be an underpinning objective of this talk? Stylistically, semantically and structurally, their accounts could be categorised as 'hortatory reports', texts that are framed as 'unordered lists' of 'evidences' (Fairclough 2003: 95), similar to those discussed in Chapter 5. As Fairclough points out, communication that simultaneously represents and advocates is indicative of the rise of 'promotional culture' in organisations (p. 112). The 'positivity' conveyed by Maggie, Fiona and Alice could thus be interpreted as a manifestation of 'promotional culture'.

Alice's reference to 'the rest of the staff' who 'get a say' reveals the subtleties of the power hierarchies at AP. The elaboration on the leadership team's activities is in stark contrast to a brief mention of 'the rest of the staff'; this contrast appears to undermine the model of distributed leadership espoused by Jenny and Sophie. 'Getting a say' implies that initiative and power belong to the leadership team and 'the rest' of the staff come last in the decision-making processes. Lynn's comment below expresses both her powerlessness and an understanding that the dominant government notion of school improvement embedded in the everyday practice at AP 'fails' some children:

> But that's the only thing that I see on a daily basis is that a few kids are failed, and we know that because they go onto high school and fail, and

we hear about it. And I think it's obviously been like that for years and years and years, but I assume that they just can't find a perfect answer. Leave that for the power that be to decide.

(Lynn, TA, AP)

It is these kinds of understandings that could contribute to the emergence of alternative local conversations about school improvement. However, conversational patterns sustained by Alice, Maggie and Fiona may confine the conversations at AP to the focus on positivity, uniformity and promotional language. An appearance of uniformity could, in turn, lead to the silencing of staff who, like Lynn, think differently. In the policy climate that promulgates the assumption that high-stakes tests results mean that children achieve their 'full potential' (Louise), alternative meanings are being discouraged, despite government rhetoric of diversity (DfE 2010a). The next section presents data which suggests that, despite sweeping changes to practice introduced with the waves of 'policy hysteria', other conversational themes can still be heard in the 'local' school.

Resistance to 'tinkering'

The most prominent themes conveying resistance at AP and GLP were frustration with, and concerns about, negative consequences of government 'tinkering' (Jenny, Sophie). While the majority of interviewees accepted the benefits of the *National Strategies* (Chapter 5), the proliferation of policies that followed was considered problematic. The 'policy hysteria' is experienced in both schools as piecemeal, often contradictory or simply impossible to introduce within the prescribed timescales:

> Every year something comes into the frame which is out of the blue, and it's new and it's completely different.
>
> (Angelika, SLT, GLP)

> Since I became headteacher, there has not been a year gone past that has not been at least one, if not more, major, I mean **major** changes.
>
> (Jenny, H, AP)

> I'm not sure how well thought through it's actually been, it seems very very quick.
>
> (Eve, AS, AP)

> I think their problem is they don't seem to get to an idea and stick to it. They're constantly changing it.
>
> (Carol, AS, GLP)

> That's all up in the air now ... they're talking about change again.
>
> (Mark, T, AP)

When referring to government discourse on change, many participants used direct speech. The following examples illustrate how professionals in both schools remember the messages from policymakers:

> They tend to sort of bring something out and say: 'This is what you've got to do'. And then two years into that they'll actually say: 'No you're wrong with that, let's change it and now you've got to do this instead'.
>
> (Carol, AS, GLP)

> The last government wanted us to be looking at creative curriculum and now that we're changing, the new government say: 'We want set subjects'.
>
> (Maggie, SLT, AP)

> 'Oh, you're not doing this anymore, you're doing that. And I want this!'
>
> (Maria, SLT, AP)

Practitioners' evaluations implicit in such reporting of government 'speak' convey an erratic, inconsistent nature of policymaking as an expression of will imposed on schools through command and control rather than a systematic, considered approach to reforming education. They also imply an absence of reasoned arguments for the sudden shifts and U-turns in policy, which, as discussed later in this chapter, are often justified through the recourse to the myth of perpetual crisis. The effects of the 'policy hysteria' reported in both schools included teacher frustration, excessive workload and waste of resources:

> The government can't say when things are going wrong, so they change it, they can't admit that they got it wrong.
>
> (Sophie, DH, AP)

> The paperwork's just growing and growing and growing.
>
> (Maria, SLT, AP)

> I think teachers get a bit fed up being told what to do. We're not completely stupid.
>
> (Sandy, T, GLP)

Irony was also used to convey frustration with 'new' changes that were often simply a re-labelling of older agendas. As Stephen pointed out, 'if you stand still long enough in primary education, you end up becoming an innovator'. Similarly, 'another one, new, OK' was Jenny's way of communicating new government initiatives to school governors:

> We joke about it in the governing body: 'OK, another one, new, OK'. In fact, this year we've been a bit twitchy because we've been waiting for the changes, and they haven't told us! (*laughs*)
>
> (Jenny, H, AP)

AP staff are 'ready for whatever they throw at them' (Jenny) and have 'that ethos of saying "Yes" when something comes along' (Sophie). In contrast, professionals at GLP drew their confidence from working together on making sense of policies, even if they were not 'fully designed and all over the place':

> I never quite understood the rationale exactly behind the revised curriculum. Never quite understood it. Eventually we got to the bottom of it and it was all about, the main message that came out of that one was to do with more flexibility. That was the message we took anyway.
>
> (Angelika, SLT, GLP)

The above articulations of resistance suggest practitioners' disconnection from government improvement agendas. The repetition of the personal pronouns 'we' and 'our' in relation to school values and practices contrasted sharply with the use of 'they' in references to policymakers. Notions of community, belonging and solidarity were evoked by such recurring phrases as 'our children', 'our ethnic mix', 'our school', 'our classes', 'our leadership team' and 'our parents'. In contrast, policymakers were referred to either as 'they' or eliminated altogether through the use of personification (Fiona and Maggie):

> I can understand why they want to do it.
>
> (Eve, AS, AP)

> They're talking about change again. Next year they could decide to bring in a new strategy.
>
> (Mark, T, AP)

> I hope they don't get rid of everything, I hope they just let it sort of bed down.
>
> (Alison, SLT, GLP)

> The new curriculum came in.
>
> (Fiona, SLT, AP)

> The new frameworks came in.
>
> (Maggie, SLT, AP)

The participants also reported examples of refusing to take up some minor government initiatives, for example Assessment of Pupil Progress (APP) (QCA

2010). Jenny's wisdom and courage to stand up for her beliefs were highly respected by her staff. As Alice admitted, 'We have made stands on things like APP, we decided it wasn't for us, because Jenny's a strong enough Head to say "No"'. Similarly, Alison understands that asking staff to change practice does not automatically guarantee compliance. Rather than confronting teachers who were 'not taking any notice', she set more realistic timeframes for staff reluctant to take up APP. Having considered the attitude of others (Mead 1934), the fact that some 'people can't see the point of it', she planned more staff meetings for voicing issues. The result was a decision made by the Leadership Team at GLP to introduce this new, time-consuming form of assessment gradually:

> Some schools have done APP for every child in reading, writing and maths, whereas we've done it gradually, and maybe if Ofsted come they will think those schools are wonderful, but we are not under the pressure. So we're not such stressed teachers for a start.
>
> (Alison, ST, GLP)

The superficiality and fluidity of the dominant discourse, the use of power to twist meanings of words in an attempt to keep schools in a state of constant mobilisation has been poignantly evaluated by Stephen as follows:

> The thing that really got under my skin . . . it was this thing about 'satisfactory isn't good enough', and there's two ways of looking at that. First, well, 'satisfactory' means 'good enough'. But the other thing, it implied that a 'good' school was then happy. If my school was judged as outstanding, I'd still want to improve. So inventing this kind of new form of words, so that schools need to improve . . . **All** schools need to improve! And if you stop feeling like that then really you've got to get off the bus! We **know** that, and it's not just because the government tells you so, it's because you want the best for the children.
>
> (Stephen, H, GLP)

Stephen refers here to a decision by Michael Wilshaw, on his appointment to the role of Ofsted Chief Inspector, to change inspection judgements so that 'satisfactory' schools would now be judged as 'requiring improvement'. The decision was based on an assertion that 'satisfactory' is 'not good enough' (Wilshaw 2012). The message here is of Wilshaw's power to redefine reality – 'power to tell others what is and what should be' (Fairclough 2003: 180). This simultaneously undermines the power, expertise and integrity of teachers and school leaders; hence Stephen's frustration at being told what he himself finds crucial, doing 'the best for the children'. When 'new forms of words' enter the dominant discourse of improvement and begin to take over the conversations at schools, they may gradually force out existing discourses. The following section focuses on significant absences (Fairclough 2003), themes that could have been present but seemed to be pushed to the margins of the conversational patterns at AP and GLP.

Significant absences: 'Hey, what exactly are we doing to our children?'

Two significant absences in the patterns of conversation at AP and GLP were child-centred orientation and political considerations. A shift in focus from educating children to enacting policy leads to more holistic and humanistic purposes of education being redefined as 'success' in tests and favourable Ofsted judgements. A preoccupation with the dominant constructions of 'school improvement' appeared to provide a distraction from what Jeanne expressed as 'sometimes stepping back and thinking: Hey, what exactly are we doing to our children?' On the contrary, the pressure to improve performance resulted in a conception of the quality of teaching as 'doing'. For example, most participants' answers to the question about what teaching meant to them consisted of lists of activities such as planning, meeting, monitoring, trying new things, restructuring, role modelling, setting direction and many more. Miriam used the image of spinning plates to describe her everyday work. Stephen talked about running on a treadmill: 'what's the next thing, what's the next thing, what's the next thing . . .' Fiona stated: 'we just want to be very active really, because this is the best way'.

The myth of perpetual crisis is supported by assertions about schools not being 'good enough' (Wilshaw 2012) and the resulting 'policy hysteria' contributes to a culture of performativity that may be pushing child-centred orientation to the margins. As pointed out by Stronach (2010), the traditional local themes of child-centredness and care have been replaced in recent years by the global theme of effectiveness. In this context, Sandy appeared to be the only participant to show a strong awareness of the attitude of the child (Mead 1956), by trying to think about what a particular experience or situation may be like for the child:

> As soon as they come to my class, I say: 'The first thing I want you to do is to have fun. Because if you're having fun, then you'll learn' . . . I keep putting myself in the kids' place and think: 'well I don't want to sit there listening to Mrs Rowling talking to me, no!'
>
> (Sandy, T, GLP)

The importance of a child-oriented approach is discussed further in Chapter 8, in the context of the educational climate that the 'policy hysteria' may create for the children.

The reluctance of practitioners to engage in political considerations was apparent in very few references to political issues. Of the twenty-seven participants, just two, Stephen and Sophie, engaged in an evaluation of educational change based on different 'party lines'. Sophie was critical of reforming education to 'fit with the policies of this or that political party'. Stephen contested the political origins of education reform, but also acknowledged the inescapable connection between policy, funding and the recognition of the value of education:

> And however cynical you are about politics, you cannot, you cannot lose sight of the fact that much more money was spent on education throughout those years [under New Labour] than had been the case before. I'm not a political animal particularly, but it was . . . there was a real recognition there that more money needed to be spent. I mean the state of state schools in the late 1990s was a national disgrace, so programmes like Building Schools for the Future send out a message that education is valued by the society.
> (Stephen, H, GLP)

Although political consideration was a 'minority' theme in the two schools, Stephen raised an important point about how the meanings gestured by policymakers may be taken up to convey messages that go beyond change to be enacted in schools. As we shall see in Chapter 8, these meanings can also be extended to how policy may gesture a (mis)recognition of the needs of children.

Perpetual crisis: 'Just sort of airbrushed out as if it doesn't matter'

The patterns of conversation in both schools revealed a range of contextual factors that have been 'just sort of airbrushed out as if it doesn't matter' (Jenny) from the Coalition discourse on school improvement. For example, several AP and GLP teachers had worked in schools in deprived areas where poverty, mental health issues and drug abuse profoundly affected children's education. The priorities in such schools included providing meals for children who came to school hungry, liaising with social services, managing serious behaviour problems and dealing with parenting issues. Schools in less deprived areas may also have parenting issues. Sophie and Jenny first met at Grange Hill School, where the lack of parental discipline was notorious. Sophie recalled this experience as follows:

> And I remember very, very vividly standing in the playground on the first day, looking at her [Jenny] and her looking at me and saying: 'We must be mad, why on earth did we do this?' Because there were parents standing over with cigarettes, there were dogs running around, bikes racing around, Year 6s in dropping earrings and high heels and we thought: 'Where do we go with this primary school?'
> (Sophie, DH, AP)

Sophie spent her first months at Grange Hill 'sorting out emergencies':

> All our focus had to be on holding the day together and when we first went there I did nothing but patrol the corridors for hours on end, because the behaviour was so out of control in places.
>
> (Sophie, DH, AP)

The contingencies of local contexts mean that the uncompromising focus of the policymakers on high-stakes tests may be meaningless and unrealistic:

> It is so much more difficult to get children coming from a home background where there's terrible things going on at home, and you're expected to get them to level 4.
>
> (Jenny, H, AP)

However, the central government's hegemonic planning mentality (Scott 1998) ignores everyday situations involving 'real' children in 'real' local contexts, where simply 'holding the day together' may be a nearly impossible achievement. No 'objective' measures can fully convey the 'gritty' experience of working in a 'real', rather than a 'hypothecated, generic, abstract' school. Research on 'school effect' highlights that just 10 per cent to 20 per cent of variation in pupil performance depends on the school factors, particularly teaching (Ainscow et al. 2010; Cook 2013). The remaining 80 per cent to 90 per cent comprises a complex dynamic of individual and socio-economic factors such as 'maternal health and wellbeing, family income, parental job security, the socio-economic mix of peers and access to thriving labour markets' (Cook 2013: 1).

This complexity is, however, 'airbrushed out' of the myth of perpetual crisis and the myth is then used as a reason for 'urgent' reform (DfE 2010a). When read as a motive rather than a reason (Barthes 2000), the myth of perpetual crisis may be motivated by its usefulness in legitimating the current transformation of 'new capitalism' through a neoliberalisation of social relations. Neoliberalism is based on an assumption that individual freedom, private property rights and unregulated markets provide a superior form of social organising (Harvey 2007). Regulation and quality control are leveraged in free markets through customer choice and competition, while the key role of the neoliberal state is to extend market values to non-market contexts such as education. These tenets are underpinned by an assumption that individuals are independent, self-reliant and self-interested, rather than interdependent (Chapter 3). Consequently, the neoliberal state promotes competition for scarce resources, entrepreneurialism, accumulation of wealth and unrestrained economic growth as 'modern', 'progressive' pursuits. The extension and acceleration of market-oriented education reforms by the Coalition is thus aligned with the neoliberal ideology and embedded within the transformation of 'new capitalism' (Fairclough 2003).

As explained by Fairclough (2003), the capitalist system transforms itself periodically in order for its expansion to continue. Characteristic of 'new capitalism' has been a 're-structuring' of relations within the economic, political and social domains and a 're-scaling' or relations between the global, the national and the local. Neoliberal ideology promotes these processes. The parallel weakening of democracy is reflected both in the global discourse of the neoliberal version of 'new capitalism' and its particularisations at the level of education systems. Neoliberal reforms discussed in this chapter have been transforming education into an '*edu-business*' and a site for training the workforce for the marketplace. As suggested by the case study data, the myth of perpetual crisis is also used to re-frame time. Paradoxically, time is being made perpetual or 'frozen' (Barthes 2000) and simultaneously accelerated in the myth of perpetual crisis. This puts schools in a state of permanent mobilisation, demanding an instant response to fast changing conditions. The policymakers' expectation of instant improvement, within the five to six years of the electoral cycle, or the three-year cycle of PISA, has made practitioners in AP 'ready for whatever is thrown at them' (Jenny). Critically, the demand for instant improvement may encourage 'thoughtlessness' (Gunter 2014: 97) in the enactment of policy, with negative consequences for the children.

Conclusion

This chapter explored how AP and GLP practitioners negotiated the dominant meaning of 'school improvement' in their everyday practice. The 'performing school' (Perryman 2009) is becoming increasingly competent at 'performing' in high-stakes tests, in tune with government prescription. It works hard on developing 'systems' and structures for enacting policy. However, the volume, timeframes, fragmentation and arbitrariness characteristic of the 'policy hysteria' constrain professionals in thinking and talking together about how the 'new orthodoxy' of transforming education may affect the children in their care, beyond improving their SATs scores. In this context, by playing the 'waiting game', in readiness for 'whatever is thrown at them', practitioners may be contributing to a distortion of educational values. Conversely, being attentive to significant absences rather than what is 'thrown at them' by policymakers may be helpful in restoring the child-centred orientation and political considerations that seem to have been lost in the maelstrom of the 'policy hysteria'. The potential to transform education resides in the 'gritty' everyday practice of the 'local' school, rather than the 'will', 'energy' and 'passion' of an Education Secretary (Cameron 2011). When the policies written by an Education Secretary have been enacted or shelved and replaced with new solutions to the perpetual crisis, school improvement may or may not be on the mind of an individual teacher or teacher assistant engaging in everyday work. As explained in Chapter 8, profound change may emerge in local interactions that value the responsiveness to, and responsibility for, others. The meaning of such a change is qualitatively different from the dominant conception of transformation and its concomitants of efficiency, free markets and self-reliant individuals. Chapter 7 discusses the latter in greater depth, suggesting that these neoliberal values 'de-form' rather than transform children's educational experience.

Notes

1   Other problems have also been reported, in relation to the schools owned by stock market companies or corporations that depend on the markets. For example, a Swedish free schools chain JB Education decided to sell nineteen and close down eight of its schools in 2013 because of financial difficulties (Orange and Adams 2013).
2   For example, as reported by the Anti Academies Alliance (AAA), Downhills Primary School was forced to become the Harris Primary Academy in 2012 after losing its legal battle in the High Court. AAA is an organisation composed of unions, parents, pupils, teachers, local councillors and MPs who oppose the Academies Programme and campaign for schools to be accountable to the local community (antiacademies.org.uk/). Under current regulations, the governance of academies is based on private arrangements between the DfE and the sponsor rather than the legal regulation applied to state schools. In effect, this makes taxpayer-funded services unaccountable to the taxpayer.
3   I refrained from using the word 'transformation' in all my interviews, referring instead to 'school improvement' and 'changes to the government approaches to education reform'.
4   The absence of critique in the empirical data could also be partly explained by the nature of 'data' as something given (Van Manen 1990). As explained in Chapter 4, research participants may choose to give or withhold their views and experiences.

References

Ainscow, M., Chapman, C., Dyson, A., Gunter, H., Hall, D., Kerr, K., McNamara, O., Mujis, D., Raffo, C. and West, M. 2010. *Social Inequality: Can Schools Narrow the Gap?* Macclesfield: BERA.

Alexander, R. 2009. *Introducing the Cambridge Primary Review.* Available at: http://esmeefairbairn.org.uk/news-and-learning/publications/cambridge-primary-review (accessed 12 April 2105).

Alexander, R. 2012. Neither national nor a curriculum? *Forum,* 54(3): 1–12.

Alexander, R., Armstrong, M., Flutter, J., Hargreaves, L., Harlen, W., Harrison, D., Hartley-Brewer, E., Kershner, R., MacBeath, J., Mayall, B., Northen, S., Pugh, G., Richards, C. and Utting, D. 2010. *Children, Their World, Their Education: Final Report and Recommendations of the Cambridge Primary Review.* Abingdon: Routledge and the University of Cambridge.

Allen, R. 2010. Replicating Swedish 'free school' reforms in England, *Research in Public Policy,* (10): 4–8. Available at: www.bristol.ac.uk/media-library/sites/cmpo/migrated/documents/researchissue10.pdf (accessed 12 April 2015).

Alvesson, M. 2011. *Interpreting Interviews.* London: Sage.

Anti Academies Alliance. 2012. *Downhills School Legal Battle Ends*. Available at: http://antiacademies.org.uk/2012/12/downhills-school-legal-battle-ends/ (accessed 12 April 2015).

Ball, S.J. 2013. *Education, Justice and Democracy: The Struggle over Ignorance and Opportunity*. London: Centre for Labour and Social Studies.

Barthes, R. 2000. *Mythologies*. (A. Levers, Trans.). London: Vintage Books.

Bassey, M. 1999. *Case Study Research in Educational Settings*. Buckingham: Open University Press.

Beckett, F. 2011. Preface. In Gunter, H. (ed.) *The State and Education Policy*. London: Continuum, xx–xxiii.

Berger, P. and Luckmann, T. 1966. *The Social Construction of Reality: A Treatise in the Sociology of Knowledge*. London: Penguin Books.

Biesta, G. 2010. 'Five Theses on Complexity Reduction and Its Politics'. In Osberg, D. and Biesta, G. (eds) *Complexity Theory and the Politics of Education*. Rotterdam: Sense, 5–14.

Cameron, D. 2011. *Speech on Education* (9 September). Available at: www.gov.uk/government/speeches/pms-speech-on-education-2 (accessed 12 April 2015).

CBI. 2012. *First Steps: A New Approach for Our Schools: End of Year Report*. Available at: www.cbi.org.uk/media/2473815/First_steps_end_of_year_report.pdf (accessed 3 March 2015).

Coffey, A. and Atkinson, P. 1996. *Making Sense of Qualitative Data: Complementary Research Strategies*. Thousand Oaks, CA: Sage.

Cook, W. 2013. *How Intake and Other External Factors Affect School Performance*. London: Research and Information on State Education Trust.

DfE. 2010a. *The Importance of Teaching: The Schools White Paper 2010*. Available at: www.ictliteracy.info/rf.pdf/Schools-White-Paper2010.pdf (accessed 15 March 2012).

DfE. 2010b. *The Case for Change*. London: Crown Copyright.

DfE. 2011. *Training Our Next Generation of Outstanding Teachers: An Improvement Strategy for Discussion*. London: Crown Copyright.

DfE. 2012. *Academies Annual Report 2010/11*. London: The Stationery Office.

DfE. 2013a. *Numbers of Open Academies and Free Schools*. Available at: www.education.gov.uk/researchandstatistics/statistics/keystatistics/a00214288/academies-and-free-schools (accessed 13 April 2015).

DfE. 2013b. *Academies Annual Report 2011/12*. London: The Stationery Office.

DfE. 2014. *Increasing the Number of Academies and Free Schools to Create a Better and More Diverse School System*. Available at: www.gov.uk/government/policies/increasing-the-number-of-academies-and-free-schools-to-create-a-better-and-more-diverse-school-system#history (accessed 13 April 2015).

DfE. 2015. *Open Academies and Academy Projects in Development*. Available at: www.gov.uk/government/publications/open-academies-and-academy-projects-in-development (accessed 13 April 2015).

Fabricant, M. and Fine, M. 2012. *Charter Schools and the Corporate Makeover of Public Education: What's at Stake?* New York: Teachers College.

Fairclough, N. 2003. *Analysing Discourse: Textual Analysis for Social Research*. Abingdon: Routledge.

Gunter, H.M. (ed.) 2011. *The State and Education Policy: The Academies Programme*. London: Continuum.

Gunter, H.M. 2014. *Educational Leadership and Hannah Arendt*. London and New York: Routledge.

Gunter, H.M. and Forrester, G. 2009. School leadership and education policy-making in England, *Policy Studies*, 30(5): 495–511.

Hacking, I. 1999. *The Social Construction of What?* Cambridge: Harvard University Press.

Harvey, D. 2007. Neoliberalism as creative destruction, *The Annals of the American Academy*, 610(1): 22–44.

Hatcher, R. 2012. Democracy and governance in the local school system, *Journal of Educational Administration and History*, 44(1): 21–42.

Higham, R. 2013. Free schools in the big society: The motivations, aims and demography of free school proposers, *Journal of Education Policy*, 29(1): 122–139.

Higham, R. 2014. 'Who owns our schools?' An analysis of the governance of free schools in England, *Educational Management Administration & Leadership*, 42(3): 404–422.

Hill, R. and Matthews, P. 2010. *Schools Leading Schools II: The Growing Impact of National Leaders of Education*. Nottingham: National College Publishing.

Mahony, P., Menter, I. and Hextall, I. 2004. Building dams in Jordan, assessing teachers in England: A case study in edu-business, *Globalisation, Societies and Education*, 2(2): 277–296.

Mead, G.H. 1934. *Mind, Self, and Society from the Standpoint of a Social Behaviourist*. Chicago, IL and London: The University of Chicago Press.

Mead, G.H. 1956. *On Social Psychology*. Chicago, IL: Chicago University Press.

Mead, S. 2006. *Education Reform Lessons from England: An Interview with Sir Michael Barber*. Available at: www.educationsector.org/publications/education-reform-lessons-england (accessed 12 April 2015).

Orange, R. and Adams, R. 2013. Swedish Free School Operator to Close, Leaving Hundreds of Pupils Stranded. *The Guardian* (31 May). Available at: www.theguardian.com/education/2013/may/31/free-schools-education (accessed 14 April 2015).

Perryman, J. 2009. Inspection and the fabrication of professional and performative processes, *Journal of Education Policy*, 24(5): 611–631.

QCA. 2010. *Assessing Pupils' Progress: Learners at the Heart of Assessment*. Coventry: CDA.

Ravitch, D. 2014. *Reign of Error: The Hoax of the Privatization Movement and the Danger to America's Public Schools*. New York: Vintage Books.

Scott, J.C. 1998. *Seeing Like a State: How Certain Schemes to Improve the Human Condition Have Failed*. New Haven, CT and London: Yale University Press.

Stronach, I. (2010) *Globalizing Education, Educating the Local: How Method Made Us Mad*. London and New York: Routledge.

Stronach, I. and MacLure, M. 1997. *Educational Research Undone: The Postmodern Embrace*. Buckingham: Open University Press.

TUC. 2014. *Education Not for Sale: A TUC Research Report*. Available at: www.tuc.org.uk/sites/default/files/Education_Not_For_Sale_Repor_Report.pdf (accessed 13 April 2015).

Van Manen, M. 1990. *Researching Lived Experience: Human Science for an Action Sensitive Pedagogy*. New York: SUNY.

West, A. 2014. Academies in England and independent schools (fristående skolor) in Sweden: Policy, privatisation, access and segregation, *Research Papers in Education*, 29(3): 330–350.

Wiborg, S. 2010. *Swedish Free Schools: Do They Work?* London: Centre for Learning and Life Chances in Knowledge Economies and Societies.
Wilshaw, M. 2012. *The End of 'Satisfactory Schools'*. Available at: www.ofsted.gov.uk/news/ofsted-announces-scrapping-of-%E2%80%98satisfactory%E2%80%99-judgement-move-designed-help-improve-education-for-mill (accessed 10 December 2012).

Chapter 7

Rethinking policy, strategy and educational leadership

> I want the children to climb trees and do things like that. I've written about that in my newsletter: 'the fifty things that children should do before they're eleven and three quarters'. It's all about going rock climbing, flying a kite, rolling down a big hill and all this sort of stuff. I've said to the parents: 'look it up, if you're not sure what to do with your children over a weekend'.
> (Stephen, headteacher, Green Lanes Primary)

> So we have to make sure that we just keep bombarding them with learning opportunities and opportunities outside of learning, so there are lots of collisions in their learning and they can develop as they need to and we can identify that and push them on.
> (Pete, headteacher, Abbey Primary)

This chapter focuses on the leadership and management of English schools in a climate of rapid and continuous change. Two main aspects of leadership and management are explored in the specific context of the case study schools. First, the perceptions of school leaders of what leadership means to them as they go about their everyday practice. Second, how educational leadership and management have been reconstructed through government policy and the collision between the values underpinning these policies and those of the educational professionals charged with implementing them in their schools. As noted in Chapter 6, school leaders have been cast as 'direct agents' of government reform (Gunter and Forrester 2009) and tasked with creating 'excellent schools' (DfE 2010: 9). The tendency to define good leadership in terms of 'Excellence As Standard' is also characteristic of the new *National standards of excellence for headteachers* (DfE 2015: 5) and leadership programmes developed under the auspices of the government-funded NCSL such as the National Professional Qualification for Headship (NPQH) (NCSL 2011). Standards for 'excellent headteachers' seem to be strongly influenced by the culture–excellence thinking underpinning mainstream management discourse, which casts managers–leaders in the role of guardians of organisational values and mores (Watson 2011). For example, one of the headteachers' standards is to 'communicate compellingly the school's vision and drive the strategic leadership, empowering all pupils and staff to excel' (DfE 2015: 5).

The case study data suggest that the headteachers at AP and GLP perceived their responsibilities in more complex and less 'spectacular' ways. Two main themes emerged from the patterns of conversation about leadership: first, the enabling role adopted by the headteachers in relation to their staff and second, the influence of the headteachers on the schools' ethos which seemed to be embedded in ordinary everyday communication rather than the rhetorical turn characteristic of the discourse on 'excellence' and 'empowerment'. As discussed in Chapter 6, everyday practice in the two schools has been destabilised by policy responses to a perceived perpetual crisis exemplified by 'PISA panic' (Alexander 2012: 4). However, a sense of crisis seemed to be absent from the patterns of conversation at AP and GLP. Instead, as pointed out by Jenny (H, AP), 'doom and gloom' in her staffroom would emerge in response to yet another government policy that her teachers were obliged to deliver. Also in tension were two contrasting notions of 'good' education, as illustrated in the epigraph to this chapter. In contrast to Stephen's (H, GLP) ethos of a more holistic, child-centred education, Pete's (H, GLP) articulation of 'good' education evoked an image of learning as a battlefield in which victory is achieved by 'pushing children on'. This conception of learning seemed to contradict Pete's conviction that 'school improvement should come from *within*' rather than the performative 'push' by the government. Similar contradictions in other interviews suggest that just as schools are 'not of a piece' (Ball *et al.* 2012), individuals are also complex. This point is developed in Chapter 8.

This chapter begins to consider an 'educational transformation' that could emerge *within* everyday practice at AP and GLP. The concept of self-organisation has been taken up by complex responsive processes theorists to explain how organisational change emerges from countless everyday local interactions that follow self-organising influences such as local values and local power relations (Chapter 3). On this account, schools would not be 'doomed to anarchy' (Stacey 2007: 197) in the absence of government improvement policies. On the contrary, this absence could provide the very conditions for creative, genuinely novel outcomes to emerge from local interactions. This chapter starts with a discussion of local patterns of conversation about the schools' ethos and leadership. When asked about the ethos of their schools and their own values, practitioners talked about sharing, ambition and hard work (AP) and responsibility and care (GLP). The case study data also revealed that a 'push' for higher standards may create a culture of exclusion. In this regard, connections are drawn between the 'emotivist culture' (MacIntyre 1985), based on an objectification and manipulation of the 'school workforce' (DfES 2002) for the ends of education policy, within the Cartesian-Newtonian rationality discussed in Chapter 2.

Educational leadership in everyday practice

Two key findings emerged from the empirical data on the meanings of leadership in everyday practice. First, the power of the headteachers in both schools was firmly rooted in their lived experience as educators. Second, the overarching responsibility the headteachers referred to was to provide 'enabling' conditions for staff to carry out their teaching and develop as professionals. The schools seemed to uphold a traditional conception of the headteacher as an 'educational leader', a lead professional or *primus inter pares* ('the first amongst equals') rather than the notions of 'executive headteachers' (Hill *et al.* 2012) promoted by policymakers. As Gunter (2004: 28) points out, post Education Reform Act of 1988, this role was recast as 'transformational' leadership and based on implementing the centrally-designed National Curriculum 'through a combination of charismatic appeal and contractualism'. This reconstruction was accompanied by changes to standards for headteachers (DfE 2015), new models of leadership promoted by the NCSL (Davies 2006; NCSL 2011), as well as more 'business-oriented' approaches of the cadre of 'entrepreneurial' CEOs of new academies and free schools. However, the conceptions of leadership at AP and GLP reflected complex personal identities resulting from professional experience and values through which government policies on standards and performance were mediated.

The power of the headteacher: 'What you say and what you do is just hoovered up by the school community'

The power of headteachers to influence organisational patterns of conversation was apparent in the discourse observed in staff meetings and interviews, as well as website texts produced by both schools for 'public view'. Whether it is 'repetition, chanting the same old mantras' (Jenny) or 'giving off signals about what you think is important, almost by osmosis' (Stephen), the ethos and values espoused by both headteachers appeared to infuse the language used by their staff. Steven appeared surprised by his personal power to influence:

> It just never fails to amaze me that what you say and what you do is just hoovered up by the school community. You have to be careful with your words . . . you have to trust that what you're thinking is based on, is based on a belief system and a value system, which has some kind of merit in our society.
>
> (Stephen, H, GLP)

Jenny articulated her influence more directly:

> Once you start appointing good people and training them up, it's not just **you** saying it.
>
> (Jenny, H, AP)

The greatest convergence in ambitions and aspirations was implicit in the discourse of those working most closely with both headteachers. For example, Stephen's wish to be 'visible' and to 'raise our profile in the local community' was taken up by Miriam, his deputy. When talking about her responsibilities, she referred to 'raising the profile of caring and community spirit', 'raising the profile of subject leaders' and 'raising the profile of partnership between parents and the school'. Visibility, high profile and good reputation were also of importance to Louise, who appreciated both Stephen and Miriam for how they would:

> turn up, be as enthusiastic as they always are and be very visible and high profile around the school, not just with the staff but with the parents. And being seen to do their job well. And they've got a good reputation, I hear other people talk about them in the Borough.
>
> (Louise, SLT, GLP)

A similar working relationship was expressed by the deputy heads at AP, Sophie and Alice. Jenny's 'mantra' of expectations was taken up by Sophie who asserted that 'we expect people to work very hard'. Alice talked about 'high expectations of all our children', 'expectations of good behaviour from pupils', 'expecting a lot from the phase and year group leaders'. Thirteen out of seventeen interview participants referred once or several times to 'high expectations', which suggests that Jenny's belief in expectations was 'hoovered up' by her staff. There were also rewards for meeting the expectation of hard work. Sophie pointed out that, as a 'great believer in developing people', Jenny offered her teachers 'fantastic' leadership development opportunities. This, in turn, raised the status of the school in the Local Authority and attracted ambitious, hard-working young teachers from local schools.

One of the last tasks that Jenny set for herself before retiring from a forty-year career in education was to 'find' a headteacher for AP who would follow in her footsteps. Having met Pete at a conference and having found that 'he thinks along the same wavelength', Jenny was determined to win him over, as suggested by Pete's account:

> I was in a conference with the head of this school who was retiring, and we were chatting about the job and about her school, and she said 'come and see it'. And I said, 'well, I'm not looking for a job', and she said 'well, see it anyway'! (*we laugh*) So that's why I'm here . . . Jenny had been here quite a while and was an outstanding head, and I've got a lot to live up to.
>
> (Pete, H, AP)

The career trajectories of the headteachers and deputy heads at both schools were firmly grounded in teaching qualifications (Qualified Teacher Status) and substantial experience of working as a class teacher (see Appendix). They thus exemplify what Gunter (2012) refers to as 'educational leadership' – leadership underpinned by the lived experience of being an educator. The importance of such experience was emphasised by Miriam, Sophie and Alice. As deputy heads, they could have chosen 'office jobs' and given up teaching. None has chosen to do so. While Miriam and Alice took on the roles of 'teaching deputy heads' at GLP and AP respectively, Sophie's teaching activities focused on the Continuing Professional Development (CPD) of teachers as a lead facilitator of esteemed *Improving* and *Outstanding Teachers Programmes*. Alice understands that regular teaching maintains her credibility:

> If you're not in the classroom teaching, very quickly other staff become a bit disillusioned with what you're saying.
>
> (Alice, DH, AP)

Miriam appreciates the 'working knowledge' that teaching gives her:

> I've got that working knowledge rather than it just being 'well I've looked on a piece of paper it says there "this level" so why haven't the children made the progress?' I've been in there and seen.
>
> (Miriam, DH, GLP)

The ethos of educational leadership articulated in both schools resonates with an emphasis on 'traditional pedagogical values', which has contributed to the success of the Finnish education system (Sahlberg 2011: 103). For example, despite increases in administrative tasks, a 'good' Finnish school principal is 'always also a teacher':

> I strive to be a good principal in my school. It means that I have to do my best as a manager, leader, director, and pedagogic guide for teachers and students . . . I want to be a good and trusted person . . . A school principal is in charge of the part of a complex social system that is continuously changing. Without experience as a teacher this work would be very difficult to fulfill successfully.
>
> (Martti Hellström, School Principal as quoted in Sahlberg 2011: 119)

As pointed out by Sahlberg, school principals in Finland protect the 'wellbeing of schools' (p. 93), taking into account the needs of students, teachers and the society rather than market-based principles. A similar protecting and enabling role of the headteacher emerged from the patterns of conversation in AP and GLP to which we now turn.

'Strategic' leadership? I don't think we've come across strategic leadership just yet, so I'm not sure

Gemma's admission above that she is 'not sure' about 'strategic' leadership 'just yet' encapsulates most participants' responses to an interview question about 'strategic' leadership. Despite strong emphasis on strategic leadership in standards for headteachers (DfE 2015), the NPQH curriculum (NCSL 2011) and literature written under the aegis of the NCSL (Hill and Matthews 2010), developing a 'strategically focused school' (Davies 2006) seemed to be a peripheral rather than key preoccupation of the headteachers at AP and GLP.

Elements of 'strategic' leadership featured in the schools' websites and other outward facing texts such as School Development Plans. For example, each school's home page displayed the vision and mission statement and a 'strap line' encapsulating its core values. The language was 'positive', pinpointing achievement, listing awards and providing links to SATs results and Ofsted reports. The schools' websites thus displayed features of 'promotional genres' in simultaneously providing information and promoting the schools (Fairclough 2003). Most references to 'strategy' and 'strategic' were used in interviews in relation to the *National Strategies* (DfEE 1998, 1999; DfE 2011). Although 'strategic' thinking and 'visioning' played a part in some of their decisions, they seemed to be peripheral in Jenny's and Stephen's approaches to headship. Despite his use of military language in relation to learning cited in the epigraph to this chapter, Pete spent his first weeks as a new head of AP talking to staff, children and parents, ordering new classroom furniture and 'messy play' tables for the infant playground. Their overarching preoccupation as headteachers was enabling their staff to focus on the everyday tasks of teaching.

Jenny referred to her approach as 'distributed leadership', based on a 'broad' senior leadership team and a culture of 'developing people'. Her approach, developed through years of experience as teacher and headteacher, resonates with the concept of self-organisation:

> No one person can do everything brilliantly, you've got to let other people help out. And different people have come on board, because you can only do so much yourself, and you get keen young people and they say 'oooh, have you heard about that? Should we be looking at that?' And I'll say 'yeah, let's do it, you're going to do it and I'll join with you'. So you gradually get people on board who want the school to be the best, and it's self-perpetuated, it grows and grows and grows.
>
> (Jenny, H, AP)

Jenny's relationships with her staff were 'matriarchal', based on her belief in high expectations: 'same as you do with a class of children in a school full of teachers'. She was perceived by her teachers as trusting and generous in rewarding hard work and initiative:

> She's very, very good. If you want to do something, and you've come up with a way to do it, she'll let you have a go. She's very good at saying: 'I don't know what's going on every day, it's a massive school, I expect one of you to know'.
>
> (Alice, DH, AP)

> And it's very much that delegation and the trust. And I suppose you need that in such a large school, Jenny can't do absolutely everything, so it's really nice she has that trust and that confidence in us.
>
> (Annabel, T, AP)

> She has trust in us really, that we can do these things.
>
> (Fiona, SLT, AP)

> At the end of the day it all falls back to the head but she's very, very good at giving, so: 'you make the decision and I'll support you'.
>
> (Maggie, SLT, AP)

Jenny's enabling approach was espoused by the 'middle leaders', who also saw their role as 'helping out' and supporting junior members of staff and sharing responsibility (Annabel, Emma, Maria, Mark). Similarly, while talking about leadership, junior members of staff referred to their year group or key stage leader as someone to 'go to and see' for support, with questions and problems (Gemma, Angie, Sylvia). The unified response of teachers to Jenny's pragmatic approach was a strong commitment to enacting policy:

> Certainly the way I've always approached it with teachers, is, because you can get this doom and gloom, whereas I said, 'well, we've got to do it, let's find the easiest way for us to do it'. No point moaning, they [the government] will make us do this, so let's find the easiest way, and the teachers will buy into that. They'll say: 'Ok, we've got to do it, but this will make it a bit easier for ourselves'.
>
> (Jenny, H, AP)

Pete's experience as a teacher, Local Authority consultant and headteacher was enhanced by a Masters course in leadership, which he completed at a local university. The course gave him 'his own personal time' to think, read and discuss issues with fellow students. As he pointed out, 'doing a high-level degree' enhanced his credibility as headteacher and developed his critical understanding of policy:

> It's the higher-level critical understanding of what was going on was probably the biggest learning thing for me. So now, whenever I read a document, especially something from government, I can first of all look at

154 'Global' policies and local interactions

> the influences on that, I can see where it's come from. Which global community has **that** come from? Did it work in Finland, did it work in Sweden? Is it going to work for us? Which I wouldn't have done before to tell you the truth. It's also given me a wider understanding with different kinds of systems and models that I can draw on if I need to. Because the theory side of things is important. If you've got the understanding, and if you're able to create a model for yourself that you can then share with your staff, that's important.
>
> (Pete, H, AP)

Pete's critical approach contributed to a new trajectory on which he took the school following his appointment as a new head of AP. Having gained an outstanding Ofsted grade, the school considered the possibility of converting to an academy, but chose instead to register for a Rights Respecting School Award (RRSA). Developed by UNICEF UK, the RRSA initiative aims at making the *United Nations Convention on the Rights of the Child* central to the school's ethos and everyday practice (Sebba and Robinson 2010).

Stephen calls himself a 'reflective democrat' and his approach has also won him great respect among his staff and put GLP on a path to improvement. Having completed the NPQH, Stephen is aware of the importance of vision, because 'the v-word is one that's always thrown at you at NPQH'. His vision is a result deep reflection, in contrast to Davies's (2006) simplistic notion of vision as 'excellent' performance standards:

> To begin with you're starting with an empty cup in front of you, you think: 'I don't think I've got a vision', but when you actually explore what's important to you, what you do on a daily basis, you can then kind of extrapolate what are the things that are at the core, the reason why you went into education. So the things that were really important to me were communication, letting people know what you're doing and why you're doing it, and not just staff but children as well. If you want the children to be fair-minded, you have to explain to them why you're doing something.
>
> (Stephen, H, GLP)

For Stephen, vision is a reason why he is an educator. It is also about enabling everyone to consider questions such as: 'What do we feel about this? What will this look like to the children here?' Unlike Jenny, who focused on developing teachers but not teaching assistants, Stephen believes in involving and listening to everyone:

> I want people, not just my senior teachers, but I want, you know, my midday supervisors to come up and say 'look, can we try doing this **this** way?' Because I think that's how schools develop and become better, when people feel that their voice matters, that they can come forward and say things.
>
> (Stephen, H, GLP)

Stephen's approach to improvement that emerges from *within* resonates with that of his staff, who define good leadership as listening, 'never making snap judgements' (Angelika) and 'taking it slowly' (Miriam). Miriam's door is 'always open':

> People do pop in, and everybody wants to speak to you about different things, and it's treating everybody whatever they want to speak to you about as just as important. So I try to make sure everybody knows I'm listening to them, and I take what they want to say very seriously. Everybody needs to be listened to. Everybody's important; everybody needs to feel that they've got the opportunity to get their voice heard.
>
> (Miriam, DH, AP)

As a leader, Angelika espouses to 'never make snap judgements':

> because a lot of what's happening is not written down, it is not obvious to see. But certain practices which I have tried to encourage over the years, I do expect to see, and I don't always see them. And it is a workload and a time element . . . and already teaching at its most basic is a huge workload . . . But the idea is generally, you know a lot of people will take the vision on board and go with it and are very, very keen to identify for themselves whether the children will thrive on that. But as I said there's lots of ways of skinning a cat and people are different, everyone has their own special talents and their own ways of doing things.
>
> (Angelika, SLT, GLP)

The model of 'responsive–responsible' leadership espoused by senior leaders at GLP has been summarised by Louise as follows:

> Leadership means you're responsible for a team and you have to lead from the front. You're leading by example and you're leading by enabling your staff to do what they do best, and showing them what they can do and appreciating what they can do. I have to be myself, I have to make sure that I'm seen to be enjoying my role, that I am good in my role, that I listen, that I act.
>
> (Louise, SLT, GLP)

Underpinning these conceptions of leadership in both schools is lived experience of being an educator and a strong 'people orientation', as suggested by references to listening, taking on the perspective of others and, at GLP, embracing difference. The patterns of conversation about leadership at AP and GLP beg a question about different forms of transformation that could emerge in the two schools without the constraints of the 'policy hysteria' (Stronach and MacLure 1997). Although answering this question might collide with the complexity concept of emergence, the ethos of the two schools suggests a reciprocity and respect in relationships that may provide an alternative to the 'calculating purposefulness' (Honneth 2006: 91) underpinning the global education policy theme of economically driven performativity. This point is developed further in Chapter 8.

The reconstruction of educational leadership

Central government's reconstruction of educational leadership has been concurrent with the *businessification* of education, based on a neoliberal belief that 'there is nothing the public sector can do that the private sector can't do better' (Beckett 2011: xxi). It relies on a new cadre of school leaders who espouse a business-oriented ethos and are not required under new legislation to have former experience as educators. For example, the requirement for headteachers to hold the Qualified Teacher Status was removed by the New Labour 'without any public debate that we can identify' (Gunter and Forrester 2009: 498). In 2012, as part of 'greater freedoms' in the 'school market', the Coalition government made the NPQH optional (NCSL 2011). Concerned about the drive for replacing headteachers with Chief Executive Officers, Sophie emphasised that:

> it's essential that the leadership team are experienced teachers. I don't at all buy into the notion that you can bring somebody out of the industry and make them headteacher of a school. Because I think first and foremost headteacher is to be head **teacher** . . . You've got to have a lead teacher in there, somebody who really knows and understands what the job is about.
> (Sophie, DH, AP)

Voices such as Sophie's are, however, drowned by the voices of policymakers and business organisations such as the CBI articulating a belief that the private sector has 'potential to transform the face of school leadership in England' (PWC 2007: 12):

> Schools should be led by chief executives who may not necessarily be teachers
> (PWC as quoted in Ball and Youdell 2008: 22)

> We should be open to the idea of leaders from outside education coming into our schools . . . two thirds of heads in England have no experience of leadership outside education, three quarters of heads in the best systems and Canada do.
> (CBI 2012)

These normative statements fail to explain why a lack of experience in education might be desirable in headship positions. Instead, the emphasis is placed on the ethos of entrepreneurialism and 'excellence'. For example, the Academies Programme discussed in Chapter 6 relies on 'outstanding' individuals such as Lord Harris, the sponsor of the Harris Federation. According to the federation website, Lord Harris's 'self-made success as a businessman is an inspiration to our students and his entrepreneurialism is thoroughly reflected in the can-do culture of our Academies' (Harris Federation, 2014). His blueprint for improvement is encapsulated as the 'Harris in a box initiative' and claimed to have led to outstanding pupil outcomes across the federation (Hill *et al.* 2012). The 'Harris in a box initiative' is 'a set of online resources about a Harris way of doing things'. Underpinned by the 'Harris philosophy', it allows individual academy principals 'freedom' to adapt the 'Harris core principles' such as data tracking to their specific academy contexts:

> So while all academies are required to use the same data tracking systems, the system is flexible enough for principals to be able to adapt it to their specific requirements. Similarly the Ofsted template of what makes for an outstanding lesson is used as the basis for assessing the quality of classroom teaching across the federation, but the forms that are used and the precise arrangements that apply vary from one academy to another.
> (Hill *et al.* 2012: 69)

The convergence between the 'Harris philosophy' and policy focus on standardisation, pupil performance data and school Ofsted grades is suggestive of a continuing faith in 'spectacular' solutions discussed in Chapter 5. However, leaving 'spectacular' solutions in the hands of business entrepreneurs is a manifestation of the ongoing privatisation of education (Ball 2013b). Only the benefit of hindsight may reveal whether blueprints such as the 'Harris in a box initiative' have the potential to transform education in England to a 'world-class' system. As argued by Ball (2013a: 172), at play here are processes of 'wearing away professional ethical regimes and their value systems' and 'their replacement by entrepreneurial-competitive regimes and their value systems'. As suggested by the case study findings discussed below, central to these processes is a recasting of standards as values. This recasting infuses standards (abstract performance indicators) with the highly personal meaning characteristic of values. The recasting can be illustrated by the following statement by Louise, in which she articulates a common taken-for-granted assumption that good SATs results mean that children achieve their potential:

> Yes, it's great for us to say: 'fantastic, our SATs results are great', but what we are saying by saying that is that our children are achieving their potential.
> (Louise, SLT, GLP)

A similar recasting is implicit in Gove's speech (2011) on the *Moral purpose of school reform*, which defines this purpose in terms of raising 'aspirations, standards, hopes' in order to 'liberate thousands from the narrow horizons which have limited mankind's vision for centuries'. 'Ambitious' standards of performance in high-stakes tests are imbued here with values associated with the emancipatory potential of education. The recasting of standards from a means for measuring school improvement to a 'moral' purpose is a manifestation of *management by values*, to which we now turn.

Standards and management by values

Following the publication in 1982 of Peters and Waterman's *In Search of Excellence*, mainstream management literature showed an increasing interest in the potential of organisational culture and shared values to improve organisational outcomes. As a result, former models of *management by instruction* and *management by objectives* gave way to *management by values* (Mowles 2011). As explained in Chapter 3, *management by values* utilises the sense of purpose and strong meaning attached to individuals' values for achieving organisational goals. Recast as values, standards become a powerful management tool that can be used by policymakers and school leaders to bind staff together in a 'moral' pursuit. Diverse values can be embraced or excluded, leading to a culture of inclusion or exclusion. Paradoxically, however, in the potential of values lies also the danger of manipulating values and excluding difference in order to foster a culture of compliance within an organisation viewed as an idealised whole. Gove's tendency to attach the emancipatory value of 'liberating thousands' to pupil performance standards is typical of *management by values*. In organisational settings, this may lead to a reconstruction of the workplace:

> as a site of spiritual engagement. It is a foil to understanding the process of organising merely as an activity [of] realising targets and outcomes, placing this activity in the expression of higher truths.
> (Mowles 2011: 126)

Defined as voluntary compulsions, values belong to the sphere of our individual choice that gives us a sense of identity and purpose. As Mowles (2011: 156) explains, values are 'voluntary compulsions', simultaneously voluntary and compelling in that we are compelled by the values we choose. This tacit understanding of values was expressed by Angelika talking about the culture at GLP:

> I think there is a sort of natural pressure, it's not an imposed pressure that's in terms of standards. I think there's a certain amount of understanding that everyone has their strengths and their special qualities and that you can't be robots as such and clocking in this time, going out that time. And I think that's an important part of why people feel comfortable here.
> (Angelika, SLT, GLP)

Standards were embraced at both schools as unquestionable and inevitable, for example:

> Raising standards is priority number one.
>
> (Stephen, H, GLP)

> I mean obviously there are the basic ideas of teaching and learning and raising standards and we're trying to work on those all of the time.
>
> (Angelika, SLT, GLP)

> And obviously, we have all our monitoring systems to ensure that our teaching is up to the correct standard. Should I see that [pupils'] results aren't up to standard, I'd go in and say 'what resources are you looking at? Obviously they're not working brilliantly; let's have a look at adapting and changing things'.
>
> (Annabel, T, AP)

There is, however, a difference in raising standards as a work task and 'basic' measure of the quality of 'teaching and learning', as articulated by Stephen and Angelika above, and 'teaching up to the *correct* standard' articulated by Annabel, suggestive of a value judgement. The difference in approach to standards seems to have to created distinctive cultures in the two schools and these will now be explored in turn.

A more relaxed approach to standards and an orientation to difference created a culture of inclusion in GLP. Participants linked the culture of inclusion to Stephen's values of caring, seeking balance and creating 'memorable' learning experiences for the children. His vision of a 'caring community' was echoed by Miriam and other members of staff, for example, Jeanne and Louise, who care about 'children being happy and safe at school'. The ethos of care included caring for the staff; both Miriam and Stephen were appreciated for their wisdom of managing the school 'without putting a lot of pressure on everybody else' (Alison). Sandy was appreciative of their realistic, balanced expectations:

> I don't think the leadership put excessive pressure on us here. I know that at some other schools planning is excessive, differentiation is near enough different for every child. Well whoever thinks they can do that, please come and show me.
>
> (Sandy, T, GLP)

Angelika's reflection summarises the 'subtle balance' valued by the staff at GLP as follows:

> And there's a subtle balance I think in keeping a happy school, between keeping your eye on standards and on monitoring and all the aspects that

cause standards to rise, but also in treating people, respecting them for their expertise and their differences and so on, and their slightly different approaches to teaching and so on.

(Angelika, SLT, GLP)

The feeling of comfort about and acceptance of difference was articulated by Stephen, Jeanne, Louise and Susan. The culture at GLP illustrates the argument by Mowles (2011) that shared values can enhance the meaning and purpose of common endeavour and thus strengthen the community in their pursuit of common goals, provided difference is embraced. It also illustrates how an understanding of the distinction between the 'natural pressure' (values) and 'imposed pressure' (standards) may enable professionals to hold on to their own diverse values, at the same time making the task of raising standards 'priority number one'.

The situation seemed to be different at AP, where the culture was articulated as 'teaching up to the correct standard' (Annabel) and 'everyone pushing in the right direction' (Mark). Fourteen out of seventeen participants referred to 'pushing' as positive and desirable, including teachers new to the school. For example within a year of working at AP, Maria appeared to have internalised the value of 'pushing for improvement'. While talking about her fast promotion to the Literacy Leader of Learning, she reflected on:

> how hard I work and how I want to push the school forward as well ... supporting staff and pushing your own subject as much as you can, not standing still.
>
> (Maria, SLT, AP)

As illustrated in the epigraph to this chapter, a 'push' on standards may lead to notions of education as a battlefield, where children need to be 'pushed on' (Pete). The Newtonian forces metaphor of pushing, pulling and stretching children abounded in the discourse of practitioners at AP. For example, the references below to 'pushing the children' are illustrative of a tendency to objectify the children discursively:

> I think in terms of behaviour we're very lucky, which helps with being able to push the children further when you're not battling their behaviour.
>
> (Gemma, T, AP)

> The parents will push us ... They want us to push the children.
>
> (Emma, T, AP)

> We have our tracking meetings here to ensure the children are making progress, and intervention comes in, so we push them on that front.
>
> (Annabel, T, AP)

These references render children, metaphorically speaking, into objects to be pushed, manipulated and measured according to predetermined categories, not unlike the 'passive nature' as the object of enquiry for the Newtonian-Cartesian scientist discussed in Chapter 2. As noted by Fairclough (2003), insights into metaphors may contribute to an understanding of how culturally shared meanings and values are not only articulated but also enacted in everyday practice. Examining the metaphors 'we live by' (Lakoff and Johnson 1980) and metaphors 'we lead by' (Alvesson and Spicer 2011) may also help professionals to reflect on how they implicitly construct and make sense of the complexities of everyday practice. As pointed out by Oberlechner and Mayer-Schönberger (2003: 6), an analysis of leadership metaphors may also reveal the 'hidden strategies of leaders' and 'metaphorical manipulations of those led or taught about leadership'.

There were also voices questioning the culture of 'pushing for results' and 'pushing children', mainly among the non-teaching staff at AP:

> A lot is pushed towards these SATs tests and that makes the school look good. And I just don't think that's right.
>
> (Sylvia, AS, AP)

> It seems very harsh for six- to seven-year olds to be sort of pushed into this kind of environment.
>
> (Eve, AS, AP)

These were, however, minority voices at AP. The common goal for the school expressed by Jenny as 'being the best that one can be' created the culture of having 'the right people on the bus' (Sophie). The 'value' of working up to the 'correct' standards created, in turn, discursive binaries of right/wrong and reward/punishment for (non)compliance:

> having the right people on the bus . . . getting the right staff and looking after them properly and making them feel valued and giving them an opportunity to take responsibility and developing them.
>
> (Sophie, DH, AP)

> I think we should expect high standards of everybody, I think we should expect everybody to be good or outstanding teachers . . . and we shouldn't be accepting less than that.
>
> (Alice, DH, AP)

> And sometimes having to be a bit tough if you've got people who are not doing the job right, because it's the children who matter. And being prepared to air it on the line and say: 'You've got to meet the standards'.
>
> (Sophie, DH, AP)

Standards were used in Jenny's 'battle' with the previous teaching team who, as Jenny maintains, were not working as well as they could – they had been allowed 'to get away with murder' by the previous headteacher:

> And there were quite a number of teachers here who did not want to work any harder than they were working and that wasn't working hard enough to get the results we wanted, so we really had to start almost from **scratch**. There was a really, really big staff turnover, there had to be
>
> (Sophie, DH, AP)

A theme underpinning the narrative of the transformation of AP from a 'coasting' to a highly successful school is that of a change in values, promotion of the 'right' values and exclusion of difference. Two questions could be asked in relation to this theme and the 'positive' accounts of the school's culture. First, is the extremely hard work, which leaves AP teachers 'exhausted' in what Maggie called the final, 'killer' term of the year, sustainable? Second, to what extent is the pressure of always 'pushing to get to the outstanding criteria' (Maggie) transferred onto AP children? A discussion of how the ethos of academic achievement can create an inclusion/exclusion dynamic in relationships with children is discussed in Chapter 8.

The reconstruction of educational leadership as *management by values* may profoundly change relationships in schools by creating patterns of inclusion and exclusion in a 'push' for a unified culture. As discussed in Chapter 6, deploying pupil performance standards as a measure of educational quality has been challenged for its narrow focus and distorting effects on pupils' experience of education (Alexander *et al.* 2010; Ball *et al.* 2012). Deploying standards as values in an attempt to create a monolithic culture of excellence is also an intrusion into the private sphere of individual values. As Watson (2011: 15–17) points out, this takes managers into 'deep and dangerous waters' raising ethical questions about the extent of managerial influence in matters as profound as 'the human need for meaning' and the questions 'concerning what is right and wrong in human behaviour'. As discussed in the following section, a deeper understanding of *management by values* can be gained in the light of the analysis of relations in modernity offered by Alasdair MacIntyre (1985).

An obliteration of the distinction between means and ends

As pointed out by Carol, 'there are always improvements to be made', because 'nothing is ever perfect enough' (AS, GLP). This statement points to one of the elements of what MacIntyre (1985) explains is a coherent, three-fold ethical scheme prevalent in Western culture until the Enlightenment. The remaining two elements were the purpose (the *telos* or end) and the means (moral principles) through which the 'perfect enough' state may be achieved. Rational justifications for moral principles were premised on an apprehension of the imperfection of 'man-as-he-happens-to-be' and 'human-nature-as-it-could-be-if-it-realised-its-*telos*' (MacIntyre 1985: 62–63). In this three-fold ethical scheme, moral principles provided the means of supporting the imperfect humans in passing from the present imperfect state to their 'true end'. Examples of such three-fold schemes can be found in Aristotelian ethics[1] and religious orders. From the Enlightenment and the rise of modern, secular perceptions of reality as subjective and the essential human nature as contested, the teleological view of humans lost its categorical status. As argued by MacIntyre:

> Since the whole point of ethics – both as a theoretical and a practical discipline – is to enable man to pass from his present state to his true end, the elimination of any notion of essential human nature and with it the abandonment of any notion of a telos leaves behind a moral scheme composed of two remaining elements whose relationship becomes quite unclear.
>
> (p. 65)

The loss of the established *telos* provided conditions for the conflation of means and ends and the dominance of instrumental reason, which characterises modern culture in general and dominant approaches to education reform in particular. For example, high scores in PISA tests are presented in the dominant discourse as simultaneously a means and end. They are constructed both as the goal of education reform in England (an end) and a lever for increasing British competitiveness in the global economy (a means). Thinking of means as separate from ends begs two questions. First, if PISA scores are to be an ultimate educational end, then how can such narrow purpose be justified? Second, if the PISA scores are a means, then to what human end? Refocusing education on the human, rather than economic ends could open up possibilities for radically different understandings of educational *telos* in the discourse on transforming education (Chapter 9).

A similar obliteration of the distinction between means and ends occurs in the recasting of standards (measures of educational improvement) as values (to be 'owned' and pursued by the school workforce as their key aim). For example, morally driven school improvement is defined by Davies (2006) in terms of consistent performance against standards. Similarly, 'excellent' headteachers '[h]old and articulate clear values and moral purpose, focused on providing a world-class education for the pupils they serve' (DfE 2015: 5). On MacIntyre's account, the conflation of means and ends has given rise to the 'emotivist culture' developed by the 'bureaucratic manager', who:

> treats ends as given, as outside his scope; his concern is with technique, with effectiveness in transforming raw materials into final products, unskilled labor into skilled labor, investment into profits.
>
> (MacIntyre 1985: 35)

The bureaucratic manager presents him/herself as a moral representative, infusing modern culture with the values of efficiency and instrumental calculation whereby effectively matching means to predetermined ends has become the *telos* of human endeavour. This, in turn, may lead to manipulative relations in which both nature and people are rendered into resources and objects to be utilised and manipulated. An example of manipulative relations in the approaches to education policy in England includes deploying school leaders as a 'generic mechanism for change' (Ball 2013a: 164). Similarly, reculturing programs to end the 'culture of underperformance' (Marshall 2013) rely on 'aligning' teachers and pupils in pursuit of 'aspirational' targets and may manipulate them into compliance through the threat of exclusion or shaming. This can be illustrated by Michael Gove's (2011) 'passionate' appeal for raising 'aspirations, standards and hopes', in which he publically lauds as 'heroes' and 'heroines' academy sponsors with a strong record of improved pupil outcomes and publically shames schools that have been 'under the floor for five years or more' (referring here to schools that failed to meet the new 'floor standard' of performance).

A host of other problems may arise from these bureaucratic modes of organising. First, if ambitious targets turn out to be unrealistic, more effort may be spent on managing the impression that targets have been met, than on the actual improvement. Second, the assumption that organisational ends are most efficiently met when people's values are 'aligned' and homogenous may not only silence alternative values and purposes but also create an illusion of consensus. As discussed in Chapter 3, a public expression of practitioner compliance with the dominant values is conveyed through the public transcript (Scott 1990), which tends to mask 'what is' with a veneer of 'what should be'. As an articulation of what subordinate groups 'really think', the private transcript is rarely spoken 'directly in the teeth of power' (ibid.: 4). As a result, however, policymakers may conclude that practitioners have willingly taken up their directives or values. This is suggestive of a disjuncture whereby appearances are taken for reality. While standards and targets as the goals of policy can be interpreted as a manifestation of the hegemonic planning mentality (Chapter 7), targets as values 'owned' by schools and 'having a visible life and meaning in the classroom' (DfES 2003: 19) take education policy to the 'deep and dangerous waters' of manipulative relations.

Conclusion

This chapter examined strategic leadership and *management by values*, connecting them to manipulative relations engendered by the loss of a coherent moral scheme in modernity. In the absence of such a coherent moral scheme, a strategic vision or an appeal to values can be utilised by leaders and policymakers for mobilising the school workforce in the cause of ongoing raising of standards. Although the 'strategies era' 1998–2011, discussed in Chapter 5, was ended by the Coalition government (DfE 2011), conversational themes in the current policy discourse continue to reflect the 'strategic' intent for the education system to become 'world-class' in order to effectively compete in the global economy. MacIntyre's (1985) analysis suggests that the roots of the increasing subordination of education to 'the economic' (Ball 2013a: 172) may reach deeper than the current, ongoing neoliberalisation of social relations. Whereas English education policymakers have increasingly turned to private sector management for solutions to educational 'crises', the 'long string of corporate scandals' seems to have shaken the public trust in the integrity of management as a profession (Khurana 2007: 364). In his study of the growth of management education in the United States, Khurana emphasises an 'unfulfilled promise of management as a profession', particularly in neoliberal times when corporate managers have 'no role-defined obligation other than to self-interest' (ibid.). The roots of this unfulfilled promise and the managerial pursuit of self-interest may lie deeper, in the emotivist culture of modernity (MacIntyre 1985) and its bureaucratic modes of management.

So what conclusions could be drawn about policy, strategy and *management by values* from the theoretical analysis and discussions of the case study data presented in this chapter? What principles could underpin a conception of educational transformation, or (simply) 'improvement that comes from *within*', as suggested by Pete? Angelika's distinction between the 'natural pressure' of values and the 'imposed pressure' of standards and her understanding of the highly individual, complex nature of values could inform a more cautious approach to *management by values*. The culture of inclusion at GLP, based on respecting and embracing difference, could be an important message to policymakers who, while passionately promoting their mission may need to also remember that leadership means: 'you're responsible . . . You're leading by example and you're leading by enabling your staff to do what they do best, and showing them what they can do and appreciating what they can do' (Louise). The more 'strategically' oriented leaders might benefit from reflecting on the 'metaphors they lead by' and how the language they use may be understood by others. And last, all of those preoccupied with a pursuit of 'ambitious' standards may need to remember Stephen's point that the 'fifty things that children should do' before they leave primary school are 'about going rock climbing, flying a kite, rolling down a big hill and all this sort of stuff'.

Note

1 MacIntyre's (1985) detailed explanation of Aristotelian ethics and the rise of manipulative relations can be found in Chapter 5 of his book *After Virtue: A Study in Moral Theory*.

References

Alexander, R. 2012. Moral panic, miracle cures and educational policy: What can we really learn from international comparisons? *Scottish Educational Review*, 44(1): 4–21.

Alexander, R., Armstrong, M., Flutter, J., Hargreaves, L., Harlen, W., Harrison, D., Hartley-Brewer, E., Kershner, R., MacBeath, J., Mayall, B., Northen, S., Pugh, G., Richards, C. and Utting, D. 2010. *Children, Their World, Their Education: Final Report and Recommendations of the Cambridge Primary Review*. Abingdon: Routledge and the University of Cambridge.

Alvesson, M. and Spicer, A. (eds). 2011. *Metaphors We Lead By: Understanding Leadership in the Real World*. Abingdon: Oxon.

Ball, S.J. 2013a. *The Education Debate* (2nd edn). Bristol: The Policy Press.

Ball, S.J. 2013b. *Education, Justice And Democracy: The Struggle over Ignorance and Opportunity*. London: Centre for Labour and Social Studies.

Ball, S.J. and Youdell, D. 2008. *Hidden Privatization in Public Education: A Report*. London: Institute of Education.

Ball, S.J., Maguire, M. and Braun, A. 2012. *How Schools Do Policy: Policy Enactments in Secondary Schools*. London and New York: Routledge.

Beckett, F. 2011. Preface. In Gunter, H. (ed.) *The State and Education Policy*. London: Continuum, xx–xxiii.

CBI. 2012. *First Steps: A New Approach for Our Schools: End of Year Report*. Available at: www.cbi.org.uk/media/2473815/First_steps_end_of_year_report.pdf (accessed 3 March 2015).

Davies, B. 2006. *Leading the Strategically Focused School: Success and Sustainability*. London: Paul Chapman.

DfE. 2010. *The Importance of Teaching: The Schools White Paper 2010*. Available at: www.ictliteracy.info/rf.pdf/Schools-White-Paper2010.pdf (accessed 15 March 2012).

DfE. 2011. *The National Strategies 1997–2011: A Brief Summary of the Impact and Effectiveness of the National Strategies*. London: Crown Copyright.

DfE. 2015. *National Standards of Excellence for Headteachers: Departmental Advice for Headteachers, Governing Boards and Aspiring Headteachers*. London: Crown Copyright.

DfEE. 1998. *The National Literacy Strategy: Framework for Teaching*. London: DfEE.

DfEE. 1999. *The National Numeracy Strategy: Framework for Teaching Mathematics*. London: DfEE.

DfES. 2002. *Time for Standards: Reforming the School Workforce*. London: DfES.

DfES. 2003. *Excellence and Enjoyment: A Strategy for Primary Schools*. London: HMSO.

Fairclough, N. 2003. *Analysing Discourse: Textual Analysis for Social Research*. Abingdon: Routledge.

Gove, M. 2011. *The Moral Purpose of School Reform*. Available at: www.gov.uk/government/speeches/michael-gove-on-the-moral-purpose-of-school-reform (accessed 28 March 2015).

Gunter, H.M. 2004. Labels and labelling in the field of educational leadership, *Discourse: Studies in the Cultural Politics of Education*, 25(1): 21–41.

Gunter, H.M. 2012. *Leadership and the Reform of Education*. Bristol: The Policy Press.

Gunter, H.M. and Forrester, G. 2009. School leadership and education policy-making in England, *Policy Studies*, 30(5): 495–511.

Harris Federation, 2014. *Welcome from the Chief Executive*. Available at: www.harrisfederation.org.uk/53/welcome (accessed 22 January 2014).

Hill, R. and Matthews, P. 2010. *Schools Leading Schools II: The Growing Impact of National Leaders of Education*. Nottingham: National College Publishing.

Hill, R., Dunford, J., Parish, N., Rea, S. and Sandals, L. 2012. *The Growth of Academy Chains: Implications for Leaders and Leadership.* Nottingham: NCSL.

Honneth, A. 2006. *Reification: A Recognition-Theoretical View.* Available at: http://tannerlectures.utah.edu/lecture-library.php#h (accessed 14 March 2014).

Khurana, R. 2007. *From Higher Aims to Hired Hands: The Social Transformation of American Business Schools and the Unfulfilled Promise of Management as a Profession.* Princeton, NJ: Princeton University Press.

Lakoff, G. and Johnson, M. 1980. *Metaphors We Live By.* Chicago, IL: The University of Chicago Press.

MacIntyre, A. 1985. *After Virtue: A Study in Moral Theory* (2nd edn). London: Bloomsbury.

Marshall, P. (ed.). 2013. *The Tail: How England's Schools Fail One Child in Five – and What Can Be Done.* London: Profile Books.

Mowles, C. 2011. *Rethinking Management: Radical Insights from the Complexity Sciences.* Farnham: Gower.

NCSL. 2011. *National Professional Qualification for Headship Competency Framework.* Available at: www.gov.uk/government/uploads/system/uploads/attachment_data/file/284573/npqh-competency-framework.pdf (accessed 05 May 2014).

Oberlechner, T. and Mayer-Schönberger, V. 2012. *Through Their Own Words: Towards a New Understanding of Leadership through Metaphors.* Available at: http://papers.ssrn.com/sol3/papers.cfm?abstract_id=357542 (accessed 29 March 2015).

Peters, T.J. and Waterman, R.H. 1982. *In Search of Excellence.* New York: Harper and Row.

PWC. 2007. *Independent Study into School Leadership.* Available at: http://webarchive.nationalarchives.gov.uk/20130401151715/www.education.gov.uk/publications/eOrderingDownload/RB818.pdf (accessed 03 April 2015).

Sahlberg, P. 2011. *Finnish Lessons: What Can the World Learn from Educational Change in Finland?* New York and London: Teachers College.

Scott, J.C. 1990. *Domination and the Arts of Resistance: Hidden Transcripts.* New Haven, CT: Yale University Press.

Sebba, J. and Robinson, C. 2010. *Evaluation of UNICEF UK's Rights Respecting Schools Award: Final Report.* Available at: www.unicef.org.uk/Documents/Education-Documents/RRSA_Evaluation_Report.pdf?epslanguage=en (accessed 27 March 2015).

Stacey, R.D. 2007. *Strategic Management and Organisational Dynamics: The Challenge of Complexity* (5th edn). Harlow: Pearson Education.

Stronach, I. and MacLure, M. 1997. *Educational Research Undone: The Postmodern Embrace.* Buckingham: Open University Press.

Watson, T. 2011. *In Search of Management: Culture, Chaos and Control in Managerial Work.* Andover, MA: Cengage Learning.

Part III

Complex responsive processes theory and educational ends

Chapter 8

'Tremendous power', ethics and responsibility

> I do have dark days. There are days when I think why on earth did I put myself in this position? And the answer that I give myself is: 'could you go back to doing what you did before?' So really, you know you feel that the extra responsibility which lives with you every second of your working day is worth it, because you couldn't go back to what you were doing before.
> (Stephen, headteacher, Green Lanes Primary)

> But, yeah, I love teaching. I love the kids they make me laugh. And hopefully I make them laugh now and again.
> (Sandy, teacher, Green Lanes Primary)

Chapter 8 focuses on how educational practice is reconfigured by policymakers from a 'labour of love' (Sandy, T, GLP) to managing children through 'data', in which the child has been conceptualised primarily as an abstract statistic. Within this approach, school leadership is defined in terms of transforming 'high aspirations' into outstanding results in high-stakes tests and teaching conceived of as a 'craft' that is 'best learnt as an apprentice observing a master craftsman or woman' (Gove 2010). A similar form of reductionism appears to inform the OECD (2013: 19) definition of a teacher as a 'person whose professional activity involves the transmission of knowledge, attitudes and skills that are stipulated to students enrolled in an educational program'. This definition confines the teacher's role within a transmission model of learning (Kelly 2009), limiting his/her responsibility to a specific, finite stage of a child's education. It also positions children as passive 'receivers' of knowledge, attitudes and skills, ignoring their contribution to social reproduction and change (Corsaro 2011).

The recent Ofsted inspection targets for GLP were displayed on the wall in Stephen's office next to the following words by Heim Ginott (1972: 13),[1] which emphasise the 'tremendous power' of teachers:

> I have come to a frightening conclusion. I am the decisive element in the classroom. It is my personal approach that creates the climate. It is my daily

mood that makes the weather. As a teacher I possess tremendous power to make a child's life miserable or joyous. I can be a tool of torture or an instrument of inspiration. I can humiliate or humour, hurt or heal. In all situations, it is my response that decides whether a crisis will be escalated or de-escalated, and a child humanized or de-humanized.

Published before the expansion of education reform in the 1990s, these words are a universal reminder of teachers' 'tremendous power' in the classroom as well as responsibility for their everyday choices. Read in 2015, in the context of reconstruction of relations discussed in Chapters 5–7, the title of Ginott's book, *Teacher and Child*, could be re-formulated as *Politician, Teacher and Child*. However, despite invasive policy influences, in the ordinary 'everydayness' of each encounter with a child, the teacher does have the 'tremendous' power to choose whether a child will be 'humanized or de-humanized'. This power can be explained by the social theory of identity formation developed by G.H. Mead and refined by Honneth (1995, 2006). According to Honneth, identity develops in and through social interactions and the formation of a psychologically healthy personality depends on the systems of interaction within the child's family home as well as those in the school and the broader community.

As suggested in the epigraph to this chapter, Stephen seems to realise this when, on his 'dark days', he feels overwhelmed by his responsibility for 'shaping young lives'. As suggested by Sandy, there are also 'light' moments in the everyday life of a primary school. The above reflections by Sandy, Stephen and Ginott (1972) capture the theme of paradoxes and contradictions that emerged from the case study data on power, ethics and responsibility. According to complex responsive processes theory, the inherently paradoxical nature of everyday life is manifested in the simultaneous existence of opposing elements that cannot be resolved or eliminated. For example, understanding power as a paradox of enabling constraint reveals how teachers, despite being constrained by an externally imposed regime of targets, can exercise power in their own classrooms. Sophie's (DH, AP) point that it is teachers and not policymakers 'who make it work for the children' resonates with Ginott's message that, ultimately, it is the teachers' response 'that decides'. The complexity concept of interdependence offers insights into issues of power and ethics in the everyday life of a school, emphasising the importance of adults in 'shaping' children's lives, as well as the meaning that children bring into the lives of adults.

Knowledge industry, targets and the *child-worker*

As noted in Chapter 1, the OECD (2009: 3) vision of education as a 'knowledge industry' is predicated on transforming educational practices by the 'knowledge about the efficacy of those practices'. The data and discussions presented in this book suggest that education policy in England seems to have made great strides towards this form of transformation. This has partly been achieved through the use of targets, introduced into education on the basis of their 'long-standing use' in industrial management and 'increasing use' in public services (Beard 2000: 10). However, numerous commentators point to negative consequences of the use of targets even in industrial settings. As abstractions mapped in the 'boardroom', targets may be disconnected from what is possible to achieve on the 'factory floor' (Seddon 2008; Mowles 2011; Stacey 2010, 2012). The notion of targets assumes that workers in organisations need to be incentivised and supervised to high performance. Consequently, target setting requires the deployment of an accompanying apparatus to monitor and control workers (Chapter 5). It may also promote gaming behaviours or subterfuge if the consequences of missing targets are too severe. The emphasis on targets in schools contributes to a reconstruction of the child as a *child-worker*, diminishing the quality of children's experience of education. As argued by Hogan (2011: 28), the 'recasting of issues of quality in educational experience as issues of indexed quantity (of grades, test scores, etc.)' has in effect pushed 'the heart of educational quality itself to the margins, or even out of the picture'. The obliteration of the distinction between educational means and ends discussed in Chapter 7 is played out in the classroom as a target-driven education in which pupil performance targets become both a means to achieving educational transformation and its core purpose.

The child-worker: 'My targets for this week are . . .'

Combined with the regime of targets, the conception of teaching as 'transmission' of knowledge, skills and attitudes (OECD 2013) also appears to reconstruct the *child-learner* as a *child-worker*. As suggested by the case study findings, the use of targets in the everyday teaching and learning activities at AP and GLP focused the patterns of conversation between children and adults on the themes of 'setting' and 'achieving' targets. The recasting of the child as the *child-worker* in the everyday practice of schools has also been accompanied by the discursive reconstruction of children as the future 'workforce' in policy discourse in which education is an 'engine' of the economy (Chapter 6). Underlying these reconstructions is a misrecognition of children's needs (Honneth 1995, 2006), with consequences that may last beyond their primary school years.

In alignment with the instruction that targets are 'owned' by children and have a 'visible life and meaning in the classroom' (DfES 2003: 19), targets were indeed 'visible' at AP, in children's books, classroom displays and whiteboard presentations for lessons. The school also involved parents in target setting, through the *Home-School Liaison Book*. A page layout for each week is presented in Figure 8.1.

Implicit in the layout of the page is a distinction between 'achieving targets' and 'learning' as well as the priority of targets over 'learning and enjoyment'. Regular weekly work on targets at home and in school throughout the primary

My targets for this week are:

1. _____

2. _____

Target	How well I feel I have achieved my target	My comments

☺ Target achieved    😐 Target partly achieved    ☹ Target still needs work

This week I have learned and enjoyed:

1. _____

2. _____

3. _____

Parent's/Carer's Comments

Figure 8.1 Page layout in the *Home-School Liaison Book*

years is likely to instil in the children a notion of learning as achieving targets. A similar institutionalisation of targets has also taken place at GLP:

> So the children have their targets, and they'll say: 'these are the level 3 targets', so they'll be able to see how they're getting on towards those. Say for example one of our year 5 classes, they'll have their targets and they'll know they need to look out for where they've done that in their work, because their teacher will be saying, 'How have you met this target? Show me in your work that you're using commas to demarcate your clauses'.
> (Miriam, DH, GLP)

Target setting is reconstructing the curriculum as a 'collection of targets' (Pring 2013: 65) and learning as 'targets talk', whereby children are expected to 'show' how they have met specific targets. Learning is externalised and children's learning experience reduced to 'getting' a target and achieving it in order to move 'onto the next one':

> So if they've learnt how to use connectives appropriately then they're onto the next one rather than having to wait until the next assessment, which might be half a term away, before they get their next target.
> (Miriam, DH, GLP)

Teaching is recast as efficient target setting based on breaking learning down into small steps where learners' responses are predetermined within a framework of predetermined, standardised answers. The shift in focus from children's learning to managing targets leads to an education that propagates a 'closure' rather than 'openness' of mind (Barnett 1997). The purpose of such education could be encapsulated as training an efficient workforce, in line with the government's economic imperative (DfE 2010a). Ironically, however, preparing children for life 'in a very different world' and not being able to 'anticipate what kind of employment they are going to have' (Sophie) calls for an education that would encourage an 'openness' rather than 'closure' of mind.

Targets also seemed to be deployed as techniques of disciplinary power (Mowles 2011; Ball *et al.* 2012). For example, six-year-old Millie wrote in her *Home-School Liaison Book*, 'I have dun my target', listing the following in her weekly targets list: 'I will set cwiot on the carpit' ('I will sit quietly on the carpet') and 'I will not bite my nais in class' ('I will not bite my nails in class'). This is one of the many examples of weekly targets found in AP children's *Home-School Liaison Books* related to self-regulation and discipline. Contrary to Michael Gove's (2011) goal to 'liberate' children from the 'narrow horizons' of thought and vision (Chapter 7), the reference to a 'target dun', written by a six year old, is a symbol of education reform that confines children's learning within the narrow horizons of predetermined outcomes. These outcomes seem to ignore the need of children to be recognised for who they are rather than for who they should become.

Children as data: 'If a plant's growing you don't pull it out of its pot, do you, to check its roots?'

The intensification of 'governing by data' in England (Lawn 2011) is premised on the notion of data as a 'lever' for school improvement. As emphasised by Lawn, 'governance by data' defines educational improvement in terms of more efficient systems of data collection and uninterrupted 'data flow'. For example, the UPN system enables officials in Whitehall to monitor SATs results of any child in the UK (DfE 2010b). This way of looking at children 'as data' was also beginning to be embedded in both case study schools. In order to meet the demands for accountability, schools need to regularly generate data that 'track' the progress of each child and this brings both target setting and assessment to the fore of teaching. It also necessitated the development of a designated role of 'assessment manager' in each school (Maggie at AP and Miriam at GLP). The assessment system at AP was extremely efficient at minimising the risk that a child might 'slip off the teacher's radar' (Maggie). Maggie's role included monitoring the use of assessment by all AP teachers, 'tracking' each child's progress in literacy, numeracy and science every six weeks and meeting class teachers to discuss targets for each child. When asked what happens when children are not 'on target', Maggie replied:

> Then we have to think and meet with the SENCO: 'are they on the SEN register?[2] Is it a learning difficulty that's stopping them from progressing?' Sometimes it could be an issue at home and we take it into account, or is it an attendance issue, is it something we need to put an intervention group in, give them extra support. Or do they just need a big kick up the backside and saying: 'Come on, we know your capability of doing it but you're just being lazy'.
>
> (Maggie, SLT, AP)

Maggie's explanation of the possible reasons for children missing their targets is linked to 'deficiencies' located *in* the child or the family home and *outside* the target- and assessment-driven practice. A deeper evaluation of what this practice means to children reveals the contradiction in using extrinsic incentives such as targets to 'motivate' children, despite children's natural curiosity and intrinsic desire to know and understand the world emphasised by lifespan psychologists (Illeris 2007). The 'pedagogy of confinement' (Gibbs and Iacovidou 2004) inherent in designing learning around predetermined outcomes and past achievements of standards constrains the breadth, flexibility and creative opportunities in learning that would support children's intrinsic desire to learn (Alexander *et al.* 2010).

When children are 'on target', it is not uncommon for teachers to 'strategically' shift support onto the children who are not yet 'on target' (Mark, T, AP). As Ball *et al.* (2012: 81) point out, all pupils are expected to improve, but some improvements are 'strategically more important than others'. Apart from the issue of equality of support highlighted by Mark, for the system of target 'tracking' to work, children need to be tested every six weeks. As pointed out by Sandy, frequent assessment disrupts learning, putting pressure on children and teachers alike:

> I think the pressures on assessment and testing are too great. I think that teaching and learning should take the high priority rather than assessment or stopping children every so often. We have assessment week, you know. You stop everything, you assess, and then you have to start again. If a plant's growing you don't pull it out of its pot, do you, and check the roots?
> (Sandy, T, GLP)

What drives the practice of looking at children 'as data' is a desire to minimise the risk of children missing their targets. As a result, however, 'targets talk' and 'assessment weeks' begin to dominate the systems of interaction within schools. This has led a reconstruction of teaching, whereby 'acquiring mastery' (Gove 2010) is associated with accurate assessment rather than a deep understanding of children and their development. A contrasting notion of good teaching was expressed by Sophie thus:

> We have to have a real understanding of children and how they develop and how they learn and you have to have an understanding of what the teaching job is all about. Because teaching is about commitment and passion and you can't be a half-hearted teacher, it's vocational.
> (Sophie, DH, AP)

However, when understanding children is replaced with looking at children 'as data', teaching becomes a matter of technique, which can lead to a loss of 'passion' and the 'heart'. It renders children as statistics that require teachers to engage in the 'cold-calculating activity' (Honneth 2006: 96) of generating and using data on the 'efficacy' of their practices (OECD 2009). The reasons why most practitioners appeared to cede their 'passion' and the 'heart' to enact target-driven education are complex. The 'ethos of saying "Yes"' (Sophie) could be one of them, as could *doing* school improvement without a deeper reflection about its complex purposes and consequences. Fiona's and Miriam's statements suggest a lack of reflexivity (Ball *et al.* 2012) in drawing on taken-for-granted assumptions about 'benefit' to children to justify both their hard work and compliance with the dominant notion of school improvement:

> If it's good for the children, if it really is, then, you know, then we'll do it.
> (Fiona, SLT, AP)

I think that's the bit about teaching being a vocation rather than just a job, isn't it? It is the children at the heart of it, and if you don't say 'Yes' it is the children who won't benefit.

(Miriam, DH, GLP)

Both schools presented themselves as 'positive', as places where 'you come in and go out of that door with a smile on your face' (Jeanne) and where teachers are ready to cope with whatever is 'thrown at them' (Jenny). However, saying 'Yes' to 'governing by data' may distort interactions within schools and de-humanise children, reducing them to 'track-able' data. The extrinsic incentives of targets and assessment tests may also stunt children's intrinsic motivation to learn (Illeris 2007). The new *Teachers Standards* attempt to address this problem and develop children's 'love of learning' by emphasising that teachers 'must set high expectations' in order to inspire, motivate and challenge pupils (DfE 2011: 10). As discussed below, however, the culture of 'high expectations' may also be problematic.

The 'dark' side of high aspirations

In response to what he perceived as a 'deeply embedded culture of low aspiration' in 'far too many communities' across England (DfE 2010a: 4), Education Secretary Michael Gove (2010–2014) set out to raise aspirations and expectations as well as standards.[3] As pointed out by Zipin *et al.* (2013), the theme of 'raising aspirations' is typical of education policies across the world and aimed at increasing economic competitiveness in the global 'knowledge economy'. Apart from casting socially disadvantaged communities as 'in deficit' through the binary of high/low aspirations, the discourses of high aspirations reduce the complexities and stark conditions in which such communities 'struggle to imagine and pursue futures' (ibid.: 2). They also shift responsibility for socio-economic disadvantage from the state to communities and individuals.

The case study data also suggest that the consequences of a 'push' on high aspirations are not always 'positive'. Since high aspirations are linked to high standards and the latter are defined in terms of 'outperforming' other schools (DfE 2010a), the expectation of teachers to raise high-stakes tests results is transferred onto the children. Teachers give a huge amount of time and effort to the children and expect a lot in return, especially at AP, where Jenny's aspiration 'to be the best that one can be' has become a shared value (Chapter 7). It is also instilled in the children, particularly through the 'golden rules' that are displayed in every classroom and often discussed in assemblies and lessons. The 'golden rules' at AP include the expectations for the children to 'listen', 'look after property' and 'work hard' as well as to 'be kind and helpful', 'gentle and honest'. Most AP children are also presented with 'family aspirations', such as achieving high levels in SATs and getting into 'good' (selective) secondary schools. Having previously worked in a school in a deprived area, Emma found AP parents 'quite pushy':

> A lot of the parents will push us to make sure that we change the reading books: 'Is this book hard enough?'
>
> (Emma, T, AP)

The 'dark' side of high aspirations was emphasised by a small number of participants in both schools (Lynn, TA, AP; Sylvia AS, AP; Eve, AS, AP; Sandy, T, GLP). High aspirations create a divide between schools and pupils who succeed and those who do not. As pointed out by Sandy, aspirations to a high position in schools' league tables may also be unrealistic:

> Well, the parents and teachers and heads are all like: 'oh we're not here, we're down here at the moment, we want to be up here. Yeah we're up here!' It's good to be on top, but what about the bottom? What if a school can't go up? I mean I'm sorry, but if I've got a Mini out there, I'm not going to be a Formula 1 racing car. It doesn't matter how I look after it or treat it, I can't do it.
>
> (Sandy, T, GLP)

Apart from creating reductionist evaluations of schools as 'bottom' or 'top' in league tables, high aspirations seem to be beneficial for 'high achievers', but not children who struggle with the academic regimes of literacy and numeracy:

> with the league tables and with the SATs, it's very 'one way is the only way' type of thing. And a lot of children that we work with, it's not beneficial for **them**. I think even when they get to high school there's still not that many choices for them other than to sit in a lesson and listen. Or become naughty and disruptive.
>
> (Lynn, TA, AP)

Where high aspirations are unrealistic, they may be destructive, they may 'humiliate', 'hurt' and 'make a child's life miserable' (Ginott 1972: 13). As Sylvia pointed out, not getting the expected level in SATs can make children 'not feel as good about themselves' as their more able peers. Sylvia's critique of labels such as 'Level 3 children' or 'Level 5 children' used by the teachers at AP also resonates with Ball *et al.*'s (2012: 78) argument about how pupils are 'objectified as talented, borderline, underachieving, irredeemable'. As noted by Ainley and Allen (2012: 24), English children are 'conditioned' early on to connect their self-esteem to their test scores.

Children's performance in SATs may have long-term consequences in relation to children's self-esteem as well as the choices available to them. For example, Eve was concerned about 'all those children nobody wants', referring to the lowest achieving children who often experience difficulty in finding secondary school places in local schools, because of low academic performance. Conversely, with high aspirations, young children may be socialised into being 'the best that one can be' (Jenny) by outperforming others. An aspiration to excellence can be interpreted as promoting the Cartesian conception of a human being as an atomised *homo clausus* (Elias 1994) discussed in Chapter 2, leading to:

> [the] loneliness we are now facing and are solemnly passing on to our children under the guise of education and the individual, manic pursuit of excellence-as-self-absorption – and with this, all the little built-in panics and terrors that come with the blind rush to be up-to-date, ahead of the game . . . the potent desire to end up 'on top'
>
> (Jardine 1998: 88)

High aspirations seemed to trigger profound changes in both schools, transforming children's experience of education and potentially changing 'the kind of person they're going to turn out to be' (Sophie). While both schools have been successful at raising standards of performance in high-stakes tests, such success may have 'little to do with education' conceived as learning what it means to be human and what is essential for living in a democratic society (Pring 2013: 64). It may also have little to do with understanding the needs of the child, an important issue to which we now turn.

The priority of recognition

As signalled in Chapter 3, recognition involves an empathetic engagement in the world arising from our assessment of the value that people 'have in themselves' (Honneth 2006: 111). In explaining the importance of recognition to psychologically and socially healthy child development, Honneth posits, first, that recognition precedes cognition ontogenetically and, second, that identity develops within and through social interactions.[4] In substantiating the claim that recognition comes before cognition, or in other words that our 'empathetic engagement precedes a neutral grasping of reality', Honneth (2006: 113) draws on the work of an English psychoanalyst and paediatrician Donald Winnicott. Winnicott (1965, 1971) demonstrated that an infant's and young child's positive relation-to-self (self-confidence) arises from being loved and cared for. Self-confidence involves emotional confidence in the experience of needs and feelings and in being able to express them without the fear of being abandoned. This basic emotional self-confidence constitutes the 'psychological precondition' for the development of 'all further attitudes of self-respect' that contribute to one's sense of self-worth (Honneth 1995: 107).[5] Infants' needs and their satisfaction by the primary carers are complex and often contradictory. This complexity is conveyed by Martha Nussbaum (2001) as the infant's need of 'holding', which includes the need to be physically held, as well as nutrition, sensitive care and an environment in which the infant's helplessness is acknowledged. Although the process of growing and being cared for always involves moments of discomfort or frustration, 'holding', which is 'good enough', provides conditions for the growth of a child's self-confidence. Since this basic self-confidence originates in a recognition of needs experienced in infancy, the crucial primary relationships with the mother and other significant carers will have run their course by the time children begin school.

The development of self-esteem, however, depends on the intersubjective experiences that occur during the school years. These are based on being recognised as a person, a 'being possessed of personal qualities' (p. 112) rather than the generic UPN child (DfE 2010b). As emphasised by Honneth (1995: 113), recognising a child as a person does not involve an application of generalised social norms but rather an appraisal of 'concrete traits and abilities' (which Mead would refer to as 'particularisation'; Chapter 3). This kind of recognition may be very difficult to realise in an education system conceived within a normative frame of high aspirations for top academic performance. This system prioritises cognition over recognition, defining teaching in terms of delivering an 'aspirational National Curriculum' (DfE 2010a: 61), target setting and 'objective' tracking of children's progress through regular assessment exercises. This, in turn, may lead to a tendency to perceive children as 'mere insensate objects' rather than individuals possessed of unique personal traits and abilities:

> in this kind of amnesia we lose the ability to understand immediately the behavioral expressions of other persons as making claims on us—as demanding that we react in an appropriate way. We may indeed be capable in a cognitive sense of perceiving the full spectrum of human expressions, but we lack, so to speak, the feeling of connection that would be necessary for us to be affected by the expressions we perceive.
>
> (Honneth 2006: 129)

On Honneth's account, the attitudes of 'cold' calculating rationality fostered within technicist approaches to teaching result in a perceptive objectification ('reification') of children that is characteristic of autism:

> forgetting our antecedent recognition ... corresponds to the result produced by a perceptive reification of the world. In other words, our social surroundings appear here, very much as in the autistic child's world of perception, as a totality of merely observable objects lacking all psychic impulse or emotion.
>
> (p. 129)

In prioritising top performance, the systems of interaction based on performance targets foster a tendency to forget the essential needs of the child to be recognised, cared for and valued as a person. They also socialise children into a world where an empathetic recognitional stance towards others is displaced with relationships dominated by instrumentalist rationality. Since self-esteem is also rooted in children being recognised for belonging to 'communities of value' (Honneth 1995: 111), the denigration of the 'culture of low aspiration' (DfE 2010a: 4) within such communities may further adversely affect children's self-esteem.

The knowledge about the 'efficacy of educational practices' necessary for transforming education into a 'knowledge industry' (OECD 2009: 3) emphasises the spectator view of knowledge, the kind of knowledge accessed through a 'neutral confrontation' with the world and others as objects. This kind of knowledge is for Honneth a manifestation of the 'forgetfulness of recognition' indicative of a loss of awareness of the self as constituted in and through relationships with others.[6] Conversely, an awareness of the interdependent self provides the basis of relationships underpinned by recognition rather than disinterested, 'objective' contemplation of others and the world, whereby 'we must be affected by other people before we can take up a more neutral stance' (Honneth 2006: 131). The responsibility of the teacher, therefore, goes beyond accountability for 'transmitting' knowledge, attitudes and skills (OECD 2013). Similarly, to be a school leader, means to be affected, not just to affect others by getting them 'to do what is asked of them' (NCSL 2011: 7). The priority of recognition provides a basis for an alternative conception of accountability, where the task of 'holding others to account' (NCSL 2011: 7) implies a mutual obligation to be accountable. While government discourse of high aspirations frames accountability in terms of children's 'high performance', Honneth's theory is a reminder of the obligation to recognise the needs of children to be cared for and respected.

Connecting interdependence to power and ethics

The concept of interdependence is central to understanding power relations as based on mutual need rather than the will to dominate (Chapter 3). Because of our needs of recognition, care, love and respect, we need others and, simultaneously, others need us. The notion of 'power figurations' (Elias 1978) refers to fluid bonds that tie people together in complex networks of such mutual dependencies. As Mowles (2015: 250) points out:

> as long as I need something from someone else more than they need it from me, or they are in a position to direct me, then power is temporarily tilted in their favour.

Power is thus an element in all human relations. It is neither 'good' nor 'bad' but rather it can be seen as a relationship which, paradoxically, constrains and enables us at the same time. This understanding of power has important implications for understanding the complexities of policymaking. Like schools and individuals working within them, policymakers are also entangled in complex power figurations. For example, the Education Secretaries and ministers in the Department for Education are simultaneously enabled by the 'power of office' to design and control school improvement policies and constrained by their time in office or decisions of their superiors. Research by Abbott (2015) emphasises difficulties encountered by government ministers in developing long term strategies for education in a rapidly changing environment. Similarly, based on interviews with policymakers, Moss (2009: 166) found that her participants felt obliged to introduce new initiatives in order to be seen as 'productive' and not to appear 'as though you've run out of steam'. These research studies shed light on the complexities of what practitioners at AP and GLP considered to be government 'tinkering' (Chapter 6). From the complex responsive processes perspective, paying more attention to processes rather than outcomes in policy design and enactment could provide conditions conducive to the emergence of new forms of interaction between practitioners and policymakers based on mutual recognition and reversibility of perspectives. Interactions that embrace an orientation to difference (Fairclough 2003) would be particularly valuable, because understanding differently is at the core of new knowledge and understanding, while entering into the attitude of others is at the heart of ethics.

Considering ethics from the complex responsive processes perspective, it is essential to understand the emergent nature of ethical choices in our ordinary everyday encounters with others rather than adherence to fixed moral universals. Interdependence means, first, that we cannot make choices as if we were atomised individuals and second, that no human can claim a detached, godlike understanding or insight. As discussed in Chapter 7, such privileged understanding is often claimed by those engaging in bureaucratic modes of management. This has led to ascribing a higher moral purpose, such as 'liberating' pupils' minds (Gove 2011), to economically driven education reform. MacIntyre (1985) links the loss of human (as opposed to economic) purpose (*telos*) to the collapse of a coherent moral scheme following the rejection of religious dogma in the Enlightenment. God as the moral guardian was subsequently replaced by the bureaucratic manager. Complex responsive processes theorists emphasise that, despite the rise of secular, scientific worldviews, a godlike view has persisted in a habit of thinking which locates explanations of our interactions in 'systems' or idealisations that lie outside these interactions. For example, the sciences of certainty discussed in Chapter 2 locate the 'scientific' manager in a privileged vantage point of an outsider observer. As argued by Griffin (2002: 9), this habit of thinking also reduces ethics to the justification of individual thought as disconnected from action:

> When we locate ethics in the intention, or thought, apart from or before the action, we are assuming that the likely outcome of the action can be known before the action is taken. It is only on this basis that we can allocate

praise and blame. However, when the intention arises in the action ... and when the outcome of the action cannot be known in advance of acting, then a different view of ethics is required.

(Griffin 2002: 15)

A recognition of uncertainty calls for ethics that are not focused on a teleological passage of humans from an 'imperfect' to 'ideal' state, but on human interaction itself and the continuing attention to the meanings of actions that could not have been known in advance. As Mead (1908: 319) points out:

> Moral advance consists not in adapting individual natures to the fixed realities of a moral universe, but in constantly reconstructing and recreating the world as the individuals evolve.

In developing a view of ethics consistent with the complexity concept of emergence, Griffin (2002: 20) focuses on ordinary everyday interactions in which 'freedom of choice and intention are experienced within the constraints of the past, in the process of movement into an unknown future'. This means that ethical responsibility is not located in 'the system' or a few individuals 'accountable' for predetermined organisational outcomes, but in the choices made by everyone engaging in day to day work. Ethics are predicated on a willingness to enter into the attitude of the other and make decisions based on the recognition of interdependence. This understanding of ethics emphasises that accountability needs to be based on a mutual obligation of policymakers and practitioners, as well as their mutual responsibility for education. Being responsible, in turn, means being equally wary of 'management by values' or adhering to fixed moral universals, but rather continuously connecting to ethical meaning that emerges in everyday interactions.

Children and renewal: 'As long as they're having fun and I'm having fun, we're both learning at the same time, hopefully'

The theme of children and renewal requires a reversal of the logic applied to analysing and reporting the case studies so far, by focusing on what children bring into adults' lives, rather than on what adults 'are doing to children' (Jeanne). The theme emerged from stories told at AP and GLP. The everyday life in both schools was richly textured with storytelling, poetry, songs, pictures and colour. One story in particular is of significance to the discussions presented in this chapter. It is a story of Aziz the weaver, a stubborn old man who would only weave white cloth. Because he was the only weaver in the village, all villagers had to necessarily wear white garments. The slow transformation of Aziz began with the arrival of a young girl, dressed in most colourful clothes, who gradually changed his mind. Unexpectedly to himself and the villagers, Aziz began weaving colourful cloth. This highly symbolic story was read by Stephen in an assembly at GLP just before the end of the school year. It was aimed in particular at encouraging Year 6 children to articulate thoughts and emotions they experienced before leaving the familiar world of the primary school to start their secondary education.

This is also a story about 'natality', the renewal and freedom that children bring into the world (Arendt 1998). According to Hannah Arendt, each birth is a miracle, a new beginning that introduces novelty and freedom in the world. Freedom means the capacity to begin, to do the unexpected, to start something anew. Such freedom cannot be given to or taken away from someone by someone else; human beings are endowed with it by virtue of being born. Natality and freedom are connected to acting:

> the new beginning inherent in birth can make itself felt in the world only because the newcomer possesses the capacity of beginning something anew, that is, of acting.
>
> (p. 9)

By virtue of being born, (wo)man is free and capable of action, which means 'that the unexpected can be expected from him, that he is able to perform what is infinitely improbable' (p. 178).

The unexpected transformation of Aziz the weaver was enabled by the young girl bringing something new into his life – colour. The story highlights the importance of being able to start anew and is as important for adults, as it is for children. Sandy seemed to understand the significance of children in adults' lives (Van Manen 1990), articulating it as a learning opportunity that 'being with the kids' provided for her:

> I love being with the kids . . . And as long as they're having fun and I'm having fun, we're both learning at the same time, hopefully.
>
> (Sandy, T, GLP)

What is it, then, that as adults we could learn from the logic that seems to enable young children to begin every day anew? It would seem to take very little for a teacher or policymaker to transform the educational experience of children by simply being open to beginning anew. Paradoxically, however, this transformation requires also a profound change in perception and a reconstruction of the past and present agendas that come with the role, office, personal belief, political considerations and career trajectory. Followed by thoughtful action and recognition of the importance of diversity. Or, as Arendt would argue, it takes:

> the courage to interrupt their routine activities, to step forward from their private lives in order to create a public space where freedom could appear,

and to act in such a way that the memory of their deeds could become a source of inspiration for the future.

(Maurizio Passerin d'Entreves 2006)

In the light of the complexity understanding of ethics, such courage is not a fixed universal but rather needs to be continually defined anew through action, the outcomes of which cannot be known in advance.

Conclusion

This chapter focused on the paradoxes and contradictions emerging from the reconstructions of teaching as a 'mastery' of target-driven education and teachers as 'transmitters' of knowledge, attitudes and skills. The resulting reconstruction of children 'as data' promotes 'cold-calculating activity' (Honneth 2006: 96) instead of empathetic engagement with children. The complexity understanding of humans as interdependent illuminates our need to be recognised and respected by others, revealing alternative meanings of power and ethics. Interdependence entails that *both* practitioners and policymakers are responsible for transforming education. Making schools alone accountable for the outcomes of policies means that policymakers may be unwilling to claim responsibility for their policies. Avoiding responsibility, however, does not absolve one from being responsible. In an interdependent world, the misuse of power in promoting instrumentalist rationality may 'come back to haunt us' (Scott 1998: 21).

The generative possibilities of 'new forms of social imagination' (Gough 2010: 52) offered by the complexity concept of interdependence may be helpful in resisting and transcending the current accountability structures. Until this happens, however, the established power inequalities between policymakers and practitioners are likely to continue the disjuncture between abstract blueprints for educational transformation and the everyday realities in which children are seen 'as data'. The price of the relentless focus on standards, targets, high expectations and high aspirations is an impoverished educational practice that constrains professionals from seeing children as they are and connecting to questions about the significance of children in our lives.

As suggested by Angelika, regardless of these reconstructions schools seem to provide 'a good enough service' (Stacey 2010: 208):

> I think that teachers are the sort of people who will just make sure that the children get a good education regardless of maybe certain things that are going on.
>
> (Angelika, SLT, GLP)

Given the 'dark' side of high aspirations, the goal of providing 'good', rather than 'excellent', education could enable the recognition of the needs of children to be cared for and respected for who they are. The findings discussed in this chapter suggest that 'good education regardless' of the 'policy hysteria' is enabled by professionals who are committed to the values of care and love. Within the constraints of education reform, they work very hard 'to reach unattainable goals with inadequate tools' (Ginott 1972: 15) and sometimes they accomplish 'this impossible task'. Paradoxically, 'good enough' education may also be possible because of the inherent gift of renewal that children represent in the world of adults.

Notes

1. Ginott was a school teacher, child psychologist, psychotherapist, parent educator and author of a book *Teacher and Child* (Ginott 1972). The quotation, written by Ginott when he was a young teacher, is included in the preface to the book.
2. 'SEN' stands for children with 'Special Educational Needs' who make 'below average' progress due to learning or behavioural difficulties or disabilities. Most mainstream schools in England keep a register of these children, and the school's SEN co-ordinator (SENCO) is responsible for provision for such children.
3. For example, the Schools White Paper 2010 makes numerous references in its eighty-five pages to 'expectations' and derivatives (75 times), '(high) aspirations' (10), 'inspiration' or 'inspire' (10) and 'excellent' or 'excellence' (25).
4. Honneth develops his argument by combining Mead's (1934) theory of the social origins of self with Winnicott's (1965, 1971) theory of psycho-social development in early childhood.
5. According to Honneth (1995: 129), psychologically and socially healthy development is predicated on self-confidence, self-esteem and self-respect, which are connected to three corresponding *modes of recognition*:

    - *emotional support*, established through primary relationships, is a foundation for self-confidence
    - *social esteem*, developed through belonging to a socially valued community, provides the basis for self-esteem
    - *cognitive respect*, linked to the individual's legal rights, provides a foundation for self-respect

    This chapter is focused on modes of recognition which are of particular significance in childhood: *emotional support* and *social esteem*. A detailed analysis of *cognitive respect* is beyond the scope of this book.
6. Honneth's insights into the 'forgetfulness of recognition' resonate with Heidegger's (1962) analysis of our 'forgetfulness of being', as well as the Heideggerian critique of Cartesian relations predicated on the dualistic distinction between the 'disengaged subject' and 'object to be manipulated'.

References

Abbott, I. 2015. Politics and education policy into practice: Conversations with former Secretaries of State, *Journal of Educational Administration and History*, 47(4): 334–349.

Ainley, P. and Allen, M. 2012. Hard times for education in England, *Educationalfutures*, 5(1): 15–28.

Alexander, R., Armstrong, M., Flutter, J., Hargreaves, L., Harlen, W., Harrison, D., Hartley-Brewer, E., Kershner, R., MacBeath, J., Mayall, B., Northen, S., Pugh, G., Richards, C. and Utting, D. 2010. *Children, Their World, Their Education: Final Report and Recommendations of the Cambridge Primary Review*. Abingdon: Routledge and the University of Cambridge.

Arendt, H. 1998. *The Human Condition* (2nd edn). Chicago, IL and London: The Chicago University Press.

Ball, S.J., Maguire, M. and Braun, A. 2012. *How Schools Do Policy: Policy Enactments in Secondary Schools*. London and New York: Routledge.

Barnett, R. 1997. *Higher Education: A Critical Business*. Buckingham: SRHE and Open University Press.

Beard, R. 2000. *National Literacy Strategy: Review of Research and Other Related Evidence*. Sudbury: DfEE.

Corsaro, W.A. 2011. *The Sociology of Childhood* (3rd edn). Thousand Oaks, CA: Pine Forge Press.

DfE. 2010a. *The Importance of Teaching: The Schools White Paper 2010*. Available at: www.ictliteracy.info/rf.pdf/Schools-White-Paper2010.pdf (accessed 15 March 2012).

DfE. 2010b. *Unique Pupil Numbers (UPNs) – Policy and Practice: Guidance for Local Authorities and Schools*. Available at: www.education.gov.uk/researchandstatistics/datatdatam/upn/a0064607/upn-policy-and-practice-guidance (accessed 27 August 2012).

DfE. 2011. *Teachers' Standards: Guidance for School Leaders, School Staff and Governing Bodies*. London: Crown Copyright.

DfES. 2003. *Excellence and Enjoyment: A Strategy for Primary Schools*. London: HMSO.

d'Entreves, M.P. 2006. 'Hannah Arendt'. In Zalta, E.N. (ed.) *Stanford Encyclopedia of Philosophy*. Available at: http://plato.stanford.edu/entries/arendt/ (accessed 10 March 2012).

Elias, N. 1978. *What Is Sociology?* New York: Columbia University Press.

Elias, N. 1994. *The Civilizing Process: Sociogenetic and Psychogenetic Investigations*. Malden, MA and Abingdon: Blackwell.

Fairclough, N. 2003. *Analysing Discourse: Textual Analysis for Social Research*. Abingdon: Routledge.

Gibbs, P. and Iacovidou, M. 2004. Quality as a pedagogy of confinement: Is there an alternative? *Quality Assurance in Education*, 12(3): 113–119.

Ginott, H.G. 1972. *Teacher and Child: A Book for Parents and Teachers*. The University of Michigan, MI: Macmillan.

Gough, N. 2010. 'Lost Children and Anxious Adults: Responding to Complexity in Australian Education and Society'. In Osberg D. and Biesta, G. (eds) *Complexity Theory and the Politics of Education*. Rotterdam: Sense, 39–56.

Gove M. 2010. *Speech to the National College Annual Conference, Birmingham* (16 June 2010). Available at: www.gov.uk/government/speeches/michael-gove-to-the-national-college-annual-conference-birmingham (accessed 30 October 2013).

Gove, M. 2011. *The Moral Purpose of School Reform*. Available at: www.gov.uk/government/speeches/michael-gove-on-the-moral-purpose-of-school-reform (accessed 28 March 2015).

Griffin, D. 2002. *The Emergence of Leadership: Linking Self-Organisation and Ethics*. London and New York: Routledge.

Heidegger, M. 1962. *Being and Time.* (J. Macquarrie and E. Robinson, Trans.). Malden, MA and Oxford: Blackwell.

Hogan P. 2011. The ethical orientations of education as a practice in its own right, *Ethics and Education*, 6(1): 27–40.

Honneth, A. 1995. *The Struggle for Recognition: The Moral Grammar of Social Conflicts.* (J. Anderson, Trans.). Cambridge: Polity Press.

Honneth, A. 2006. *Reification: A Recognition-Theoretical View.* Available at: http://tannerlectures.utah.edu/lecture-library.php#h (accessed 14 March 2014).

Illeris, K. 2007. *How We Learn: Learning and Non-Learning in School and Beyond.* Abingdon: Routledge.

Jardine, D.W. 1998. *To Dwell with a Boundless Heart: Essays in Curriculum Theory, Hermeneutics, and Ecological Imagination.* New York: Peter Lang.

Kelly, A.V. 2009. *The Curriculum: Theory and Practice* (6th edn). London: Sage.

Lawn, M. 2011. Governing through data in English education, *Education Enquiry*, 2(2): 277–288.

MacIntyre, A. 1985. *After Virtue: A Study in Moral Theory* (2nd edn). London: Bloomsbury.

Mead, G.H. 1908. The philosophical basis for ethics. *International Journal of Ethics*, 18, 311–323. Available at: www.brocku.ca/MeadProject/Mead/pubs/Mead_1908b.html (accessed 10 April 2105).

Mead, G.H. 1934. *Mind, Self, and Society from the Standpoint of a Social Behaviourist.* Chicago, IL and London: The University of Chicago Press.

Moss, G. 2009. The politics of literacy in the context of large-scale education reform, *Research Papers in Education*, 24(2): 155–174.

Mowles, C. 2011. *Rethinking Management: Radical Insights from the Complexity Sciences.* Farnham: Gower.

Mowles, C. 2015. 'The Paradox of Stability and Change: Elias' Processual Sociology'. In Garud, R., Simpson, B., Langley, A. and Tsoukas, H. (eds) *The Emergence of Novelty in Organizations.* Oxford: Oxford University Press, 245–271.

NCSL. 2011. *National Professional Qualification for Headship Competency Framework.* Available at: www.gov.uk/government/uploads/system/uploads/attachment_data/file/284573/npqh-competency-framework.pdf (accessed 5 May 2014).

Nussbaum, M.C. 2001. *Upheavals of Thought: The Intelligence of Emotions.* Cambridge: Cambridge University Press.

OECD. 2009. *Creating Effective Teaching and Learning Environments: First Results from TALIS*, TALIS, OECD Publishing. Available at: http://dx.doi.org/10.1787/9789264068780-en (accessed 28 April 2014).

OECD. 2013. *Teaching and Learning International Survey TALIS 2013: Conceptual Framework.* Available at: www.oecd.org/edu/school/TALIS%20Conceptual%20Framework_FINAL.pdf (accessed 7 May 2015).

Pring, R. 2013. *The Life and Death of Secondary Education for All.* London and New York: Routledge.

Scott, J.C. 1998. *Seeing Like a State: How Certain Schemes to Improve the Human Condition Have Failed.* New Haven, CT and London: Yale University Press.

Seddon, J. 2008. *Systems Thinking in the Public Sector.* Axminster: Triarchy Press.

Stacey, R.D. 2010. *Complexity and Organisational Reality: Uncertainty and the Need to Rethink Management after the Collapse of Investment Capitalism* (2nd edn). London: Routledge.

Stacey, R. 2012. *Tools and Techniques of Leadership and Management*. Abingdon: Routledge.

Van Manen, M. 1990. *Researching Lived Experience: Human Science for an Action Sensitive Pedagogy*. New York: SUNY.

Winnicott, D.W. 1965. *The Maturational Processes and the Facilitating Environment: Studies in the Theory of Emotional Development*. London: Hogarth Press and the Institute of Psychoanalysis.

Winnicott, D.W. 1971. *Playing and Reality*. London: Tavistock.

Zipin, L., Sellar, S., Brennan, M. and Gale, T. 2013. Educating for futures in marginalized regions: A sociological framework for rethinking and researching aspirations, *Educational Philosophy and Theory*, 47(3): 1–20.

Chapter 9

Educational beginnings and ends

> This school, I think when I pass it onto someone else, is going to look and feel very different. And I just hope that the positives outweigh the negatives. In terms of legacy, I think that's all you can hope for.
>
> (Stephen, headteacher, Green Lanes Primary)

Chapter 9 seeks to synthesise the main themes of the book and consider them in relation to the 'new orthodoxy' of educational 'transformation' and the myths constructed to sustain it. The enduring appeal of the idea of 'transformation' seems to be premised on our human desire to live meaningful, purposeful lives and to leave a 'positive legacy' (Stephen, H, GLP). The 'mythical' imagination inspiring approaches to education policy and leadership discussed in this book may thus be linked to the human need for purpose, or *telos*. The myths sustaining contemporary education policies based on the sciences of certainty are designed to provide greater purpose to what are essentially normative and technicist applications of scientific knowledge. Therefore, despite the advances in scientific ways of understanding the world, humans are still a myth-making species (Chapter 3). Paradoxically, myth is an enabling constraint: it enables us to make the meaning and purpose of our lives intelligible but simultaneously constrains us by imposing a particular normative order onto the universe we inhabit. Accordingly, the myths of control, 'spectacular' solutions and perpetual crisis appear to have been deployed by English policymakers to simultaneously inspire and command practitioners to deliver a particular version of school improvement. Reading myth as a motive (rather than a reason) suggests that government declarations about transforming education into a 'world-class' system (DfE 2010) may be motivated by the political aim of affirming economic efficiencies as the ultimate educational *telos*. As evidenced by research in England and beyond, a *businessification* of education has become a dominant theme in the global discourse on education reform (Chapter 6).

Based on the empirical data discussed in Chapters 5–8, this chapter starts from a premise that problems arise when myth-making tendencies in education policy lead to 'unrealistic expectations' (Sophie, DH, AP) placed on a 'local' school. Myth making reduces complex realities to essences or necessities (Barthes 2000) and has in effect narrowed the curriculum and confined pedagogy to target setting and teaching to the test for the purpose of raising standards. The narrow definition of standards as pupil test results may facilitate the 'data flow' (Lawn 2011) between schools and education ministers, but greater efficiency in data production is not the same as providing a better educational experience for pupils. As suggested in the epigraph to this chapter, practitioners working in AP and GLP expressed a modest intention of leaving a legacy whereby 'the positives outweigh the negatives' (Stephen, H, GLP). No grandiose claims to 'transformation' were made in either school, with patterns of conversation not only focused on improving pupils' SATs scores, but also improving the buildings and play spaces as well as a 'more rounded' education. This is despite the 'tremendous power' of teachers to 'shape young lives' (Stephen, H, GLP) discussed in Chapter 8. The policy approach to accountability was addressed by some practitioners within a much broader view of responsibility for the children in their care and not simply a matter of performance statistics. From the complex responsive processes perspective, responsibility is premised on trying to continually connect to a deeper ethical meaning that emerges from our willingness and ability to enter into the attitude of others.

As signalled in Chapter 1, an increasing influence of supranational organisations such as the OECD on reforming education in line with economic priorities of efficiency and global competitiveness raises three unsettling questions. First, what are the implications of an industrial model of education for children and their teachers? Second, what is meant by 'knowledge' deployed in transforming education? Third, does creating 'modern' education necessitate breaking with tradition? These questions are revisited in this chapter in the light of complex responsive processes theory and the case study findings to consider *educational* beginnings and ends as alternatives to the dominant *economic* means–ends approach to transforming education.

Education as a 'knowledge industry'

The OECD (2009) metaphor of education as a 'knowledge industry' conveys a notion of education that can be manufactured, packaged and sold. In alignment with this notion, teaching has been defined as 'transmission' of knowledge, attitudes and skills that reduces learning to their passive acquisition by learners. As discussed in Chapter 8, the case study data suggest that an industrial, target-based model of education may lead to a recasting of the child-learner as a *child-worker* and a misrecognition of his/her needs. In the English context, after years of 'policy hysteria' (Stronach and MacLure 1997), standards as a means for improving educational quality appear to have become an end in itself. This obliteration of the distinction between means and ends results in a subjugation of *educational* aims to *economic* aims.

The relentless focus on raising standards appears to constrain the patterns of conversation at AP and GLP within the themes of 'setting', 'achieving' and 'owning' targets. The pressure of performing to standards of 'excellence' is leaving a legacy of exclusion for staff who do not display the 'right' work ethos and for pupils who perform below the statistical norm. As pointed out by Lynn (TA, AP), the problem of being labelled as underachieving or failing 'gets bigger and worse' when pupils move on to secondary schools. Lynn's point resonates with what Prigogine (1996) refers to as the 'arrow of time', or the complexity understanding of time as irreversible. Iterated over and over again, the failures, panics and misrecognitions defining the educational experience of children who struggle in the culture of 'high aspirations' may lead to a loss of self-esteem. Unlike policy and PISA cycles, which may reverse unworkable reforms, the time spent in primary education cannot be reversed and the damage to children recently assigned the derogatory label of the 'underperforming tail' (Marshall 2013) cannot easily be undone.

From the teachers' perspective, the reality of conforming to unrealistic policy expectations may result in game playing, a strategic focus on 'borderline' children, teaching to the test, managing impressions or performing in ways that 'please' Ofsted inspectors (Miriam, DH, GLP). The fundamental problem here is that the imposed system of improvement and the policy apparatus of performativity may sever an empathetic connection to a child as a person possessed of a full range of personal traits and potential (Honneth 1995, 2006). An industrial-type education may irreparably reduce the opportunities for a more holistic development of children. The espoused rhetoric of a culture of 'high aspirations' and 'liberating' children from 'narrow horizons' of thought (Gove 2011) is thus undermined by the instrumental rationality and highly technicist solutions ostensibly designed to bring these conditions about.

The myth of perpetual crisis sustains the urgency with which education in England is being transformed into a 'knowledge industry'. A Barthes-based reading of this myth reveals how it reduces the complexity of school improvement and creates an ideological account of reality, while at the same time disowning ideology (Barthes 2000). For example, the neoliberal logic of quasi-markets provided a rationale for New Labour's (1997–2010) modernisation of education, simultaneously articulating the policy intention of providing 'better life chances' for children (DfES 2004). New Labour's modernisation resulted in the spread of managerialism, the creation of an *edu-business* under the influence of private sponsors and the extension of private sector relations into public services (Gunter 2012; Ball 2013a). These processes were subsequently accelerated by the Coalition government (2010–2015), who stated their intentions in terms of economic efficiency and 'high aspirations'. These policies, however, have contributed to a gradual dismantling of public education through academisation and opening of free schools (Pring 2013; Ball 2013b; Higham 2014; West 2014). Both New Labour's and

Coalition's definition of educational transformation as extending market relations to non-market spheres of public life offers a narrow neoliberal view of human behaviour driven primarily by self-interest in order to maximise material well-being. By constructing all social relations as transactions of exchange, the neoliberal discourse erodes social bonds. From Honneth's (1995) perspective, education is not about self-interest but self-development. The latter is rooted in empathetic social relations as the basis for the development of children's self-confidence and self-respect.

As discussed in Chapter 6, the moral ambiguity of schools competing in league tables and the inequalities that can arise from the conversion to academy status have caused concern in the two case study schools. However, research data also pointed to a significant lack of political interest among AP and GLP practitioners. This seemed to lead to an absence of contestation of the dominant reform agendas and reluctance to challenge authority, especially among the younger generation of teachers and leaders. On the contrary, the commitment, hard work and ambition of 'doing your job properly' (Fiona, SLT, AP) seemed to be based on an assumption that a target-based education is the 'proper' approach to improving schools. As the culture of 'aspirational' targets (Marshall 2013) gets 'inside our heads and our souls', schools educate the workforce for the marketplace, encouraging 'both an active docility and depthless productivity' (Ball 2012: 31). By enacting the dominant transcript of school improvement, teaching professionals sustain its power.

Power depends on consent or acquiescence rather than the use of force and this makes language a crucial instrument of power (Fairclough 2003). In acquiescing with the dominant discourse practitioners often cede their own professional authority. Consistent with the complex responsive processes theory, it is impossible to predict the long term consequences of practitioner compliance with the dominant discourse. Of immediate concern is the possibility that what is communicated to children may not only affect their sense of self but also construct particular versions of the world that they may take for granted. The imposing façade of the neoliberal world is not inevitable or predetermined but constantly co-constructed and needs, therefore, to be critically examined if education is to be preserved as a public good. A critical awareness of the political and ideological agendas at play in education is, therefore, an important theme currently missing in the patterns of conversation in the two schools. For example, understanding how educational expert outsiders stake their claims to knowledge and power through hortatory reporting and use of nominalisation to promote their agendas could shine a different light on the policymaker, a CEO or school inspector (Chapter 3). It could help teachers to reclaim their own professional knowledge and expertise, which arises from *within* their everyday practice. It is to these complexities of knowledge production and application that we now turn.

Whose knowledge? Which transformation?

Transforming education through the knowledge about the efficacy of educational practices (OECD 2009) raises questions about how 'knowledge' is defined, produced and applied. Chapters 2 and 4 have emphasised the provisionality of scientific knowledge, arising from the entanglement of fact/value, subject/object and knowledge/knower. This, in turn, highlights the problematic nature of the assumption that it is possible to precisely predict long term outcomes of policies and changes to educational practice.

The privileged knowledge of policymakers and school inspectors to act on the world of schools to bring about change is a thread connecting mainstream understandings of educational transformation to Ovid's myth of creation. It is premised on godlike power to predict the outcomes of disentangling, moulding, operating on objects and people in order to leave 'each in its place and all in harmony' (Ovid AD8/2004: 16). In this paradigm, sustained through the myth of control, transformation often amounts to taking up already existing ideas to produce novelty (Mowles 2015). This approach has been illustrated in Chapter 2 by Michael Barber's (1997) blueprint for an education 'revolution', based on the existing blueprint for 're-engineering' organisations (Hammer and Champy 1993), as well as the now global phenomenon of utilising international comparisons as a policy driver in diverse educational systems (OECD 2009). Short of producing genuine innovation, these approaches also institutionalise a hierarchy of expertise in matters of school improvement, privileging the knowledge of outsider observers over the knowledge and understanding of practitioners. The expertise of these outsider observers enhances an instrumental approach to others. As argued by Patricia Shaw (2002: 4–5) in the context of the corporate world:

> Decades of a certain kind of business education and writing; the rise and rise of expensive management consulting focused on packaging 'best practice' and promising to provide expertise that will 'deliver' desired future success; the professionalization of all kinds of human communication into codified behavioural notions of 'coaching', 'counselling', 'teamwork' or 'leading' – all these have given us a curiously rational, instrumental approach to ourselves.

These ideas have been imported into education through the TLP (Thomson et al. 2014). The TLP focuses on codifying leadership traits, behaviours and interactions in schools. The dominant conceptualisations of school leadership encourage the organisation of our encounters with others around sophisticated planning tools and activities such as 'visioning', strategy formulation, target setting and data generation, which may have little to do with educating children. These approaches also appear to ignore the fact that the knowledge of what works in a specific education system is a generalisation. As such, it needs to be 'applied', or particularised in the unique, complex contexts by individuals who work with specific children and, in addition, have their own understandings of what it means to be a teacher or an educational leader. For example, an understanding of leadership articulated by the headteachers and senior leaders at AP and GLP, especially of the 'older generation', was focused on enabling and supporting teachers, being there, listening and leading by example (Chapter 7). This understanding resonates with the complexity view of knowledge not only as provisional, but also particular and situated. Such complex knowledge, generated *within* practice (Pete, H, AP), is lost in the abstractions, generalisations and idealisations of policy. As Merleau-Ponty (2002: xviii) reminds us, there is a difference between the real and the abstract worlds, the real world is the world we 'live through' rather than the world we 'think'.

Mainstream approaches to trans*form*ation are rooted in Cartesian thinking, which locates us in a world of *forms*, predetermined prior to experience and transformed through subject–object manipulations. By contrast, from the complexity perspective, transformation is not only dynamic but also generative in the sense of opening new possibilities, unknown in advance. Complex responsive processes scholars draw on G.H. Mead (1956) to explain the emergent, evolutionary nature of such a transformation. For Mead, at the core of 'trans*form*ation' viewed as profound social progress is the evolution of human consciousness, which, over time, finds its '*form*-al' expression in institutional and other social structures. Because of our essential interdependence, this process is predicated on our ability to enter into the attitude of others. It is this ability to take on multiple perspectives, to try to understand rather than act on others that constitutes a profound, progressive social change. This transformation has little to do with 'spectacular' solutions or quick fixes. Quite the opposite, it consists of gradual changes to our consciousness and operates at a mundane day-to-day level, within the domain of local interactions. It may even pass unnoticed until it becomes a global pattern of interaction.

This evolutionary perspective on educational transformation highlights the importance of emergence in changing the course of events. By definition, the emergent cannot be predetermined in advance, but by leading to novel elements, it is about unlimited possibilities. Mead's (1956) alternative to reform through 'spectacular' solutions and command and control is 'intelligent social control'. Intelligent social control is based on accepting uncertainty and interdependence as well as paying attention to processes rather than outcomes. Instead of seeking compliance, intelligent social control is based on seeking encounters with those who have different understandings, because such encounters offer generative possibilities for the novel to emerge. As pointed out by Mowles (2015), novelty emerges from local interactions that abandon predetermined agendas, visions or strategies in order to explore and better understand 'gritty' everyday realities. Reflecting on two contrasting narratives of innovation, a 'managerial narrative' of designed innovation and a narrative of innovation as 'practical, everyday politics', Mowles observed that:

It was the negotiation and exploration of the blockages, misunderstandings, lacunae, the intersection of stability and change, that led to the possibility of new things emerging. One of the most profound changes occurring, then, was in the way that people understood themselves and what they were doing.

(Mowles 2015: 100)

The intersection of stability and change is a point at which change may emerge at the same time as stability is maintained. This paradox of continuity and change occurring simultaneously is examined in the following section.

'Modern' education and the paradox of continuity and change

Education policies developed within the paradigm of certainty tend to break away from tradition in order to modernise, re-engineer or even revolutionise education (Chapters 2 and 5). They are premised on a view of schools as abstract, homogenous units that should automatically abandon 'old' practices, take up new ways of working exactly as intended by policymakers and efficiently deliver predetermined outcomes. This approach is both unrealistic and detrimental, because an understanding of practice is anchored in a system of meaning developed in the past and continued in the present.

By contrast, transformation, understood as profound progressive change in the minds of individuals and the quality of social relations, evolves over much longer timeframes than those typically defined in terms of electoral cycles or successive rounds of PISA. The paradox of continuity and change means that we are always in the midst of both continuity and change. For example, despite delineating timeframes for change, such as the 'strategies era' of 1998–2010 discussed in Chapter 5, the introduction of the *National Literacy Strategy* in 1998 was simultaneously the beginning of the 'strategies era', a continuation as well as outcome of processes started before. The 'strategies era' could also be viewed within a longer timeframe of the neoliberalisation of social relations discussed above. Timeframes for change enable us to make sense of events from which particular global patterns emerge. As argued by Elias (1991), the 'modern' tendency to refer to our own time span as a main frame of reference has two implications. First, we can 'hardly understand ourselves' (p. 30) and second, we are unable to comprehend the subtle interplay between structural innovation and processual continuity. As a result:

> The whole of history has so far amounted to no more than a graveyard of human dreams. Dreams often find their short-time fulfilment; but in the long run, they virtually always seem to end up drained of substance and meaning and so destroyed. The reason is that aims and hopes are so heavily

saturated with fantasy that the actual course of events in society deals them blow after blow, and the shock of reality reveals them as unreal.

(p. 28)

As suggested by the research findings, policies for transforming education in England tend to be constructed around an idealised vision of a 'world-class' system. Viewed within their 'short' lifespan of 1998–2010, the *National Strategies* for literacy and numeracy were evaluated by practitioners at AP and GLP as a 'double-edged sword' (Stephen, H, GLP). Although they enabled 'raising standards' (Angelika, SLT, GLP), they also constrained teachers to delivering a curriculum that often failed to meet the needs or interests of the children. More importantly, the *National Strategies* and the 'policy hysteria' are changing the way teachers talk about their work and cede their authority to educational expert outsiders. The emergence of an 'expertocracy' (Bauman 2005) seems to have led to negative consequences for the educational professional. Because modernity privileges the '*techne*' of the sciences of certainty, the increasing technological sophistication, especially in the area of assessment, has led to 'teaching by data'. Encouraged by experts such as Ofsted inspectors, the focus on data as the most valid measure of learning severs a more empathetic connection to the child as a person.

Viewed within a 'timeframe of humanity' (Elias 1991), the rise of 'expertocracy' is not a phenomenon of recent years, but can be traced back to the Enlightenment, the rise of the sciences of certainty and the primacy of an autonomous, detached observer. The disconnection between the observer and the observed leads to the objectification of human and other resources. Viewed within this timeframe, therefore, the contemporary English school with its pupils and teachers has become an object to be changed, a territory to be governed by expert outsiders: policy entrepreneurs, bureaucratic managers and school inspectors.

What could be termed as a paradoxical 'darkness' of the Enlightenment is rooted in Cartesian thinking. Although it transformed the natural sciences and led to colossal advances in technology, which flourished as a result of rigorous, reductive-analytical pursuit of universal laws, there is a dark side to the Cartesian method. As discussed in Chapter 2, the Cartesian universe is inhabited by the '*homo clausus*' (Elias 1994), an independent individual confronting others with cold-calculating purposefulness. *Homo clausus* seeks understanding in order to manipulate and control events. Compelled to perform, transform and continually act on the world and others, *homo clausus* is also disconnected from being-in-the-world (Heidegger 1962). This disconnection from others and a 'forgetfulness of being' (ibid.) is passed onto children through parenting, education and social relations that prioritise doing over being, cognition over recognition and idealisations over the world as encountered in the immediate everyday experience.

Far from being 'modern', the vision of education as a 'knowledge industry' seems to represent the 'old' reductionist Cartesian epistemology, which, as pointed out by Barad (2007), has a relatively limited set of applications. Far from being neutral and value free, the reliance of the 'knowledge industry' on technicist expertise has also important ethical implications.

'Let them be children' and educational beginnings and ends

As discussed above, transformation understood as evolutionary changes in our consciousness that make us more attuned to others is lost in the calculative relations concerned with efficiency, competitiveness and economic priorities. It is also lost in the abstractions and idealisations of education policy which view the child as a *child-worker*. The demands placed on the *child-worker* to be in control of his/her targets, increasingly independent and rational deny him/her the right to be a child. 'Let them be children' was a statement articulated by Fiona (SLT, AP) and shared by Early Years teachers in AP as well as the support staff in both schools. Allowing children to be children means paying attention to children as they are, rather than as what adults aspire them to achieve or become in the future. As Nussbaum (2001) points out, to be a child is to have needs rather than be self-sufficient, independent and rational.

Educational ends, therefore, may emerge from our recognition of children's need and right to be children. From the complex responsive processes perspective, such recognition is not a fixed universal that can be codified as a set of behaviours or attitudes to be enacted, controlled and measured. It may arise from interactions that are oriented towards children, that allow children to be children. As emphasised by Honneth (1995), these interactions are likely to be paradoxical: harmonious and conflictual, loving and rejecting, giving and withdrawing care, successful and unsuccessful – complex and 'good enough' rather than idealised as 'excellent'. In the light of the complexity assumption of human interdependence, these interactions are realised not just through what adults bring into children's lives but also through what children bring into the lives of adults. Educational ends are thus rooted in the recognition of children's needs and rights enacted in everyday interactions with children. Complex responsive processes theory emphasises our responsibility for how we respond to others as an ethical choice made in our day-to-day encounters with others.

The theory challenges taken-for-granted modes of being in the world, paying attention to local interactions in order to develop deeper understandings of the complexities of organisational and social change. It emphasises sensitivity to how we communicate with others. This sensitivity was exemplified by Stephen (H, GLP), who appeared to be amazed at how his communications were 'just hoovered up by the school community'. For Stephen this meant being responsible for listening – having 'one mouth and two ears'. Jenny was puzzled by her own use of personal pronouns:

> When we started ... when I started ... that's the other thing I do all the time, say 'we', very, very seldom do I say 'me', always 'we'. If there's something that I've done, it's 'we'. I think that's important.
>
> (Jenny, H, AP)

What Jenny appears to mean here is inclusion, acknowledging the common purpose and achievement. Using the personal pronoun 'we' in place of 'I', however, can also gesture a suppression of difference, or a sense of an idealised 'we'. A shared sense of purpose enables individual selves to be transcended through connecting to something larger than ourselves. It may, simultaneously, constrain our individuality, subduing it to the values of the community. The idealised 'we' is dynamic and paradoxical, leading to patterns of inclusion and exclusion, integration and division (Mowles 2015). Meaning-making is thus complex and subtle, it depends both on what is explicit and implicit, on what we say, which semantic and syntactic categories we use, on the assumptions we make, intentions we have and how they play out in the complex contexts of a school, neighbourhood and society. As Fairclough (2003) points out, there is scope for further research into the interdependencies between the micro- and macro-interactions (the school and policy domains) and how they may lead to transformational change. Attending to the complexities and subtleties of the discursive choices we make, often implicitly or subconsciously, as we talk about everyday practice, can enable us to enter into the attitude of others. Paradoxically, it is ambiguity and not knowing that can lead to the emergence of the novel. As explored in Chapter 6, conversations about school improvement in both schools seemed to be 'stuck' on standards and targets. However, the ambiguity implicit in participants' articulations of school improvement at GLP could provide conditions for more child-oriented approaches to educational transformation to emerge.

To conclude ...

As emphasised throughout this book, in the world of complex responsive processes, there are neither 'spectacular' solutions nor groundbreaking instruments that can determine once and for all 'what works' in achieving the desired ends. On the contrary, in the complex processes of interdependent people relating to one another, beginnings may be more important than ends. While *economic* means–ends have become central to the grand narrative of transforming education, educating children inevitably begins with children, with the novelty, freedom and renewal that each child brings into the world (Arendt 1998). An end is *educational* when it connects to *telos*, an end pursued for the sake of a human life (MacIntyre 1985). For children, this end is inherently linked with becoming adults, human beings rather than globally competitive 'workforce'. As discussed above, however, children have a need and a right to be children before they become adults. From the complex responsive processes perspective, pursuing *educational* ends for the sake of a human life cannot be given as a fixed moral universal, or a set of values introduced into a school by a policymaker to be 'owned' by practitioners. *Educational* ends begin in ordinary everyday encounters, in which both the child and the adult simultaneously affect and are affected by each other. Taking everyday practice seriously is, therefore, at the heart of complex responsive processes theory. Paying attention to *what is*, what is encountered every day, in its complexity, tension, conflict and paradox, is also a basis for leaving behind the myths, abstractions and idealisations about *what ought to be*. As Elias (1991) reminds us, focusing on fantasy-congruent knowledge, abstractions and idealisations leads straight to the graveyard of human dreams. This is not to say that dreaming or hoping for a better future is wrong, but that problems arise when this disconnects us from the here and now, or when compliance with one's dreams and hopes is imposed on others through an apparatus of control.

Before I bring my writing to the end, I wish to reflect on what I have and have not managed to write in this book. As signalled in Chapter 1, this book has sought to guide the reader into the world of complex responsive processes as they have played out in the life of two 'local' schools in England. Consistent with complex responsive processes theory, the intention underpinning this book has been to explore the 'gritty' reality of working in a primary school, rather than providing solutions or recommendations. In presenting the case studies of AP and GLP, I sought to convey at least a glimpse of the world of schools as it is 'lived through' in its 'average everydayness' (Heidegger 1962). While feeling extremely grateful to my research participants for the gift of their data, I would also like to think that the interviews enabled them to articulate thoughts and reflections that may not have been expressed otherwise. By focusing on the patterns of conversation that emerged in the data collected in the two schools, I have tried to depict the dynamic interplay between the global and the local, while at the same time trying to hold on to the 'real' people.

However, I am also aware that the research process would be impossible without a degree of abstraction (Chapter 4). Furthermore, as a qualitative case study researcher (Stake 1995; Simons 2009, 2015), I can make but tentative claims to the generalisability of this study. If some of the insights gestured in this book strike a familiar chord with the reader, then it could be because I have managed to convey some generalised understandings of how practitioners make sense of education policy, while simultaneously trying to remain connected to the context in which these generalisations arose. As pointed out by Simons (2015: 174), an in-depth understanding of policy enactment and its consequences is more likely to be gained from an in-depth study of the particular than from methodologies utilising quantitative measures, which deliver 'greater "certainty" . . . on limited measures of worth'. One of the most notable findings that emerged from this research has been the theme of hope and renewal, which every new birth brings into the world (Arendt 1998). Gestured by children, this message may pass unnoticed by adults if they are unwilling or unable to enter into the attitude of the child.

What is at stake in transforming education is interpreted differently by different actors involved in education reform. For policymakers, it may be raising standards in literacy and numeracy, or embedding the culture of 'high aspirations' as the best solutions to enduring educational problems. For primary school teachers and leaders who participated in this research, it seems to be driving up standards and, at times, coping with the 'doom and gloom' (Jenny, H, AP) arising from the demands of the 'policy hysteria'. For more critically minded educators and researchers, it may be thoughtful action (Arendt 1998) to defend education as a public good and a site of renewal rather than an industry for training a workforce for the marketplace. What is important for all of us may also depend on the timeframe. Thinking in the 'timeframe of humanity' is difficult to conceive without the benefit of hindsight and even more difficult to express in words. Gadamer's (1975) words capture the uncertainty of the future, continuing from the past, through the present of modernity:

> When science expands into a total technocracy and thus brings on the 'cosmic night' of the 'forgetfulness of being', . . . then may one not gaze at the last fading light of the sun setting in the evening sky, instead of turning around to look for the first shimmer of its return?
> (Gadamer 1975: xxxiv)

As suggested by Gadamer, it is painful to contemplate the idea that it may be impossible to reverse the consequences of the 'forgetfulness of being' that arise from the expansion of the technicist–scientific paradigm. The manifestations of this paradigm can be discerned in the 'new orthodoxy' for transforming education and its legacy of interactions characterised by instrumentalism, *businessification* and the misrecognition of children's needs. To create the 'cosmic night', to erase the possibilities of renewal is unforgivable, whether done by a policymaker, parent, teacher or anyone else. In hoping for tomorrow to be a new beginning, in looking forward to the 'first shimmer' of the rising sun, we simultaneously claim responsibility for our role in the educational lifeworld. This responsibility begins with a remembrance of being and only the future can tell what may emerge from such a beginning.

References

Arendt, H. 1998. *The Human Condition* (2nd edn). Chicago, IL and London: The Chicago University Press.
Ball, S.J. 2012. *Global Education Inc.: New Policy Networks and the Neo-Liberal Imaginary*. London and New York: Routledge.
Ball, S.J. 2013a. *The Education Debate* (2nd edn). Bristol: The Policy Press.
Ball, S.J. 2013b. *Education, Justice and Democracy: The Struggle over Ignorance and Opportunity*. London: Centre for Labour and Social Studies.

Barad, K. 2007. *Meeting the Universe Halfway: Quantum Physics and the Entanglement of Matter and Meaning*. Durham, NC and London: Duke University Press.
Barber, M. 1997. *The Learning Game: Arguments for an Education Revolution*. London: Indigo.
Barthes, R. 2000. *Mythologies*. (A. Levers, Trans.). London: Vintage Books.
Bauman, Z. 2005. 'Afterthought: On Writing; on Writing Sociology'. In Denzin, N.K. and Lincoln, Y.S. (eds) *The Sage Handbook of Qualitative Research* (3rd edn). Thousand Oaks, CA: Sage, 191–215.
DfE. 2010. *The Importance of Teaching: The Schools White Paper 2010*. Available at: www.ictliteracy.info/rf.pdf/Schools-White-Paper2010.pdf (accessed 15 March 2012).
DfES. 2004. *Five Year Strategy for Children and Learners*. Norwich: The Stationery Office.
Elias, N. 1991. *The Symbol Theory*. London: Sage.
Elias, N. 1994. *The Civilizing Process: Sociogenetic and Psychogenetic Investigations*. Malden, MA and Abingdon: Blackwell.
Fairclough, N. 2003. *Analysing Discourse: Textual Analysis for Social Research*. Abingdon: Routledge.
Gadamer, H.G. 1975. *Truth and Method*. (J. Weinsheimer and D.G. Marshall, Trans.). London and New York: Continuum.
Gove, M. 2011. *The Moral Purpose of School Reform*. Available at: www.gov.uk/gov ernment/speeches/michael-gove-on-the-moral-purpose-of-school-reform (accessed 28 March 2015).
Gunter, H.M. 2012. *Leadership and the Reform of Education*. Bristol: The Policy Press.
Hammer, M. and Champy, J. 1993. *Reengineering the Corporation: A Manifesto for a Business Revolution*. New York: HarperBusiness.
Heidegger, M. 1962. *Being and Time*. (J. Macquarrie and E. Robinson, Trans.). Malden, MA and Oxford: Blackwell.
Higham, R. 2014. 'Who owns our schools?' An analysis of the governance of free schools in England, *Educational Management Administration & Leadership*, 42(3): 404–422.
Honneth, A. 1995. *The Struggle for Recognition: The Moral Grammar of Social Conflicts*. (J. Anderson, Trans.). Cambridge: Polity Press.
Honneth, A. 2006. *Reification: A Recognition-Theoretical View*. Available at: http://tannerlectures.utah.edu/lecture-library.php#h (accessed 14 March 2014).
Lawn, M. 2011. Governing through data in English education, *Education Enquiry*, 2(2): 277–288.
MacIntyre, A. 1985. *After Virtue: A Study in Moral Theory* (2nd edn). London: Bloomsbury.
Marshall, P. (ed.). 2013. *The Tail: How England's Schools Fail One Child in Five – and What Can Be Done*. London: Profile Books.
Mead, G.H. 1956. *On Social Psychology*. Chicago, IL: Chicago University Press.
Merleau-Ponty, M. 2002. *Phenomenology of Perception*. (C. Smith, Trans.). Abingdon: Routledge Classics.
Mowles, C. 2015. *Managing in Uncertainty: Complexity and the Paradoxes of Everyday Organizational Life*. London and New York: Routledge.
Nussbaum, M.C. 2001. *Upheavals of Thought: The Intelligence of Emotions*. Cambridge: Cambridge University Press.
OECD. 2009. *Creating Effective Teaching and Learning Environments: First Results from TALIS*, TALIS, OECD Publishing. Available at: http://dx.doi.org/10.1787/978926 4068780-en (accessed 28 April 2014).

Ovid. AD8/2004. *Metamorphoses: A New Verse Translation*. (C. Martin, Trans. and ed.). New York and London: W.W. Norton & Company.

Prigogine, I. 1996. *The End of Certainty: Time, Chaos and the New Laws of Nature*. New York: The Free Press.

Pring, R. 2013. *The Life and Death of Secondary Education for All*. London and New York: Routledge.

Shaw, P. 2002. *Changing Conversations in Organizations: A Complexity Approach to Change*. London: Routledge.

Simons, H. 2009. *Case Study Research in Practice*. London: Sage.

Simons, H. 2015. Interpret in context: Generalising from the singe case in evaluation, *Evaluation*, 21(2): 173–188.

Stake, R.E. 1995. *The Art of Case Study Research*. Thousand Oaks, CA: Sage Publications.

Stronach, I. and MacLure, M. 1997. *Educational Research Undone: The Postmodern Embrace*. Buckingham: Open University Press.

Thomson, P., Gunter, H, and Blackmore, J. 2014. 'Series Foreword'. In Gunter, H.M. *Educational Leadership and Hannah Arendt*. London and New York: Routledge, vi–xii.

West, A. 2014. Academies in England and independent schools (fristående skolor) in Sweden: Policy, privatisation, access and segregation, *Research Papers in Education*, 29(3): 330–350.

Appendix
Case study schools and research participants

'Abbey Primary' (AP)

Pseudonym	Position	Over 15 years' experience in education	7–15 years' experience in education	Less than 7 years' experience in education
Alice	Deputy head (DH)		✓	
Angie	Early Years teacher (T)			✓
Annabel	KS2 teacher			✓
Emma	KS1 teacher		✓	
Eve	School bursar – administrative staff (AS)			
Fiona	Early Years teacher, Senior Leadership Team (SLT)		✓	
Gail	Midday supervisor and teacher assistant (TA)		✓	
Gemma	Early Years teacher			✓
Jenny	Headteacher (H)	✓		
Liz	KS2 teacher			✓
Lynn	Teacher assistant		✓	
Maggie	KS2 teacher, Senior Leadership Team (SLT)		✓	
Maria	KS2 teacher, Senior Leadership Team (SLT)		✓	
Mark	KS2 teacher			✓
Pete	New headteacher	✓		
Sophie	Deputy head	✓		
Sylvia	Receptionist (AS)			

'Green Lanes Primary' (GLP)

Pseudonym	Position	Over 15 years' experience in education	7–15 years' experience in education	Less than 7 years' experience in education
Angelika	KS2 teacher, Senior Leadership Team (SLT)	✓		
Carol	Administrative staff (AS)			
Alison	KS2 teacher, Senior Leadership Team (SLT)	✓		
Jeanne	Receptionist (AS)			
Louise	School bursar, Senior Leadership Team (SLT)			
Miriam	Deputy head (DH)	✓		
Sandy	KS1 teacher (T)		✓	
Susan	KS1 teacher	✓		
Stephen	Headteacher (H)	✓		

Note: Those without ticks have only worked in administrative roles.

Index

NB Numbers in **bold** refer only to the figure or table on the relevant page(s). When 'n' is used, please see the corresponding note.

abstraction 3, 57–59, 63, 67n2, 78–79; 'abstract child' 8, 16, 61, 171, 199; and context 25; in models of education reform 53–54, 88, 125, 197; *see also* 'real' children

academies 103, 113; Academies Programme 16n3, 121, 123–125, 127–129; academy status 6, 16; **117**; Anti Academies Alliance 142n2; and Lord Harris 157; and privatisation 193–194

Alexander, R. 88, 99, 115, 116, 117n3, 124–126, 129, 148, 176; *see also* Cambridge Primary Review (CPR)

Alvesson, M. 81, 129, 133, 161

ambiguity 27, 32, 48, 60, 122, 130, 131–132, 194, 200

American charter schools 6, 123–124

Angrosino, M.V. 82

Arendt, H. 13, 185, 200, 201–202

Aristotle, 28, 31, 60, 163

aspirations 5, 47, 61, 106, 150; aspirational targets 164; **194**; 'dark' side of aspirations 178–180, 181–182, 186; high aspirations 171, 187n3, 193, 202; raising aspirations 157

assessment 37, 61, 121–122, 126, 132, 175–178, 180, 181, 198; Assessment of Pupil Progress (APP) 136–137; levels 102, 106, 116n1, 130, 131, 140, 151, 175, 178–179; and Ofsted 157; *see also* Standard Assessment Tasks (SATs)

Ball, S.J. 11; academisation 124; policy enactments 7, 17n7, 82, 89, 148, 176, 177, 179; 'policy entrepreneurs' 36, 41n4; policy sociology 14, 164, 165, 194; privatisation 86, 157, 193; self-improving system 103

Barad, K. 14; ambiguity 33; conceptual cut 36, 37; entanglement 22; ethics 39–40, 85; Newtonian science 38, 90n1, 199; 'passive nature' 32; quantum science 30–31, 41n2, 73; scientific processes 14, 30, 48, 76; transdisciplinary approach to knowledge 29, 50

Barber, M. 34–37, 40, 41n4, 54, 64, 73; 'education revolution' 34, 51, 195; and *National Literacy* and *Numeracy Strategies* 97, 101, 103–104, 108–109, 112; quasi-markets 127; *see also* 'deliverology'

Barthes, R. 9, 11, 16, 61, 140–141, 192, 193

Bassey, M. 85, 90, 129

Beard, R. 34, 100–101, 110, 173

Berger, P. and Luckmann, T. 76, 79, 91n9, 129

Biesta, G. 25; 'complexity reduction' 38, 50, 72, 75, 122

Blackmore, J. 6; *see also* Transnational Leadership Package (TLP)

Bohr, N. 29–32

Burr, V. 76–77, 80

Index

businessification of education 100, 156, 191, 202; *see also* 'edu-business'
Byrne, D. and Callaghan, G. 73, 77, 91n4

Cambridge Primary Review (CPR) **99**, 117n3, 125–126
Cameron, D. 121, 123, 141
case study: findings 16, 85, 112, 122, 126, 141, 148, 157, 173, 178, 192; 'fuzzy' generalisation **74**, 90, 129; generalising from case studies 85, 201; research 15, 80, 83, 84, 86, 88, 89; schools 17n5, 97, 127, 176
causality 14, 22; complex causality 23, 72, **74**, 75, 77; efficient causality 57–58, 60, 72; simple causality 35, 38, 40, 47, 87
certainty 26, 39, 55, 98, 122, 132, 197, 201; sciences of certainty 13–14, 21–24, **25**, 26, 30, 34, 38–40, 57–58, 61–62, 71–72, **74**, 91n7, 183, 191, 198; *see also* uncertainty
Chia, C.H. and Holt, R. 58, 63
children 4, 7; abstraction 13–16; child-learner 16, 173; child-worker 173–175; as data 176–178; marginalisation of 8; and the priority of recognition 59–61; and targets 34, 102–103; 175; *see also* 'real' children
Cilliers, P. 25, 39, 91n4
Coalition government 5, 99, 104, 121–129; academies and free schools 6, 16n3, 103; education in crisis 10, 15; privatisation of education 86, 156, 193–194
Cohen, L., Manion, L. and Morrison, K. 14, 72, 75, 82, 90n2
command and control 12, 34, 98, 103, 109, 111, 116, 129, 135, 196
complexity sciences 13–14, **25**; butterfly effect 23; complex adaptive systems 48–52, 66–67; complex knowledge 75, 87–90; complex responsive processes theory 3, 12–13, 50–51, **52**, 53–55, 60–63, 65–67; complexity reduction 22–23, 38–40, 50, 75, 82, 87–91; complexity thinking 24; *see also* emergence
Confederation of British Industry (CBI) 122, 156

consultants 6, 16n1, 47, 99, 102, 103–104, 116, 125; consultocracy 103
context 8, 9, 27; decontextualised policies 48, 59, 71, 139; English education policy context 5, 15, 16n1, 17n4, 172, 192, 200; global educational reform context 6, 40, 88; and knowledge production 33, 40, 89, 201; local school context 59, 71, 80, 97, 104, 147; organisational context 23, 48, 56, 57, 79, 82, 87
conversation of gestures **52**, 53–54, 90, 108, 127; *see also* patterns of conversation
Copernicus, 28; Copernican worldview 72
Critical Discourse Analysis (CDA) 63; CDA tools **83**, 84, 122, 130; and complex responsive processes theory 80; global education policy discourse 65; hortatory reporting **83**, 98, 102, 111, 116, 133, 194; metaphor 160–161; nominalisation 64–65, **83**, 84, 194; orientation to difference **83**, 130, 159, 183, 200; 'significant absences' 125, 137, 138, 149; *see also* Fairclough
culture 39, 59, 106, 125, 152, 158–162; emotivist culture 148, 163–165; of excellence 15, 147; organisational culture 56, 82, 157, 133, 138, 148, 158, 178, 182, 193, 202; target-driven culture 16, 194; Western mass culture 9, 14, 21, 61, 162; *see also* values
curriculum 15, 58, 175, 181, 135–136, 192, 198; National Curriculum 17n3, 99, 100–102; 121, 124–126; NPQH curriculum 152; *see also National Literacy* and *Numeracy Strategies*

data: and children 176–177; and complexity reduction 122; data tracking 157, 178, 186; 'governing by data' 176, 178; performance data 6, 7, 61, 71–72, 88, 113; teaching by data 198; and the sciences of certainty 34
Davis, B. and Sumara, D. 24, 75
'deliverology' 35–38, 40, 49–50, 61, 88; *see also* Delivery Unit
Delivery Unit 34, 36, 108–109
Department for Children, Schools and Families (DCSF) 99

Index

Department for Education (DfE) 16, 17, 35, 64, 98, 125, 142, 183
Department for Education and Skills (DfES) 5, 10
Descartes, R. 22, 26, 75; Cartesian *homo clausus* 26, 29, 60, 79, 180, 198; Cartesian method 26, 40, 61, 196, 198, 199; *see also* Newtonian-Cartesian paradigm
dialectic 60; Hegelian dialectic **52**
discourse 5, 7; dominant discourse 56, 131, 132, 137, 194; education policy discourse 9, 11, 63, 103, 124–125, 139, 141, 165, 173, 182, 191; global educational reform discourse 65–66, 141,191; mainstream discourse 8, 147; *see also* Critical Discourse Analysis (CDA)

economic: competitiveness 10–11, 40, 65, 122, 126, 178; efficiency 11, 16, 34, 191, 193; ends 16, 163, 183, 192, 200; necessity 66; priorities 192, 199; reality 10, 64–66; well-being 37, 99
'edu-business' 36, 43, 119, 125, 141
Elias, N. 13, 26, 27, 40; homo clausus 26, 41, 51, 60, 79, 180, 197, 198; knowledge 62, 201; power **52**, 55, 182
emergence i, 12, 19, 24, 35, 48–54, 74, 89, 134, 156, 184
Enlightenment 22, 26, 75, 162–163, 183, 198
entanglement 21, 22, 25, 27, 30, 32, 38, 40–41, 51–52, 85, 98, 183, 195
entrepreneurialism 15, 36, 140, 157; CEOs 149; *see also* 'policy entrepreneurs'
ethics 16, 30, 33, 36, 38, 39, 40, 62, 66, 172; complexity understanding of ethics 182–184, 186, 192, 194; ethical loss 16, 162–163; research ethics 85
evidence-based: policy 72, 78, 87; reform 4, 9, 13, 14
excellence 15, 147–148, 157, 162, 180 , 193; *Excellence and Enjoyment* (DfE 2003) 99, 101–102
'expertocracy' 198 *see also* consultants

Fairclough, N. 63–64, 83–84, 93, 102, 125, 133; discourse and power 137, 194; globalisation 126; new capitalism 140–141; time depth 111; transformational change 200
Fenwick, T., Edwards, R. and Sawchuk, P. 14, 38, 39, 75
Forrester, G. 6, 16n1, 53, 129, 147, 156
Foucault, M. 30, **52**, 55
free schools 6, 16, 103, 123–125, 142, 149, 193
Fullan, M. 39, 100

Gadamer, H.G. 202
Galileo, 22, 28, 31
generalisation 13, 63 71, 97, 121, 181, 195; generalising and particularising 55
Ginott, H.G. 171–172, 179, 187
Global Educational Reform Movement (GERM) 6, 13, 16, 53, 116
global orthodoxy i, 3, 6 15; *see also* 'new orthodoxy'
global patterns 48, **52**, 53, 63, 65, **83**, 89, 196, 197; *see also* local patterns
globalisation 10, 65, 106
Gough, N. 51–52, 186
Gove, M. 122; free schools policy 124; moral purpose of reform 157–158, 164, 175, 178; teaching as a 'craft' 171, 177
Griffin, D. 12, 13, 48, 50–51, 62, 183–184
Guba, E.G. and Lincoln Y.S. 73, 90n2
Gunter, H.M. 6; Academies Programme 16n1, 123, 125; 'consultocracy' 103–104; top-down government control 35, 53, 103, 129, 147; leadership for transformation 6, 103, 149; workforce re-modelling 7, 156; *see also* Transnational Leadership Package (TLP)

Hacking, I. 77, 85, 91n6, 129
Hall, D. 103–104
Hammersley, M. 71, 87
Harris, Lord 142, 157
headteacher role 6, 35, 53, 103, 105–106, 108, 115, 134, 147–151, 152-3, 162, 163; Chief Executive Officers (CEOs) 15, 149, 156; headteacher standards 147, 149, 152
hegemonic planning mentality 58–59, 125, 140, 164

Heisenberg, V. 29, 31–33; *see also* quantum physics
high-stakes tests 5, 15, 50, 84, 113, 116, 116n1, 122, 140, 141, 158, 171, 178, 180; as the best measure of quality 34, 129, 134
Honneth, A. 8, 12, **52**, 60–61, 173, 177, 180–182, 186, 194, 199; his sources 172, 187n5; modern capitalist relations 65, 156

idealisation 57, 67n2, 71, 79, 87, 158, 183, 196, 198, 199–201; idealised leadership models 14, 15
interdependence 16, 60, 66, 172, 182–186, 196, 199
International Association for the Evaluation of Educational Achievement (IEA) 37, 117n4; *see also* Purves
international comparisons 4, 5, 15, 21, 38, 71, 72, 88, 126, 195; *see also* Programme for International Student Assessment (PISA)

Kauffman, S. 24, 48, 49, 60, 62, 71
knowledge 8, 13, 14, 22, 24, 30, 32, 34, 40; as 'accurate representation' 2, 32, 75–76, 91n5; complex knowledge 38, 72, 81, 196; knowledge application 33, 39, 58, 77, 33; knowledge economy 64–65, 178; knowledge industry 4, 7–8, 172, 182, 192–193, 199; knowledge production 73, 77, 81; leadership knowledge 53, 67n4, 88, 103, 195; local knowledge 59, 71, 104, 116, 157, 194
Kuhn, T. 25, 27–29, 32, 38, 72, 81

Lawn, M. 61, 176, 192
leadership 6, 8, 9, 53, 88, 103, 147–153, 154–157, 159, 161–162, 164–165; distributed leadership 133, 152; leadership tools 48, **52**, 57–60, **83** *see* Transnational Leadership Package; transformational leadership 10–11, 149; *see also* management
league tables 104, 106, 122, 126, 127, 131, 179, 194
learning 5, 16, 75, 99, 101, 111, 126, 147–148, 173, 175–177, 181, 198; learning environment 8–9;

organisational learning 10, 11; 67n2; teaching and learning 6, 58, 159, 173; transmission model of learning 171, 192
Lingard, B. 14, 65, 87–88, 116
Local Authority 7, 17n6, 35, 99, 100, 103, 107, 117
local interactions 10, 12, 13, 14, 17, 41, 48, 49
local patterns **52**, 66, 80, 148; *see also* local interactions
logic 184, 185; of appearances 102; Aristotelian 60; binary 21; 'fuzzy' 85; lack of 11; neoliberal 193; paradoxical 60, 102; of performativity 57; of simplification 58

MacIntyre, A. 13, 26, 62, 148, 162–164, 165, 183, 200
MacLure, M. 11, 122, 155, 192; *see also* 'policy hysteria'
Maguire, M. 82
management 6, 22, 34–36, 55, 67, 78, 100, 165, 173; impression management 81, 133; management consultancy 6, 16, 34, 36, 47, 99, 100–104, 116, 125, 195; management by values 15, 56–57, 158, 162, 164, 165, 184; managerialism and New Public Management (NPM) 88, 193
manipulative relations 164–165
Maturana, H.R. 24
Mead, G.H. 13; conversation of gestures 53–54, 108, 111, 127, 137, 138; discourse 89; emergence 50, 132; ethics 184; generalisation and particularisation 55, 181; transformation 12, 59–60, 90, 196; values **52**, 56
Merleau-Ponty, M. 47, 66, 71, 79, 196
metaphor 51, **52**, 64, 75, **83**, 160–161, 165, 192
Meyer, H.D. and Benavot, A. 34, 37, 47, 71
Mills, C. 103–104
Mowles, C. 9, 12, 90; alternative approaches to management 57, 60; complexity sciences 41n1, 73; everyday organisational interactions 78, 197, 200; mainstream management techniques 22, 39, 47, 62;

management by values 56, 158, 160; novelty 195, 196; power figurations 182; reflexive narrative enquiry 67n4
myth 8–9, 16; of control 14, 22, 40–41, 47, 50, 61, 66, 191; of perpetual crisis 10–11, 15, 122, 123, 135, 138, 140–141, 193; of 'spectacular' solutions 9–10, 11, 98, 116; Ovid's myth of creation 4, 9, 10, 12, 21, 27, 30, 195; *see also* Barthes

National College for School Leadership (NCSL) 53, 67n1
National College for Teaching and Leadership (NCTL) 16n1
National Curriculum 17, 34, 99, 121, 124, 149, 181
National Literacy and *Numeracy Strategies* (NLS and NNS) 34, 86, 97–98, **99**, 100–101, 110, 127
National Professional Qualification for Headship (NPQH) 147, 152, 154, 156
New Labour government 5, 15, 34, 64, 67, 86, 98–99, 103, 117, 139, 156; and the Academies Programme 123; and quasi-markets 121, 127, 193
'new orthodoxy' 3, 5–8, 12, 14–15, 21–22, 40, 47, 50, 64, 66, 86–87, 89, 122, 202
Newton, I. 22–23, 28; Newtonian science 22, 24, 26, 31, 41n5, 51, 73, 90n1, 160
Newtonian-Cartesian paradigm 14, 22, 26, 27, 30, 40, 49, 72
Nussbaum, M.C. 180, 199

Office for Standards in Education (Ofsted) 53, 86, 97, 100, 102, 124, 133, 137–138, 154, 157, 171, 193, 198; and 'element of chance' 112–113, **114**, 115–117; *see also* Wilshaw
Organisation for Economic Co-Operation and Development (OECD) 4, 7–9, 21, 27, 30, 37, 65, 88, 171, 172–173, 177, 182, 192, 195
Osberg, D. 22, 24, 25, 38, 39, 50

paradox 11, 16, **52**, 55, 60, 82, **83**, 89, 91, 185; of abstracting 78–79, 85; of continuity and change 197–200; of enabling constraint 48, 172, 182, 191; of local interactions 122; of values 57, 158
particularisation 55, 85, 97, 121, 141, 181, 195
patterns of conversation 15, 48, 51–54, 56, 57, 59, 63, 65, 66, 80, 82–84, 89, 122, 138–139, 148–149, 151, 155, 173, 192–194, 201; of inclusion and exclusion 130, 162, 200; *see also* global patterns
pedagogy 75, 86, 100, 104, 116, 126, 176, 192
performativity 3, 57, 66, 122, 138, 156, 193
policy 6, 7, 55; policy discourse 64, 65, 84, 136, 173; policy enactment 13, 14, 17n7, 49, 53, 58, 66, 89, 97, 98, 127, 140–141, 153, 172, 186, 191, 201; 'policy entrepreneurs' 36–37, 41, 198; policymakers 3, 4, 5, 9, 16n1, 21, 111, 183; 'policy takers' 129
'policy hysteria' 11–12, 122–123, 127, 134–135, 138, 141, 155, 187, 192, 198, 202
power 10, 12, **52**, 79, **83**; disciplinary power **52**, 55, 88, 175; of the headteacher 149; power relations 15, 16, 48, 53, 55–63, 66, 67n4, 78, 98, 115; 'tremendous power' 171–172
practitioners (teachers, headteachers and other adults in school) i, 6, 15–16, 17n4, 37, 48, 86; and everyday practice 79, 89, 98, 109, 110; practitioner accounts 84, 98, 111–112, 130, 135, 148, 160, 192, 198; practitioner compliance 53, 66, 164, 194; practitioner responses to policy 109, 121–122, 127, 136, 138, 183, 201; as a subordinate group 56, 128–129, 141, 177, 191; *see also* headteacher role
pressure 11, 86, 113, 122, 137, 138, 158–160, 162, 165, 177, 193
Prigogine, I. 22, 24, 30, 50, 51–52, 62, 71, 193
private transcript **52**, 55–56, 164; *see also* public transcript
Programme for International Student Assessment (PISA) 4, 5, 11, 37, 88, 122, 141, 148, 163, 193, 197

public transcript **52**, 55–59, 66, 82, 164
Purves, A. 37–38, 39, 49

Qualified Teacher Status (QTS) 6, 150, 156
quantum physics 14, 24, 29–33, 41n3, 73, 85, 90n1; quantum 'revolution' 29, 60; 'quantum leaders' 35

rationality 22, 26, 37; instrumental rationality 21, 26, 52, 57–58, 181, 182, 186, 193, 195
Ravitch, D. 6, 34, 123–124
'real' children 13, 16, 123, 125, 140; 'real' people 12, 58, 61, 65, 201
recognition 12, **52**, 59–61, 199; and misrecognition 8, 139, 173, 192–193, 198, 202; modes of recognition 187n5; priority of recognition 61, 180–182; *see also* Honneth
reductionism 7, 22–23, 38, 74, 123, 131, 171, 179, 199
reflection 66, 76, 90, 108, 110, 114, 133, 154, 159, 160, 172, 177, 201
reflexivity 66, 67n4, 76, 78, 85–86, 88, 177
research: case study 15, 58, 85, 89; and complexity 52, 67; paradigms 72–73, 74, 76, 90n2; RCTs 87; and reflexivity 85–86; the researcher 9, 21, 77–82, 91, 201; on 'what works' 71, 87–88, 100, 195, 200
resistance 11, 14, 48, **52**, 55–57, 58, 59, **83**, 134, 136, 186
Rizvi, F. 14, 65
Rorty, R. 29, 75

Sahlberg, P. 6, 13, 34, 37, 47, 53, 151
School Effectiveness and School Improvement (SESI) 5, 14
Scott, J.C. **52**; hegemonic planning mentality 125, 140; negative consequences of centralisation 66, 186; public and private transcripts 56, 82, 164; Soviet central planning 58–59
self-organisation 24, 25, 35, 48–49, 51, 59, 62, 66, 148, 152
Sellar, S. 87–88, 116
Simons, H. 15, 80, 85, 87, 89, 201
Shaw, P. 12, 48, 51, 62, 63, 67n4, 86, 195

Smith, J. and Jenks, C. 23
Spicer, A. 161
Stacey, R.D. 12, 13; abstraction 67n2; challenging the sciences of certainty 22, 27, 41, 50, 72, 58, 60; complex adaptive systems 48; leadership tools 57–58; local and global interactions 14, 49, 51, 54–55; novelty 148; and research methodology 62, 67n4, 78, 86; uncertainty 23, 24, 48, 71
Stake, R.E. 80–81
Standard Assessment Tasks (SATs) 84, 113, 121–122, 129, 131–132, 141, 152, 157, 161, 176, 179, 192; *see also* high-stakes tests
standardisation 3, 6, 13, 34, 35, 53, 57, 58, 98, 100, 116, 117n5, 157, 175
Stewart, I. 22, 23, 24
Stronach, I. 11, 122, 138, 155, 192; *see also* 'policy hysteria'

Teaching and Learning International Survey (TALIS) 4, 7, 8–9, 13, 14, 21, 37
targets i, 6, 36, 122; as abstractions 58, 178–9; ambitious targets 86, 123, 97, 99, 130; apparatus of 53, 126; and erosion of educational quality 59, 158, 173, 178, 181, 186, 195; in everyday practice 84, 113–114, 131–2, 115, 171, 173–177, 192–193, 199; and improvement 58; as industrial practice 34, 100, 172; for literacy and numeracy 116n1; target setting 101, 102; *see also* culture
telos 162–164, 183, 191, 200
Thomson, P. 6, 14, 36, 47, 71, 88, 195; *see also* Transnational Leadership Package (TLP)
time 9, 10, 17; change over time 22, 24, 40, 51, 53, 63, 97; timeframes 12, 25–28, 29, 38, 86, 110, 111, 134, 137, 141, 197–198, 202
transformation 3–4; alternative meaning of 12, 13, 14, 25, 28, 41, 48, 51, **52**, 59–61, 63, 66, **83**, 107, 132, 148, 165, 184–185, 196–197, 199–200; as a global orthodoxy, 5, 34, 64, 140, 172; mainstream meaning 6, 21, 25, 36, 40, 50–51, 54, 87, 103, 124–125,

194, 196; and myth 8, 11, 16, 191, 195; *see also* leadership
Transnational Leadership Package (TLP) 8, 36, 47, 71–72, 88, 195
Tsoukas, H. 52, 71, 81, 87

uncertainty 7, 3, 15, 21, 48, 62, 73, 128, 132, 184, 202; and complementarity principle 31; sciences of uncertainty 24, 40, 71–72
Unique Pupil Number (UPN) 7, 8, 13, 176, 181
unpredictability 12, 23, 27, 40, 51, 53, 59, 89, 121

values 6, 27–28, 29; as complex 15, 57, 60–62, 158, 200; in discourse **83**, 136; distortion of educational values 141–142, 157, 163–164; fact/value 14, 22, 39, 195; in local interactions 48, **52**, 53, 55, 97, 106–108, 121, 148, 159–162, 178; market values 140; policymakers' values 15, 125–126, 147, 201; and recognition 61, 65, 180, 182; traditional educational values 4, 36, 86, 149, 151; *see also* management by values
Van Manen, M. 79, 81, 91n8, 98, 142n4, 185
Varela, F.J. 24

Watson, T. 147, 162
Wilshaw, M. 137–138
Winnicott, D.W. 180, 187n4

Taylor & Francis eBooks

Helping you to choose the right eBooks for your Library

Add Routledge titles to your library's digital collection today. Taylor and Francis ebooks contains over 50,000 titles in the Humanities, Social Sciences, Behavioural Sciences, Built Environment and Law.

Choose from a range of subject packages or create your own!

Benefits for you
- Free MARC records
- COUNTER-compliant usage statistics
- Flexible purchase and pricing options
- All titles DRM-free.

Benefits for your user
- Off-site, anytime access via Athens or referring URL
- Print or copy pages or chapters
- Full content search
- Bookmark, highlight and annotate text
- Access to thousands of pages of quality research at the click of a button.

REQUEST YOUR FREE INSTITUTIONAL TRIAL TODAY

Free Trials Available
We offer free trials to qualifying academic, corporate and government customers.

eCollections – Choose from over 30 subject eCollections, including:

Archaeology	Language Learning
Architecture	Law
Asian Studies	Literature
Business & Management	Media & Communication
Classical Studies	Middle East Studies
Construction	Music
Creative & Media Arts	Philosophy
Criminology & Criminal Justice	Planning
Economics	Politics
Education	Psychology & Mental Health
Energy	Religion
Engineering	Security
English Language & Linguistics	Social Work
Environment & Sustainability	Sociology
Geography	Sport
Health Studies	Theatre & Performance
History	Tourism, Hospitality & Events

For more information, pricing enquiries or to order a free trial, please contact your local sales team: www.tandfebooks.com/page/sales

Routledge Taylor & Francis Group

The home of Routledge books

www.tandfebooks.com